Catastrophic Coastal Storms

Catastrophic Coastal Storms

Hazard Mitigation and Development Management

David R. Godschalk, David J. Brower, and Timothy Beatley

Duke University Press   *Duke Press Policy Studies*

Durham and London 1989

Library of Congress Cataloging-in-Publication Data
appear on the last printed page of this book.
The information presented in this report is based
upon research funded by the National Science Foundation under Grant No. CEE-8217115, Hurricane
Hazard Reduction Through Development Management. The findings and opinions are solely those
of the authors and do not necessarily reflect the
views of the National Science Foundation.

Contents

Tables and Figures

Tables

Figures

Preface

This book grows from years of collaborative work on growth management and hazard mitigation by faculty and students of the Department of City and Regional Planning and staff of the Center for Urban and Regional Studies at the University of North Carolina at Chapel Hill. In a real sense that line of work, which continues to influence planning theory and practice, is responsible for the ideas and research presented here.

Our motivation for this study rose from countless discussions about how to improve coastal management through applying the techniques of development management. The coastline, with its sharp contrasts between the pressures for growth and the needs to safeguard people and property from storm hazards, is a critical policy arena. We believe that public and private decisionmakers will welcome a development guidance approach which enables them to balance these competing demands. We are heartened by the empirical evidence from this research that supports our belief.

This is not a book about the history of coastal storms, although it does include case studies of some notorious hurricanes. Rather, it is about famous, or infamous, *future* storms and how to anticipate and avoid their potential catastrophic impacts.

Many people contributed directly to this study. Among our University of North Carolina faculty colleagues, Bill Rohe played a major role in the design, coding, and analysis of the survey of vulnerable coastal localities, and Ray Burby shared his experience in conceptualizing issues of floodplain hazard mitigation, permitting us to draw upon his extensive previous surveys. Our energetic student assistants included Karen Allenstein, Scott Bollens, Jane Hegenbarth, John Hodges-Copple, and Kathleen Leyden.

Bill Anderson of the National Science Foundation provided stable project management. Many valuable suggestions were provided by our distinguished project advisory panel, listed below with their professional affiliations at the time of the study:

Jay Baker, professor of geography, Florida State University
Raymond Fox, professor of civil engineering, George Washington University
Neil Frank, director, National Hurricane Center
Jim Murley, Department of Community Affairs, State of Florida
David Owens, director, Office of Coastal Management, State of North Carolina
William Petak, professor of safety and systems management, University of Southern California
John Seyffert, director of environmental services, State of Maryland
William Spangle, William Spangle and Associates, Portola Valley, California
Larry Zensinger, chief, Mitigation Assistance Branch, Federal Emergency Management Agency, Washington, D.C.

During the preparation of the manuscript we received a number of helpful substantive recommendations from two other hazard scholars: Rutherford Platt of the University of Massachusetts at Amherst and Philip Berke of Texas A & M. We are also indebted to the many public officials and others who responded to our requests for information during the case studies, surveys, and report preparation. Finally, we appreciate the help of the staff of the Center for Urban and Regional Studies, especially Carolyn Jones and Lee Mullis.

The interpretation of the information provided is our responsibility. We hope that it will contribute to a safer coast for future generations.

1 Coastal Storm Risks as a Policy Problem

At the heart of American urban growth trends is a disturbing paradox. The areas most attractive to new development are often those most dangerous to life and property. People are drawn to the natural beauty of living on beachfronts, river shores, and mountainsides, despite threats of hurricanes, floods, and landslides. Yet public policy does little to discourage development in hazardous areas, and sometimes it even unwittingly encourages it. Government officials charged with protecting people and property from such natural hazards face political limits on their ability to affect the operations of private development markets, which tend to discount future hazard risks.

This book describes the implications of this paradox for coastal areas. Coastal storm hazards pose a major and growing threat to public health, safety, and welfare. This threat is an unsolved public policy issue. After an examination of past and present approaches to mitigating coastal storm hazards, we recommend a practical solution to this critical problem through the integration of hazard mitigation measures with the workaday tools used by governments to manage urban development.

Our thesis is that land use planning and development management offer government officials a practical and feasible way to mitigate the destructive effects of hurricanes and other severe coastal storms. We agree with those who advocate these approaches as among the most promising weapons in the mitigation arsenal (White et al. 1976; Simpson and Riehl 1981). On the basis of our national study of hurricane hazard reduction through development management, we disagree with the pessimists who say that such approaches, while potentially effective, are not politically feasible (Rossi, Wright, and Weber-Burdin 1982). On the contrary, although we recognize powerful obstacles blocking effective hurricane and coastal storm mitigation, we believe that the potential for coordinated intergovernmental programs, in which local development management programs are encouraged and reinforced by strong federal and state mitigation policy, is now greater than ever. The problem is clear, and a solution is at hand; motivated decisionmakers can avert coastal catastrophe if they will take up the challenge.

The Coast as a Risky Commons

Americans view the coast as a national commons where we can find bountiful recreation opportunities and, if we are lucky, sites for retirement or second homes. Images of coastal enjoyment are deeply ingrained in our collective psyche. Coupled with steeply rising coastal real estate values, the combined visions of fun and profit are powerful lures to visitors and investors. Demographic statistics indicate that population growth within five miles of Gulf and Atlantic coastal areas has been three times as fast as that of the nation as a whole (Baker 1979). And during the summer, which is also the annual hurricane season, tourists swell the coastal population manyfold. As of 1984, 66.5 million people (over 28 percent of the nation's population) lived in counties within fifty miles of the hurricane-prone Atlantic and Gulf coast shorelines, at densities much greater than the national average (U.S. Bureau of the Census 1986, 9). Although not all people within these counties face the same storm risks as those on the immediate shorelines, the flooding and tornadoes that accompany a major hurricane can reach far inland.

Few of today's coastal residents understand how a hurricane can damage their beautiful shorefront commons. Some three-quarters of the 1985 population in counties facing the Atlantic and Gulf coasts have moved there since the last direct hit by a major hurricane. According to the National Hurricane Center, this includes almost thirty-two million of the approximately forty-three million residents in these hurricane-prone counties (Hebert et al. 1984; Hebert 1987). Table 1.1 shows the distribution of state population increases since the last direct hit.

Our dominant coastal images involve enjoying sunny skies and sandy beaches rather than fleeing from hurricane winds and storm surges. Yet

Table 1.1   Percentage of Atlantic and Gulf Coastal County Population
Never Experiencing a Direct Hit by a Major Hurricane (by state)

State	1985	At Last Major Hurricane[a]	Increase	% of 1985 Total
Texas	4,317,800	1,991,525	2,326,477	53.9
Louisiana	1,658,900	1,145,440	513,460	31.0
Mississippi	324,700	324,700	0	0.0
Alabama	469,100	452,027	17,073	3.6
Florida	8,939,600	1,189,073	7,750,527	86.7
Georgia	353,800	0	353,800	100.0
South Carolina	580,300	344,700	235,600	40.6
North Carolina	543,400	379,627	163,773	30.1
Virginia	1,407,000	28,901	1,378,099	97.9
Maryland	2,395,000	0	2,395,000	100.0
Delaware	622,000	0	622,000	100.0
New Jersey	3,818,000	0	3,818,000	100.0
New York	10,764,400	2,311,384	8,453,016	78.5
Connecticut	1,978,300	1,108,374	869,926	44.0
Rhode Island	968,000	818,933	149,067	15.4
Massachusetts	3,003,100	926,619	2,076,481	69.1
New Hampshire	214,000	0	214,000	100.0
Maine	580,500	0	580,500	100.0
All	42,937,900		31,916,799	74.3

Source: Hebert 1987.
Note: Direct hits were calculated by the National Hurricane Center based on the extent of maximum winds in the hurricane center at time of landfall. Major hurricane: ≥3 on Saffir/Simpson Hurricane Scale.
a. State totals are based on individual county populations at time of last major hurricane since 1900 (different years).

these negative and often downplayed dangers of coastal life are increasingly significant, precisely because they are underestimated in urban development policy. Coastal development plans, public or private, rarely account for the costs of rebuilding after a hurricane; yet these costs can be staggering to affected individuals, governments, and insurers. By the year 2000 hurricane winds and storm surges are expected to become the leading source of natural hazard per capita property losses, due to the migration of population and investment capital into hazard-prone areas (Petak and Atkisson 1982, 199). Concerned about the accumulation of catastrophic risk and its consequences for insurance losses, the insurance industry has conducted a study examining the effects of two $7-billion-loss hurricanes, seen as a possibility because of the large concentrations of property located along the Atlantic and Gulf coastlines (All-Industry Research Advisory Council 1986). The study concluded that although the existing private insurance system works well in spreading risk among U.S. and international underwriters and reinsurers, two successive $7 billion losses would severely damage the property-casualty insurance industry, resulting in numerous bankruptcies.

Property loss is not the only risk from future coastal storms. Although hurricane-caused fatalities since the tragic 6,000 deaths recorded in the 1900 Galveston hurricane have declined to an average of less than ten per storm in recent years, there is an alarming potential for another killer hurricane due to the increasing population in exposed urban areas. Meteorologists appear to have reached the limits of their hurricane warning capability and thus are no longer able to increase the average warning time of an expected hurricane strike. But while warning times are leveling off, the time required to evacuate people from the path of a hurricane continues to rise by as much as an hour per year in major at-risk metropolitan areas due to continuing urban growth (Griffith 1985). A recent article from the National Hurricane Center (Sheets 1985) stated that evacuation of only the vulnerable residents of exposed communities such as the Tampa Bay area, the Fort Myers area, the Florida Keys, and Miami and Fort Lauderdale, Florida, as well as Galveston, Texas, and Hilton Head, South Carolina, requires evacuation lead times of twenty to thirty hours or more. According to Baker (1979, 263), "The United States may be on the verge of a hurricane disaster involving losses of life not experienced since the turn of the century."

The coastal storm hazard policy problem thus can be defined as continuing urban growth in high-risk coastal areas without a corresponding growth in our ability to protect developed property or to evacuate exposed populations in threatened areas. While some coastal developers may recognize the threat (Miller and Bachman 1984), government action is needed to ensure that a comprehensive policy is put in place. Unless an effective solution is found, the sum of the individual decisions to exploit the coastal commons could add up to a series of unparalleled national disasters. A study of natural hazard management in coastal areas concluded the following:

> The disproportionately rapid growth of population in coastal areas makes coastal areas more vulnerable to disaster than many inland areas.
>
> The opportunities to reverse the trends by encouraging coordinated land and water management are more promising than in other parts of the nation.
>
> How these opportunities are grasped will influence whether future events will include a series of national catastrophes . . . or conversely, a gradual reduction in national vulnerability to disaster. (White et al. 1976, I-1)

Coastal Hazard Mitigation as a Policy Issue

Both public officials and private developers accept the public interest in keeping the coast open to the people while protecting them from the dangers of coastal storms. The policy challenge lies in striking the appropriate balance between coastal development and hazard mitigation, between economic growth and public safety. Conflict occurs when governments attempt to implement programs that intervene in the market in order to guide development into safe patterns.

Why is this a public policy issue? A hurricane or severe coastal storm in an undeveloped area affects only the natural environment; for a disaster involving injury, death, and property destruction to occur, there must have been human decisions to develop hazard-prone areas in the path of this storm. Otherwise these natural events would have few consequences. Three types of coastal storm impacts argue for government intervention into coastal development processes: threats to public health, safety, and welfare; costs to taxpayers for disaster relief and protection; and losses of irreplaceable natural resources. All of these impacts could be reduced by enacting and implementing effective public coastal storm hazard policy.

Health, Safety, and Welfare Threats
Coastal storm threats to public health, safety, and welfare result from the high winds, storm surges, flooding, and erosion that accompany severe

Table 1.2   Expected Annual Natural Hazard Losses: 1970 and 2000

Hazard	Per Capita ($) 1970/2000	Annual (mil$) 1970/2000	Deaths 1970/2000	Housing Units 1970/2000
Hurricane[a]	8.36/22.92	1697.2/5869.2	99/256	56,406/95,994
Tornado	8.12/20.38	1656.0/5219.1	392/920	36,212/52,119
River. Flood	13.57/12.40	2758.3/3175.3	190/159	—/—
Earthquake	3.83/6.07	781.1/1553.7	273/400	20,485/22,868
Expans. Soil	3.93/3.89	798.1/997.1	—/—	—/—
Landslide	1.82/3.40	370.3/871.2	—/—	—/—
Severe Wind	.06/.19	18.0/53.4	5/11	547/748
Tsunami	.07/.16	15.0/40.4	20/44	234/335

Source: Petak and Atkisson 1982, tables 5.3, 5.8, 5.9, 5.10. All in 1970 dollars.
a. Hurricane losses are combined hurricane winds and storm surge, calculated separately by Petak and Atkisson.

storms. Hurricanes, although not the only type of coastal storm, are the most severe storms, and those with the most commonly measured damages. As shown in table 1.2, between 1970 and 2000 property losses from hurricanes are expected to become the most serious of all natural hazard losses (Petak and Atkisson 1982). Hurricane losses in the year 2000 are expected to top all other natural hazards in terms of per capita ($22.92) and annual ($5.9 billion) dollar losses, as well as housing units lost (96,000). Hurricanes thus replace riverine flooding as the top source of per capita and annual losses and maintain their position as the top source of housing units lost. Only in terms of expected deaths are hurricanes not the most serious natural hazard, ranking third behind tornadoes and earthquakes in death loss estimates for the year 2000. Even so, hurricane deaths are expected to rise over 150 percent by the end of the century, indicating the substantial risks to life faced by coastal residents and emergency crews.

These estimated year 2000 losses are not inevitable. Changes in public policy can substantially reduce the expected future losses. By requiring increased wind resistance and floodproofing and by prohibiting new construction in high-risk areas, hurricane losses can be cut drastically. (Petak and Atkisson 1982, ch. 6) However, even the expected high property losses have not been sufficient to motivate individuals or developers to avoid or mitigate on their own the hazards of high-impact but low-

Table 1.3   National Flood Insurance Program:
Losses and Premiums in Hurricane-Prone States, 1978–1986

	Loss Payments		Premium Payments
	No.	Amount ($000)	Amount ($000)
Alabama	7,228	87,473	20,783
Connecticut	5,588	34,054	22,958
Delaware	421	1,909	8,512
Florida	25,191	163,530	794,528
Georgia	1,249	8,232	21,293
Hawaii	710	10,344	15,233
Louisiana	62,728	497,265	257,485
Maine	1,022	5,713	7,752
Maryland	2,344	21,803	24,483
Massachusetts	5,888	33,679	42,282
Mississippi	12,646	102,845	40,702
New Jersey	17,666	113,285	147,220
New York	28,527	101,770	98,041
North Carolina	2,173	12,711	41,160
Rhode Island	837	7,690	13,860
South Carolina	1,268	4,070	46,037
Texas	54,507	567,188	355,076
Virginia	3,898	55,110	36,736
Total	233,891	1,828,671	1,994,141

Source: Federal Insurance Administration 1987.

probability events such as hurricanes. Thus the responsibility falls on governments to act in order to protect the public health, safety, and welfare.

Disaster Costs

Coastal storms cost the federal and state treasuries millions of dollars annually, spreading the costs of protecting coastal development among all U.S. taxpayers. One indicator of the public costs is the amount of federal flood insurance loss claims: over $1.8 billion paid in hurricane-prone states between 1978 and 1986 (see table 1.3). While not all of these losses were due to hurricanes or coastal storms, many of them were. About 73 percent of the national flood insurance coverage is in coastal communities, and coastal claims made up 54 percent of claims payments from 1968 to 1984 (Platt 1985). Another indicator of public costs is the amount paid in disaster assistance. Coastal flooding accounted for 49 percent ($265 million of $539 million) of 1981–1984 federal disaster aid obligations (Platt 1985). And this does not include losses to the local tax base and hence losses in state and local tax revenues resulting from flood damage.

These costs can be reduced by policy changes designed to remove development incentives from hazardous areas. For example, the Coastal Barrier Resources Act of 1982 withdraws federal flood insurance and financial assistance to infrastructure such as roads and bridges within designated "undeveloped" areas of Atlantic and Gulf coastal barriers. This act could save the federal treasury $5.4 billion over twenty years (Godschalk 1984). State and local governments also can realize significant cost savings if intensive development is prevented in high-hazard areas.

Loss of Natural Resources

Coastal areas are rich in natural resources, which are lost through counterproductive efforts to protect development in hazard areas from coastal storms. Beaches, dunes, and wetlands are destroyed both by construction of poorly planned and located public and private projects and by construction of protective works such as seawalls to armor these projects from coastal erosion and storm surges (Pilkey et al. 1983). Construction in these areas interferes with the geological and ecological processes that maintain the natural protective and productive coastal systems. Estuarine wetlands have been damaged by dredge-and-fill activities and by contamination from runoff and wastes. Seawalls and groins have provided localized storm protection but have caused loss of beaches and dunes due to increased erosion from wave action and interference with normal patterns of sand transportation by ocean currents (Platt 1985).

Coastal area management programs can prevent the loss of natural resources through development regulations. By combining preventive measures such as shorefront building setbacks with restrictions on coastal armoring, governments can protect the natural resource systems necessary to maintain the beaches, as well as to safeguard future coastal development. For example, North Carolina has enacted setback regulations that require all major structures in locations subject to ocean erosion to be setback sixty times the annual erosion rate and has prohibited the further construction of seawalls and other permanent protective structures.

Development is not the only cause of natural resource damage, however. Ongoing coastal erosion, hastened by storms, is continually pushing back the coastline. Recent scientific studies have shown a major acceleration of sea level rise, probably caused by the gradual warming of the earth's atmosphere due to the "greenhouse effect" (Titus 1986). The buildup of gases in the atmosphere traps radiant energy that would normally pass outward into space, heating the atmosphere and speeding up glacial and ice sheet melting, which in turn raises ocean levels. While the average sea level rise over the last century has been less than a foot (10 to 15 centimeters), an increase of that much or more (10 to 20 centimeters) is projected by 2025 and of between 1.5 and 6.5 feet (50 to 200 centimeters) is projected by the year 2100. Using the average of one meter of shoreline erosion for each centimeter of sea level rise, the resulting average erosion by 2025 would be 10 to 20 meters (32.8 to 65.6 feet)! According to Titus (1986, 241), "A substantial rise in sea level would permanently inundate wetlands and lowlands, accelerate coastal erosion, exacerbate coastal flooding, and increase the salinity of estuaries and aquifers." He notes that erosion caused by sea level rise could wipe out recreational beaches and greatly increase the costs of flood protection and flood insurance. While Titus concludes that the adverse impacts of sea level rise could be ameliorated through anticipatory land use planning and structural design changes, sea level rise remains to be incorporated into local land use plans in most areas (National Research Council 1987).

Coastal Storm Threats

Coastal storms fall into two types: hurricanes and other severe storms. Both cause coastal erosion and flooding, but hurricanes add two additional threats—destructively high winds and storm surges. Hurricane winds range from 75 mph to as much as 200 mph. Their storm surges are domes of water forty to fifty miles across and from four to twenty feet above sea level which move onto the shore when the hurricane strikes land. Up to 90 percent of hurricane-related deaths and property damage are caused by storm surges.

Table 1.4   The Saffir/Simpson Hurricane Scale

Scale No. 1:   Winds of 74 to 95 miles per hour. Damage primarily to shrubbery, trees, foliage, and unanchored mobile homes. No real damage to other structures. Some damage to poorly constructed signs. And/or: storm surge 4 to 5 feet above normal. Low-lying coastal roads inundated, minor pier damage, some small craft in exposed anchorage torn from moorings.

Scale No. 2:   Winds of 96 to 110 miles per hour. Considerable damage to shrubbery and tree foliage; some trees blown down. Major damage to exposed mobile homes. Extensive damage to poorly constructed signs. Some damage to roofing materials of buildings; some window and door damage. No major damage to buildings. And/or: storm surge 6 to 8 feet above normal. Coastal roads and low-lying escape routes inland cut by rising water 2 to 4 hours before arrival of hurricane center. Considerable damage to piers. Marinas flooded. Small craft in unprotected anchorages torn from moorings. Evacuation of some shoreline residences and low-lying island areas required.

Scale No. 3:   Winds of 111 to 130 miles per hour. Foliage torn from trees; large trees blown down. Practically all poorly constructed signs blown down. Some damage to roofing materials of buildings; some window and door damage. Some structural damage to small buildings. Mobile homes destroyed. And/or: storm surge 9 to 12 feet above normal. Serious flooding at coast and many smaller structures near coast destroyed; larger structures near coast damaged by battering waves and floating debris. Low-lying escape routes inland cut by rising water 3 to 5 hours before hurricane center arrives. Flat terrain 5 feet or less above sea level flooded inland 8 miles or more. Evacuation of low-lying residences within several blocks of shoreline possibly required.

Scale No. 4:   Winds of 131 to 155 miles per hour. Shrubs and trees blown down; all signs down. Extensive damage to roofing materials, windows, and doors. Complete failure of roofs on many small residences. Complete destruction of mobile homes. And/or: storm surge 13 to 18 feet above normal. Flat terrain 10 feet or less above sea level flooded inland as far as 6 miles. Major damage to lower floors of structures near shore due to flooding and battering by waves and

Table 1.4   (Continued)

floating debris. Low-lying escape routes inland cut by rising water 3 to 5 hours before hurricane center arrives. Major erosion of beaches. Massive evacuation of all residences within 500 yards of shore possibly required and of single-story residences on low ground within 2 miles of shore.

Scale No. 5:   Winds greater than 155 miles per hour. Shrubs and trees blown down; considerable damage to roofs of buildings; all signs down. Very severe and extensive damage to windows and doors. Complete failure of roofs on many residences and industrial buildings. Extensive shattering of glass in windows and doors. Some complete building failures. Small buildings overturned or blown away. Complete destruction of mobile homes. And/or: storm surge greater than 18 feet above normal. Major damage to lower floors of all structures less than 15 feet above sea level within 500 yards of shore. Low-lying escape routes inland cut by rising water 3 to 5 hours before hurricane center arrives. Massive evacuation of residential areas on low ground within 5 to 10 miles of shore possibly required.

Source: Charles J. Neumann et al. 1981.

The major focus of this book is on mitigating hurricane damage because it is potentially the greatest due to the threat of shoreline wind and water surge atop rising floods. However, we recognize that the aggregate effects of a season of "northeasters" or other severe coastal storms can be significant, especially in terms of erosion. Because the mitigation actions taken for hurricanes also reduce damage from other coastal storms, our analysis applies to the full range of coastal storm threats.

Hurricanes are cyclonic storms formed by the release of latent heat from ocean water condensation (Simpson and Riehl 1981). U.S. hurricanes are characterized by counterclockwise, circular hurricane-force winds ranging out some 100 miles around a calm eye averaging 15 miles in diameter and by unusually low barometric pressure which generates sea level rise. Atlantic hurricanes generally occur between June and November, with the largest concentrations between August and October. They

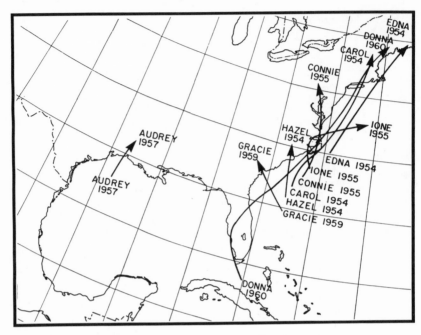

Figure 1.1   Major U.S. Hurricanes, 1951–1960 (hurricanes in category 3 or greater). *Source*: Hebert 1987.

are classified according to their wind speed on the Saffir/Simpson Hurricane Scale, which is summarized below (see table 1.4 for the complete scale description).

Category	Wind Speed (mph)	Surge (ft)	Damage
1	74–95	4–5	Minimal
2	96–110	6–8	Moderate
3	111–130	9–12	Extensive
4	131–155	13–18	Extreme
5	over 155	over 18	Catastrophic

Hurricanes are high-intensity, low-probability events. Their strikes are not predictable on a small area basis, although their regional occurrence within the Atlantic and Gulf states is an annual event. Figures 1.1 through 1.4 show the paths of hurricanes striking this region since midcentury.

Since the turn of the century, on the average two major hurricanes

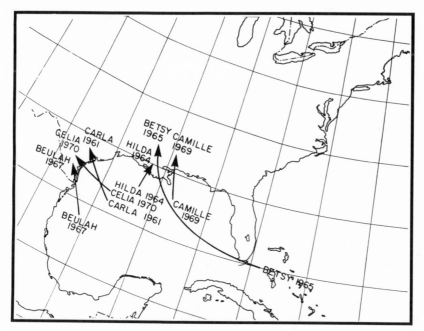

Figure 1.2   Major U.S. Hurricanes, 1961–1970 (hurricanes in category 3 or greater). *Source*: Hebert 1987.

(capable of causing billions of dollars of damage and killing hundreds) cross the U.S. coast somewhere *every three years* (Hebert, Taylor, and Case 1984, 10). Between 1900 and 1982, 136 hurricanes, including 55 major hurricanes, affected the U.S. coast (see table 1.5).

Hurricanes approach land with some warning. Their speed of onset is usually a matter of days, unlike rapid onset hazards such as tornadoes. Their length of forewarning varies with the particular hurricane, but forecasters seek to provide twelve daylight hours of warning time for the predicted strike area. Their duration of strike is typically a matter of hours. Their impact areas are large, affecting a broad swath of coastline as well as substantial areas of inland flooding. Hurricanes are not controllable, in the sense that riverine floods are, but their effects can be mitigated by prestorm actions. Their destructive potential is high but varies with the amount of population and development in the strike area.

Hurricanes damage the built environment through direct hurricane

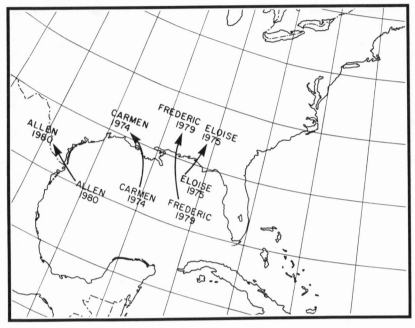

Figure 1.3   Major U.S. Hurricanes, 1971–1980 (hurricanes in category 3 or greater). *Source*: Hebert 1987.

wind forces, flying debris and materials, penetration of wind-driven water and rain into structural interiors, hydrodynamic forces (direct wave attack), hydrostatic forces (stillwater flooding), water-based battering ram effects, and tornado forces (wind and pressure effects) (Collier et al. 1977). The destructive forces of coastal storms and hurricanes pose major threats to people and property in their path. Most public policy for coping with these threats has been reactive, aimed at enhancing emergency management capabilities. With the growth in exposed populations and property, however, proactive policy increasingly is needed to anticipate and mitigate potential risks.

The Dynamic and Vulnerable Shore

Hurricanes and coastal storms have different effects, depending on the type of shore they strike. According to coastal geologists, coasts can be

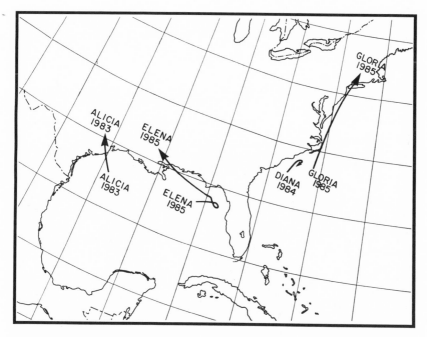

Figure 1.4 Major U.S. Hurricanes, 1980–1987 (hurricanes in category 3 or greater). *Source*: Hebert 1987.

classified as either "primary" coasts resulting from nonmarine processes such as glacial scour and delta buildup or "secondary" coasts resulting from marine processes such as wave erosion (Pilkey et al. 1983). Maine's rocky coast typifies a primary shore. Cape Cod typifies a secondary shore.

Barrier islands, formed by depositional marine processes at the end of the last ice age, are a secondary type. Much of the Atlantic coast is fronted by barrier islands, which have a natural tendency to migrate landward in response to sea level rise. These barrier islands, with their sandy beaches, are extremely attractive to coastal developers, but attempts to stabilize them to protect development often wind up destroying the beaches.

Beaches include the entire zone of mobile sand along the shore, extending seaward to a water depth of about thirty feet. Beaches exist in dynamic equilibrium controlled by wave energy, beach shape, beach sand supply, and sea level. When one of these factors changes, as during a storm, the

Table 1.5   Number of Hurricanes Affecting United States
and Individual States, 1900–1982

Area	Category Number (Saffir/Simpson Hurricane Scale)					All	Major Hurricanes ($\geqslant$3)
	1	2	3	4	5		
U.S. (Texas to Maine)	48	33	40	13	2	136	55
Texas	9	9	8	6	0	32	14
North	4	3	2	4	0	13	6
Central	2	2	1	1	0	6	2
South	3	4	5	1	0	13	6
Louisiana	5	5	7	3	1	21	11
Mississippi	1	1	4	0	1	7	5
Alabama	4	1	4	0	0	9	4
Florida	16	14	15	5	1	51	21
Northwest	9	6	5	0	0	20	5
Northeast	1	7	0	0	0	8	0
Southwest	5	3	5	2	1	16	8
Southeast	4	10	7	3	0	24	10
Georgia	1	4	0	0	0	5	0
South Carolina	5	4	2	1[a]	0	12	3
North Carolina	9	3	6	1[a]	0	19	7
Virginia	1	1	1[a]	0	0	3	1[a]
Maryland	0	1[a]	0	0	0	1[a]	0
Delaware	0	0	0	0	0	0	0
New Jersey	1[a]	0	0	0	0	1[a]	0
New York	3	0	4[a]	0	0	7	4[a]
Connecticut	2	1[a]	3[a]	0	0	6	3[a]
Rhode Island	0	1[a]	3[a]	0	0	4[a]	3[a]
Massachusetts	2	1[a]	2[a]	0	0	5	2[a]
New Hampshire	1[a]	0	0	0	0	1[a]	0
Maine	4	0	0	0	0	4	0

Source: Hebert, Taylor, and Case 1984.
Note: State totals will not equal U.S. totals, and Texas and Florida sectional totals will not
equal state totals.
a. Indicates all hurricanes in this category were moving more than 30 mph.

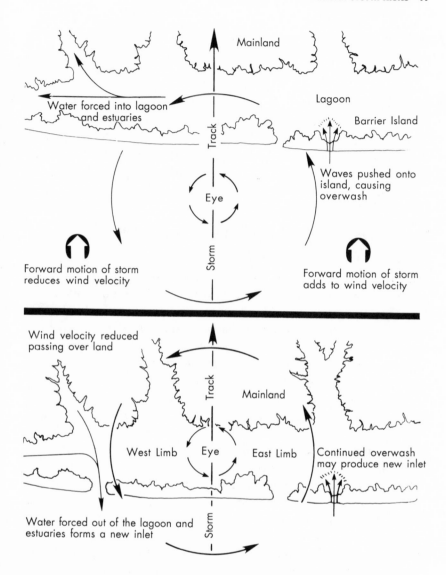

Figure 1.5   Hurricane Impacts: The Forward Progress of a Typical Hurricane across a Hypothetical Barrier Island Chain. *Source*: Pilkey et al. 1983, adapted from figure 8.2, p. 166.

other three shift in response. The natural beach responds to a storm by flattening itself or building offshore sandbars or both. These changes dissipate the force of massive storm waves. Beaches also change in response to normal erosion from wave action. This is, however, a much more gradual process than the radical changes wrought by hurricane forces.

Hurricanes massively alter the equilibrium of beaches and barrier islands. As figure 1.5 illustrates, they can overwash narrow barrier islands, flatten dunes and man-made structures, cut new inlets, and flood lagoons and estuaries. They concentrate all of nature's power on particular stretches of shoreline.

The Mitigation Gap in Coastal Storm Hazard Policy

Concern with natural hazard mitigation policy is relatively recent. Mitigation is included in the floodplain management and flooded property purchase provisions of the National Flood Insurance Act of 1968 and in the hazard mitigation planning provisions of Section 406 of the Disaster Relief Act of 1974, but federal emphasis on mitigation dates largely from the 1980s (May and Williams 1986). Some state and local governments have incorporated natural hazard mitigation into their development policies, but the majority have not. According to one analyst, "the lack of success that federal mitigation policy has enjoyed to date must lead to questions about the capacity and/or willingness on the part of state and local governments to undertake strong mitigation measures" (Clary 1985, 22). In fact, the lack of mitigation success can be attributed to problems at all levels of government, including the federal level.

To understand the relationship of mitigation to other disaster management activities, it is necessary to review the accepted natural hazard management model. This conceptual model consists of a four-stage process centered on an emergency event or disaster, such as a storm (see figure 1.6). Those stages taking place before the disaster are termed the mitigation and preparedness stages, those after the response and recovery stages. In practice the stages are not distinct. For example, mitigation overlaps preparedness and recovery.

Mitigation includes long-term actions to prevent, avoid, or reduce the impacts of a hazard. Mitigation takes place both before a disaster strikes and during the recovery phase after a disaster in anticipation of the next

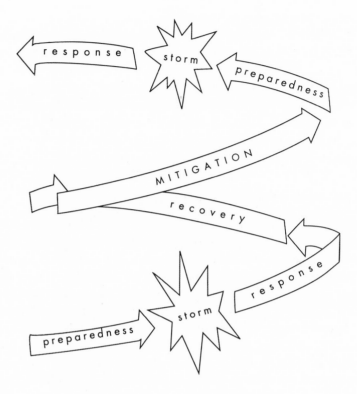

Figure 1.6   Disaster Response Stages

disaster. It is aimed at reducing the vulnerability of both people and property to injury from the hazard.

Preparedness includes the short-term activities undertaken after a disaster warning is received, such as evacuating exposed populations and attempting temporary property protection to save lives and reduce disaster damage.

Response includes the short-term emergency aid and assistance actions following the disaster strike. It is aimed at search and rescue, provision of food, shelter, and medical facilities, restoration of public services, removal of health hazards, and clearance of debris.

Recovery includes the immediate support necessary to restore minimum operating conditions and the longer-term actions to return the community to normal. Recovery combines rebuilding with opportunities for community change and improvement.

Until recent years, federal, state, and local coastal storm hazard policies have focused on the emergency management function embodied in the preparedness and response stages. Much less attention has been given to the longer-term hazard mitigation function focused on improving capabilities to withstand future disasters. Hazard mitigation has gained ground during the 1980s, but there is still a commitment and capability gap in state and local implementation. This book seeks to outline a strategy for filling this critical gap.

The Intergovernmental Mitigation Arena

Coastal storm hazard mitigation policy is created by a complex of intergovernmental actions and actors. A number of state and federal laws influence mitigation, and a number of public agencies play roles in mitigation programs. May and Williams (1986) term this "shared governance," in which responsibilities and decisionmaking are spread among federal, state, and local government agencies. Their analysis, taking a "top-down" view, points out federal disaster policy implementation gaps. Our analysis takes a "bottom-up" view, focusing on *local* disaster mitigation in the context of the overall intergovernmental system. We start with the local level where mitigation action occurs, but we recognize the critical influence of state and federal policy on that action.

Balancing competing demands for coastal development versus disaster mitigation is complicated by fragmentation of governmental authority. The shoreline falls under overlapping local, state, and federal agency jurisdictions. Over half the respondents to a survey of coastal barrier local governments reported that at least one other municipality shared jurisdiction over the same barrier, and about two-thirds said that conflict among planning goals, policies, and laws was a primary concern (Platt and Callahan 1987). What may appear to be a coastal commons is in fact a complex patchwork quilt of organizational turfs.

To understand the dynamics of mitigation policy and practice, it is necessary to understand this institutional shared governance framework, as well as the technical side of mitigation. The organization of this book is based upon the need to grasp both the institutional and the technical aspects in order to appreciate the feasibility and logic of our recommendations.

The increasingly serious policy problem of the rise in urban growth in coastal hazard areas has been stated in this chapter. The major alternative approaches to mitigating hurricane and coastal storm hazards are reviewed in chapter 2. To illustrate the evolution of U.S. mitigation policy and practice, and its remaining gaps, case studies of redevelopment following three major hurricanes during the past two decades are presented in chapter 3. Current federal mitigation programs and policies are discussed in chapter 4, and chapter 5 describes present mitigation programs and policies at the state level, with particular focus on the coastal management programs of two leading states: North Carolina and Florida. Local mitigation tools and techniques, the elements of an integrated development management and hazard mitigation strategy, are covered in chapter 6. The current mitigation practice of high-risk coastal localities, as revealed in a survey conducted by the authors, is analyzed in chapter 7. Causal influences on the perceived priority, adoption, and effectiveness of mitigation are identified and modeled in chapter 8. Finally, chapter 9 summarizes the conclusions of the research and presents recommendations for changes in mitigation policy and practice at local, state, and federal governmental levels.

References

All-Industry Research Advisory Council. 1986. "Catastrophic Losses: How the Insurance System Would Handle Two $7 Billion Hurricanes." Oak Brook, Ill.

Baker, Earl J. 1979. "Geographical Variations in Hurricane Risks and Legislative Response." *Coastal Zone Management Journal* 5, no. 4: 263–283.

Beatley, Timothy, David Brower, and David Godschalk. 1984. *The Hurricane Hazard: A Literature Review and Conceptual Framework*. Chapel Hill, N.C.: University of North Carolina, Center for Urban and Regional Studies.

Clary, Bruce. 1985. "The Evolution and Structure of Natural Hazard Policies." *Public Administration Review* 45 (January): 20–28.

Collier, Courtland A., et al. 1977. *Guidelines for Beachfront Construction with Special Reference to the Coastal Construction Setback Line*. Gainesville, Fla.: Florida Sea Grant Program.

Federal Insurance Administration. 1987. Personal correspondence with Claudia Murphy, Office of Insurance Support Services, November 30, 1987, providing premium and claims information by state.

Godschalk, David R. 1984. *Impacts of the Coastal Barrier Resources Act: A Pilot Study*. Washington, D.C.: Office of Ocean and Coastal Resource Management, U.S. Department of Commerce.

Godschalk, David R., and David J. Brower. 1985. "Mitigation Strategies and Integrated Emergency Management." *Public Administration Review* 45 (January): 64–71.

Griffith, David. 1985. "Hurricane Preparedness: Progress and Prognosis." Talk at Emergency 85, May 21, 1985, Washington, D.C.

Hebert, Paul J., Glenn Taylor, and Robert A. Case. 1984. *Hurricane Experience Levels of Coastal County Populations—Texas to Maine*. Miami, Fla.: National Hurricane Center.

Hebert, Paul J. 1987. Personal correspondence, updating data on hurricane experience levels to 1985. Miami, Fla., National Hurricane Center. July 15.

May, Peter J., and Walter Williams. 1986. *Disaster Policy Implementation: Managing Programs under Shared Governance*. New York, N.Y.: Plenum Press.

Miller, Christopher, and Geraldine Bachman. 1984. "Planning for Hurricanes and Other Coastal Disturbances." *Urban Land* 43, no. 1, (January): 18–23.

National Research Council. 1987. *Responding to Changes in Sea Level: Engineering Implications*. Washington, D.C.: National Academy Press.

Neumann, Charles J., et al. 1981. *Tropical Cyclones of the North Atlantic Ocean, 1971–1980*. Asheville, N.C.: National Climatic Center.

Petak, William, and Arthur Atkisson. 1982. *Natural Hazard Risk Assessment and Public Policy*. New York, N.Y.: Springer-Verlag.

Pilkey, Orrin H., Sr., et al. 1983. *Coastal Design*. New York, N.Y.: Van Nostrand Reinhold.

Platt, Rutherford. 1985. "Congress and the Coast." *Environment* 27, no. 6 (July/August): 12–17, 34–40.

Platt, Rutherford, and Keane Callahan. 1987. "The Political Geography of Developed Coastal Barriers." In *Cities on the Beach: Management Issues of Developed Coastal Barriers*, edited by Rutherford Platt, Sheila Pelczarski, and Barbara Burbank. Chicago, Ill.: University of Chicago, Department of Geography.

Rossi, Peter, James Wright, and Eleanor Weber-Burdin. 1982. *Natural Hazards and Public Choice: The State and Local Politics of Hazard Mitigation*. New York, N.Y.: Academic Press.

Sheets, Robert. 1985. "The National Weather Service Hurricane Probability Program." *Bulletin of the American Meteorological Society* 66, no. 1 (January): 4–6.

Simpson, Robert H., and Herbert Riehl. 1981. *The Hurricane and Its Impact*. Baton Rouge, La.: Louisiana State University Press.

Titus, James G. 1986. "The Causes and Effects of Sea Level Rise." In *Effects of Changes in Stratospheric Ozone and Global Climate*, edited by James G. Titus, 1:219–248. Washington, D.C.: U.S. Environmental Protection Agency.

U.S. Bureau of the Census. 1986. *Statistical Abstract of the United States, 1986*. Washington, D.C.: U.S. Department of Commerce.

White, Gilbert F., et al. 1976. *Natural Hazard Management in Coastal Areas*. Washington, D.C.: National Oceanic and Atmospheric Administration.

2 Alternative Approaches to Mitigating Coastal Storm Hazards

Major Types of Mitigation Approaches

The policy problem of coping with coastal disasters is not new. Two thousand people were killed in a hurricane at Charleston, South Carolina, just before the turn of the century, and 6,000 were killed in the Galveston hurricane in 1900. But the *scope* of the problem has grown as more urban development has taken place in the exposed hazard areas so that exposures of large amounts of property and human populations to hurricane threats are no longer rare and isolated events. As the problem has increased, so has the variety of mitigation approaches devised to cope with it.

Early approaches attempted to hold back storm forces through seawalls and dikes. For example, following the disastrous 1900 hurricane in Galveston, a 15.5-foot-high seawall extending for ten miles was constructed to protect the developed portions of the island. Later approaches added floodproofing and windproofing of buildings exposed to hazards, warning systems, comprehensive evacuation plans to move people to safety, and insurance to compensate property owners for disaster losses. Experiments in seeding hurricanes with silver iodide to reduce windspeed were attempted with inconclusive results (White et al. 1976).

More recently, land use or development management has been advocated as a comprehensive approach to hazard mitigation (Godschalk and Brower 1985; White and Haas 1975). Under this approach the type, location, rate, public cost, and quality of development and redevelopment within hazard areas are managed so as to promote sound urban

Table 2.1 Primary Approaches to Reducing Coastal Storm Hazards

---

A. Alteration of Coastal Environment
  1. Sand-trapping Structures
    a. Groins
    b. Jetties
  2. Sand-moving Programs
    a. Beach nourishment
    b. Sand-scraping
  3. Shoreline Protection Works
    a. Seawalls
    b. Revetments
    c. Bulkheads
    d. Terraces
    e. Breakwaters
  4. Flood Control Works
    a. Dams
    b. Dikes and levees
    c. Retaining ponds
    d. Flood channels

B. Strengthening Buildings and Facilities
  1. Strengthening Buildings
    a. Floodproofing
    b. Elevating
    c. Windproofing
  2. Srengthening Facilities
    a. Floodproofing
    b. Burial
    c. Elevating

C. Evacuation
  1. Horizontal
  2. Vertical

D. Development Management
  1. Planning
    a. General comprehensive planning
    b. Storm hazard mitigation and poststorm reconstruction plans

Table 2.1   (Continued)

---

   2. Development Regulation
     a. Zoning
     b. Subdivision regulations
   3. Land and Property Acquisition
     a. Fee-simple acquisition of undeveloped land
     b. Relocation of existing development
     c. Purchase of development rights/easements
     d. Transfer of development rights
   4. Taxation, Fiscal, and Other Incentives
     a. Differential taxation
     b. Special assessments and impact fees
   5. Capital Facilities Policy
   6. Information Dissemination

---

patterns while reducing the exposure of people and property to hazard risks. Hazard mitigation becomes one of several public objectives of development management, which also seeks efficient, equitable, and environmentally conserving land use patterns.

Coastal storm mitigation has been applied to all the potential goals of hazard reduction:

1. *Decreasing the vulnerability* of people and buildings to storm forces through armoring, stabilizing, conserving, and rebuilding the coastline and strengthening coastal buildings and facilities to withstand high winds and waters
2. *Reducing the exposure* of people and buildings to storm forces through providing for warning and evacuation of people in threatened areas, relocating existing houses at risk in hazardous locations, and guiding new growth and poststorm redevelopment to safer sites
3. *Modifying storm forces* themselves through experiments with cloud seeding aimed at reducing wind speeds within hurricanes

With the exception of storm modification, all of the mitigation approaches are in current use, though in different combinations and degrees of effectiveness.

In this chapter both the traditional and the newer mitigation approaches are described and their respective strengths and limitations identified. The four primary approaches discussed are: alteration of the coastal environment so that it better withstands storm forces, strengthening of buildings and accompanying facilities, evacuation of exposed populations, and hazard mitigation integrated with development management (see table 2.1). Since flood insurance is primarily after-the-storm compensation rather than before-the-storm mitigation, it will not be covered in this chapter beyond its effects on the primary approaches, but it is fully discussed in the chapter on federal programs.

These mitigation programs and techniques are applied both in *pre-storm* development and *poststorm* reconstruction stages. For instance, special storm-resistant building standards may be adopted in advance of a hurricane or coastal storm to apply to new construction, or they may be applied to the reconstruction and repair of structures damaged or destroyed by a storm. While these two mitigation stages obviously blend together, there are important differences between them, and where appropriate these will be discussed below.

Alteration of Coastal Environment

A traditional approach to protection against hurricanes and coastal storms is to strengthen, reinforce, or replenish the natural environment so that it is less susceptible to the physical forces exerted by storms. The two main measures are structural stabilization and beach nourishment. Four types of environmental alteration are described here: sand-trapping structures, sand-moving programs, shoreline protection works, and flood control works.

Coastal beaches are continuously in motion. Geologists have shown that beaches rely on a finite sand budget whose distribution is controlled by four factors (Pilkey et al. 1983):

1. Wave energy, which increases during storms, flattening the beach and building offshore sandbars
2. Beach shape or profile, which tends to flatten out during storms and grow steeper in calm weather
3. Sand supply, which varies in grain size (with coarser grains allowing

steeper beach slopes and more stable beaches) and in overall amount (with a constant need for replacement of the supply lost from winds, waves, and man-made structures)

4. Sea level, whose vertical rise pushes the shoreline landward, especially on low-lying coastlines, and accelerates beach erosion

Approaches to coastal environmental alteration seek to stabilize the moving beaches, holding back erosion and rising sea level. In the short run structural measures can keep man-made structures from falling into the sea, but they nearly always result in the ultimate narrowing and destruction of the beach. Nourishment maintains the beach but may be only a temporary solution.

Sand-trapping Structures

Sand-trapping structures are designed to protect, maintain, or enhance beaches and dunes which absorb storm impact and energy. They dam up the river of sand, changing the natural flow. *Groins* are structures extending into the ocean at right angles to the coast, typically constructed of concrete, timber, steel sheetpiling or riprap. Groins induce deposition of sand on the updrift side and in turn block lateral deposition in downdrift areas. *Jetties* are also built at right angles to the shore but generally extend further into the ocean and are often constructed in pairs to prevent shoaling in coastal inlets.

Sand-moving Programs

Natural processes of beach erosion and accretion can be supplemented through programs designed to move sand to "starved" areas from other areas where it is in greater abundance. *Beach nourishment* programs transport large amounts of sand to an area experiencing high rates of erosion, using pumps, dredges, and/or trucks. In this way existing beach and dune profiles are preserved by redistributing sand resources to correct for "sand budget" imbalances. Large scale nourishment programs can be very expensive and in areas of high erosion may require constant replenishment even to maintain existing shoreline levels. The recent Miami Beach replenishment project cost $64 million for fifteen miles of new beach sand (Pilkey et al. 1983, 150). *Sand-scraping* is a less expensive but more temporary way to reinforce a beach structure, for example, by filling-in behind protective seawalls and bulkheads using bulldozers and other earth-moving machinery.

Shoreline Protection Works

Shoreline protection works are structures designed to protect buildings and property from wave and water forces. *Seawalls* are vertical walls embedded in the earth to absorb wave energy, typically constructed from heavy concrete sheetpile, with a stepped-down or curved face (see U.S. Army Corps of Engineers 1981; Yasso and Hartman 1976; Walton and Sensabaugh 1983). *Bulkheads* are smaller vertical walls used to protect headland areas and inlet channels. *Revetments* have a similar purpose but may be angled and typically use riprap or interconnecting concrete blocks to protect dunes and beaches from erosion. *Terraces* are used in cliff areas and involve the insertion of vertical pilings and planks at different levels. *Breakwaters* are fixed or floating structures that parallel the coast, serving to reduce the energy of waves before they hit the shoreline.

Flood Control Works

Flood control works are designed to manage and reduce the damaging effects of flooding. They range from relatively small projects such as the construction of *retaining ponds* to hold excess storm water to the undertaking of large *dams* to control the movement of water in river systems. *Dikes* and *levees* are elevated earthen works used to protect against rising floodwaters. *Flood channels* are used to funnel and divert floodwaters away from developed areas. Flood control works have been a primary technique advocated by the U.S. Army Corps of Engineers in addressing hurricane and coastal storm risks. A series of levees and locks has been constructed on Lake Pontchartrain (New Orleans) to protect against and manage hurricane flooding (U.S. Army Corps of Engineers 1980). Kiawah Island, South Carolina, has developed a storm water management plan which includes a lagoon system, which can be emptied prior to a storm landfall (S.C. Water Resources Commission 1982). Texas City (near Galveston, Texas) has built a sixteen-mile long, earthen levee system (maximum height of twenty-three feet above mean sea level), along with a concrete floodwall drainage system, a closure gate, and pumping drainage stations designed to provide protection from fifteen-foot storm surges (Texas Department of Public Safety 1984). A similar project found in

Freeport (also near Galveston) includes thirty-eight miles of earthen levees, as well as drainage and pumping facilities, and a tide control gate.

Benefits and Limitations of Environmental Alteration

Environmental alteration measures have been used successfully to protect investments in existing coastal development from both ongoing erosion and sea level rise and from concentrated storm forces. Often where practical alternatives cannot be provided, such measures are the last defense against abandoning major buildings (such is the case for the major in-place investments at Miami Beach or Virginia Beach or Galveston), but these measures have high costs, both in monetary and environmental terms.

Structural reinforcement of the coast can be especially expensive. Seawalls, revetments, and other forms of protection walls can cost millions to build and are subject to costly maintenance. Though costs vary by location, Pilkey et al. (1983, 155) estimate seawalls to cost $300 to $800 per foot of shoreline, with bulkheads and revetments costing from $100 to $300 per foot. Once built, these protective structures then become themselves in-place public investments, vulnerable to damage or destruction by hurricanes and coastal storms. Perhaps most importantly, such shoreline protection devices serve to interrupt the natural dynamics of beach and dune systems and are frequently the direct cause of erosion and loss of beach. Moreover, as Pilkey et al. observe (1980, 45), once such investments in shoreline armor are made, they commit us to continual public investments well into the future.

> The emplacement of a seawall is an irreversible act with limited benefits. By gradually removing the beach in front of it, every seawall must eventually be replaced with a bigger ("better"), more expensive one. While a seawall may extend the lives of beach-front structures in normal weather, it cannot protect those on a low-lying barrier island from the havoc wrought by hurricanes; it cannot prevent overwash or storm-surge flooding.
>
> The long-range effect of seawalls can be seen in New Jersey and Miami Beach. In Monmouth Beach, New Jersey, the town building inspector told of the town's seawall history. Pointing to a seawall he said, "There were once houses and even farms in front of that wall. First we built small seawalls and they were destroyed by the storms

that seemed to get bigger and bigger. Now we have come to this huge wall which we hope will hold." The wall he spoke of, adjacent to the highway, was high enough to prevent even a glimpse of the sea beyond. There was no beach in front of it, but remnants of old seawalls, groins, and bulkheads for hundreds of yards at sea.

Beach nourishment represents a gentler, less environmentally obtrusive, approach to shoreline reinforcement. Yet, sand-moving programs are also very expensive and may provide relatively short-lived benefits. New Hanover County, North Carolina (1982), has estimated that the total annual cost to replace all of the sand eroded from county beaches would be over $5.2 million. In addition to the costs of transporting the sand, jurisdictions may have trouble finding an adequate source of sand. Dredging sand from sound areas, for instance, may have serious environmental repercussions. Moreover, if sand grain size is not matched correctly, transported sand may be lost very quickly through normal wave and tidal processes. Because nourishment programs rarely supply sand to the extent seaward they should, the beach profile is typically steepened (Pilkey et al. 1980). This in turn induces further coastal erosion, which may average up to ten times that of the natural system.

Sand-trapping structures, similarly, attempt to replenish beach areas by redirecting the natural flow of sand. Unfortunately, by interrupting normal patterns of littoral drift, groins and jetties typically cause erosion in down-current areas. Induced accretion in some coastal areas is usually at the expense of erosion in other areas. For example, in Westhampton Beach, New York, a system of groins has built up the beach in front of the houses on the east side, but west of the last groin the natural beach has been depleted, and houses there are washing away (Long Island Regional Planning Board 1984).

Perhaps more importantly, from the perspective of hurricane and coastal storm hazards, these types of programs provide little protection. While they may cause incoming waves to break further seaward, actual exposure to storm surges will not be reduced. Ocean City, Maryland, considered a co-operative state-local program to build a system of groins to protect and enhance its beach areas. A consulting report on hurricane hazard mitigation prepared for the city cautioned against considering the groin system as an effective storm hazard reduction program (Humphries and Johnston 1984).

It is imperative that the public, and particularly the property owners, recognize that the groin plan is designed to provide a wider
beach (if cells are filled to capacity) for recreational purposes and
perhaps reduce the frequency of beach nourishment. The groin plan
is not an effective means of protecting buildings from coastal flood
damages. A wider beach may cause storm waves to break further
seaward, but levels of flooding will not be reduced. In addition,
updrift accretion and downdrift erosion caused by groins is more of a
rule than an exception. Both have occurred locally because of the
North Jetty; it can occur on a smaller scale. On a more positive side,
the wider beach will contribute to a more successful dune stabilization effort.

Strengthening Buildings and Facilities

Rather than relying on improvements to stabilize the surrounding coastal
environment, building and facility strengthening efforts seek to reinforce
the structure of exposed buildings, along with accompanying "lifeline"
facilities such as sewage collection lines, water and power distribution
lines, and roads. These programs apply to all new construction in coastal
flood hazard areas, as well as to buildings rebuilt following major storm
damage. Thus, they ensure a minimum standard of resistance to storm
forces, including flooding, storm surge, high winds, and erosion. Building standards are spelled out in building codes, which must be met in
order to receive building permits from local government building inspection departments. Facility standards are spelled out in state and local
engineering design regulations.

Building code requirements and National Flood Insurance regulations
are parallel efforts. Although some communities and states have individual building codes, most have adopted one of the three model building
codes: (1) Standard Code, published by the Southern Building Code Congress International and commonly used in the South; (2) BOCA Code,
published by the Building Officials and Code Administrators International and commonly used in the Midwest and East; and (3) Uniform
Code, published by the International Congress of Building Officials and
commonly used in the West.

Under the National Flood Insurance Program (NFIP), communities subject to flooding must regulate new construction in flood hazard areas. These areas include all land subject to inundation by the "base flood" or "100-year flood," defined as the flood with a one percent chance of occurrence in any given year. In coastal communities the 100-year floodplain is divided into two zones based on the degree of hazard present: the V-(velocity) zone is that part of the 100-year floodplain that would be inundated by tidal surges with velocity wave action (defined as a 3-foot breaking wave), and the A-zone is that part of the 100-year floodplain not subject to severe wave action. In V-zones new construction and substantial improvements to existing structures must be elevated on pilings or columns so that the bottom of the lowest floor structure is at or above the base flood elevation, the building must be securely fastened to the pilings or columns, and the space below the lowest floor must be free of obstructions or enclosed with breakaway walls intended to collapse under wind and water load without damaging the elevated building or foundation. In A-zones the lowest floor must be elevated to or above the base flood elevation on pilings, columns, fill, or raised foundations (Federal Emergency Management Agency 1986).

In addition, some state and local governments have adopted coastal construction codes to supplement their standard building codes. The Federal Emergency Management Agency (hereinafter FEMA) has issued a sample coastal construction code, based on standards for wind-loading relationships prepared by the American National Standards Institute (ANSI) and for water loading from the *Shore Protection Manual* prepared by the Corps of Engineers (FEMA 1986, appendix G).

Strengthening Buildings

The adoption of building codes and construction standards to *floodproof* and *elevate* buildings in flood-prone areas above the projected level of the 100-year flood has been the most widespread response to hurricane and coastal risks. These building strengthening actions are required by the National Flood Insurance Program (see chapter 4). Along with *wind-proofing* requirements in building codes, these types of actions seek to decrease the vulnerability of buildings exposed to storm forces.

Some communities have mandated building elevation in excess of that required under the 100-year base flood elevation (BFE). Referred to as "freeboard" elevation, this can further minimize the impacts of wave and surge forces. East Providence, Rhode Island, for example, has enacted provisions which differentiate a high- and low-hazard zone. In the high-hazard zone (near the beach) residential buildings must be elevated to fifteen feet above mean sea level, rather than the ten feet required under the NFIP requirements (Kusler 1982, 46).

Building codes vary widely in the resistance they provide to hurricane forces. Depending on the state and the code in use, storm strengthening requirements may be either local option or state-mandated, or some combination. Some standard codes may not have been updated to include adequate requirements. And the definition of "adequacy" is the subject of a continuing debate. For example, the proposed (but not adopted) Texas model Hurricane Resistance Building Standards (Texas Coastal and Marine Council 1981) required stringent wind-loading standards to protect against storm winds of 140 mph (as compared with the 105 mph requirement in the Standard Code).

Strengthening Facilities

Inhabited structures located in hazard areas must also be served by basic support facilities. These facilities, like the structures themselves, can be strengthened to better resist storm forces. Primary among these are wastewater collection, water distribution, electric and telephone lines, and roads. Sewer and water lines and pumps can be *floodproofed*, while electric and telephone utilities can be placed *underground* for better protection. Roads are best protected through *elevation*, which may require moving the road to a location farther inland.

Benefits and Limitations of Strengthening Programs

Damage surveys following major hurricanes consistently report on the protective value of following recommended building standards (FEMA 1986). In addition to including adequate structural strength, designers of coastal buildings must anticipate the effects of erosion and scouring of sand from under the building which can weaken foundations and move the shoreline inland. While following coastal construction standards can improve survival rates for exposed buildings, there are no guaranteed means of "hurricane proofing."

More stringent building standards are often opposed on the grounds that such requirements will serve to increase substantially the costs of construction. While such measures do increase costs, the actual extent of increase is debatable. Lesso (1979) has examined the potential cost increases that would have resulted from enactment of the Texas Model Building Standards, which could have required new coastal construction to withstand minimal wind speeds of 140 mph. He estimated that the proposed standards would create an additional 3–8 percent increase in the structural costs of the building and a 1–3 percent increase in the overall cost of the structure. He also calculated the expected reduction in wind damages to result from these standards using a Monte Carlo simulation model. Considering, as well, the expected savings from reduced insurance rates, Lesso concluded that the increased building/wind standards would be very economical.

> An approach is to consider this option in terms of adding extra insulation to a home. There is a high initial cost with the expectation of reduced heating and cooling bills in the future. It was this approach that was used. An example involving a $50,000 structure on a $15,000 lot was used. The added investment would be $500 to $1500 and this could be amortized over the economic or ownership life of the structure by reduced insurance rates. This was done for periods of 5 to 30 years and interests rates of 6, 9, and 12 percent. The nominal results show that there should be about $.07 to $.80 per $100 valuation reduction in insurance rates.

Under certain circumstances, stringent local building codes could have the effect of displacing development and economic activity. For instance, if a particular locality is the only one in a state's coastal area to impose high elevation requirements, builders and investors may choose to locate in adjoining localities where equally high development profits can be obtained at reduced costs. This displacement will depend on a number of factors, such as the strength of the relevant development markets (typically very high in coastal areas) and the availability of comparable sites. Displacement effects are unlikely in situations where a uniform state building code exists.

The effectiveness of building codes and construction standards is intimately tied to the enforcement program which accompanies their adoption. Many coastal localities do not have budgets or personnel sufficient to ensure that such standards are adhered to. The nature of the building process also makes it difficult to verify, after considerable construction has occurred, if required standards have been satisfied (for example, are pilings embedded to the required length?). The adoption of more stringent hurricane-resistant building standards may also not be a very viable mitigation alternative where local personnel qualified to develop such measures do not exist. It is also important to note that localities may simply not have the option of adopting more stringent measures. For instance, under North Carolina's statewide building code, more innovative and stringent local codes are generally discouraged and must be approved by a state building code council.

Several studies have attempted to assess the economic effects of the elevation and floodproofing requirements of the NFIP. Cheatham (1979) studied these effects for a coastal area in Mississippi through a survey of building contractors and real estate professionals and an analysis of economic and construction data. Contractors specializing in residential development estimated that NFIP requirements increased the cost of new residential structures by an average of 21 percent. Contractors specializing in commercial structures estimated that these additional costs were only 5 percent for commercial structures. In case studies of inland communities French et al. (1980) report that similar flood protection programs raised construction costs by 10–25 percent.

Debate has been brisk over the effects of NFIP requirements on encouraging or discouraging new development in flood hazard areas. On the one hand, it is argued that the increased construction costs from building standards serve as a disincentive. On the other hand, the availability of subsidized flood insurance (see chapter 4) is likely to serve as a positive incentive for such building. In the Cheatham study, for instance, about 70 percent of the residential contractors believed that NFIP requirements (elevation primarily) served as a deterrent to growth in floodplain areas. Even among those who argue that on balance the flood insurance requirements discourage floodplain development, there is general agreement that such programs will not reduce the overall quantity of development occurring in floodplains. Sheaffer and Roland (1981, 9–10) state that compliance with existing floodplain regulations did not deter development in floodplains of the twenty-one case study communities they analyzed, noting that increased costs of floodproofing were more than offset by anticipated reductions in future flood losses or insurance costs. Burby and

French (1981) point out that the same factors which stimulate the adoption of floodplain land use management programs also stimulate encroachment on the hazard area, which in turn limits program effectiveness—a paradoxical result of the high priority of floodplain management in communities with significant proportions of their developable land in the floodplain.

Evacuation

A traditional approach to hurricane hazards is to plan for the evacuation of people in the event that such storms threaten. The objective of this approach is to save lives, and it offers no protection to public or private property. The National Weather Service, and specifically the National Hurricane Center in Miami, tracks hurricanes and tropical storms and issues warnings which are used by local and state officials to initiate evacuation from threatened coastal hazard areas.

The most common form of evacuation is to move people to higher ground away from the path of the storm; usually evacuation refers to this horizontal movement. A new concept currently under study is to move people to hurricane-resistant vertical shelters above the floodwaters but not necessarily out of the hazard areas; this is termed vertical evacuation or vertical refuge. Both horizontal and vertical evacuation are discussed here.

Horizontal Evacuation

Coastal localities are increasingly involved in developing and implementing hurricane evacuation plans (see, for example, Tampa Bay Regional Planning Council 1981 and 1984; Rogers, Golden, and Halpern 1981; Southwest Florida Regional Planning Council 1981 and 1983; Ruch 1981). Evacuation planning efforts have been aided significantly through the development and application of computer simulations of hurricane effects. The most advanced of these is SLOSH (Sea, Lake, and Overland Surge from Hurricanes), which is able to take into account the effects of sounds, bays, and other material and man-made irregularities of the coastline (see Allenstein 1985). Among other things, these computer simulations will generate maximum surge penetration levels, time histories of surges at selected geographical points, computed wind speeds at selected points, and computed wind directions at selected points, under different assumptions about hurricane size, direction, and so on. This information permits evacuation officials to identify areas that should be evacuated, the safest routes for this evacuation, and the periods of time before landfall that these routes can be used. SLOSH information, for example, can indicate the number of hours before landfall that a causeway will become flooded and unusable for evacuation purposes (see Ruch 1981).

Evacuation plans typically also involve behavioral analyses which estimate the proportion of the population expected to leave, the likely routes they will take, and the number and types of vehicles they are likely to use. This information is collected through a survey of residents. An analysis of hurricane shelters and appropriate evacuation destinations is also usually conducted as part of an evacuation study. Finally, the capacity and characteristics of the roadway system in place are analyzed. Ideally, the resulting evacuation plan permits public officials to issue evacuation notices in sufficient time, to direct and regulate evacuating traffic in the most expeditious manner, and generally to allocate resources and personnel most efficiently. Evacuation plans and studies, of course, also have the potential of identifying deficiencies in the existing road and transportation system from the point of view of safe and expeditious evacuation. Such an analysis may indicate, for example, that an additional bridge to the mainland is needed to accommodate predicted evacuation demand (DCRP 1983; DCRP 1984).

One of the most important products of an evacuation plan is its estimate of the time it would take to evacuate threatened residents from an approaching hurricane. This period, termed *evacuation time*, represents the amount of time before the projected hurricane eye strikes land that is necessary for issuance of an evacuation order that will allow threatened residents to move to safety. Evacuation time includes two major elements: (1) *clearance time*, composed of the "mobilization time" needed by households to get ready to evacuate, the "travel time" they need to escape the hazard area, and the "queueing delay time" that occurs when traffic is slowed due to inadequate road capacity, and (2) *prelandfall hazards time*, composed of the "surge roadway inundation time," before the hurricane eye landfall when evacuation routes are inundated by storm surge, and the "arrival of gale force winds time," before landfall when high winds would prevent safe evacuation (Tampa Bay Regional Planning Council 1984).[1]

Vertical Evacuation (Refuge)

In many heavily populated coastal regions evacuation of the complete at-risk population horizontally (that is, by automobile) is problematic under certain storm conditions. Alternatives to traditional evacuation are "vertical refuge" and "vertical evacuation" (Berke 1987). Vertical refuge is the emergency relocation of people who are unable to evacuate from high-hazard areas threatened by hurricanes to structurally reinforced multistory buildings as a last resort prior to a storm landfall. Vertical evacuation is the organized, planned relocation of people at risk to vertical shelters. Some high-risk localities are considering vertical shelters, primarily as a supplement to rather than a replacement for horizontal evacuation. Vertical shelters have the advantage of reducing the exposure of evacuating individuals to storm forces (for example, storm flooding of a bridge to the mainland).

Benefits and Limitations of Evacuation

Evacuation has saved many people from hurricanes. For most built-up urban areas in threatened locations there is no other apparent alternative to protecting the populations from storm forces. Yet evacuation is not a completely dependable solution in all threatened areas.

Most coastal officials recommend that full evacuation in the face of a hurricane be conducted. Yet, heavy reliance on evacuation is problematic for a number of reasons. The National Hurricane Center has indicated that it can provide only 12 hours of "high confidence" warning time before hurricane landfall. This is far exceeded by the actual times required to evacuate residents in heavily populated and growing coastal regions. Estimated time to evacuate Galveston is 26 hours (Ruch 1981) and for the Florida Keys is 31.5 hours (Post, Buckley, Schuh, and Jernigan 1983). In many coastal localities, then, complete evacuation will not be a feasible alternative.

Moreover, evacuation can be very costly, both in terms of personnel and public expense and in terms of the disruption it causes to people's lives. Evacuation also raises the possibility that evacuees will end up more exposed to the forces of hurricanes along congested evacuation routes than they might have had a public evacuation not been initiated.

One solution to the problem of overlong evacuation times is to initiate the evacuation process far in advance of an imminent hurricane landfall. However, such a practice increases tremendously the chances that a false evacuation will be called (the storm's path takes it elsewhere), which decreases the public's confidence in emergency officials and reduces the number of individuals who will heed the next hurricane warning (the "cry wolf" syndrome). In many cases the sudden strengthening and landfall of a hurricane may even preclude this type of cautious strategy.

Evacuation is at best only a partial solution to the problem of human risk. Many individuals, even if ordered to evacuate under threat of criminal prosecution, will not evacuate. Some believe they can ride out the storm; others fear looting or vandalism to their property during evacuation. The now infamous story of the hurricane party at the Richileau Apartments in which twenty-seven people were killed by Hurricane Camille illustrates this point. As a further example, nearly 30 percent of the respondents in a phone survey of the Nags Head/Kitty Hawk area of the North Carolina coast (on a barrier island) indicated that they would not evacuate if another hurricane such as Diana (1984) were to threaten the coast (Beatley and Brower 1986). In a recent mail survey of residents of the town of Southern Shores, North Carolina, over 30 percent of the respondents expressed uncertainty about evacuating if a hurricane warning were issued (Coastal Resources Collaborative 1985).

Vertical evacuation can overcome some of the problems of horizontal evacuation, including the long clearance times required to move people to safety along congested roads. And since vertical shelters make use of existing engineered buildings (medium- and high-rise) that are already better able to withstand storm forces and only need some modifications to accommodate evacuees, most vertical evacuation proposals do not involve structural modifications to buildings. Consequently, under this assumption the costs involved in vertical evacuation will tend to be relatively small.

However, Salmon (1984) identifies a number of practical and political problems associated with vertical evacuation. Perhaps of most importance is whether a sufficient number of hurricane-resistant structures exist in coastal localities to accommodate this method. In many highly vulnerable coastal jurisdictions, when low-density residential uses are predominant, few engineered structures appropriate for such refuge exist. Secondly, there is the question of how safe refuge in such structures ultimately is under hurricane conditions. The issue here is one of balancing the risks of horizontal evacuation (for example, being caught on the causeway) against the potentially catastrophic results of a building failure.

> There is no evading the fact that horizontal evacuation, if properly carried out, can virtually be guaranteed to avoid catastrophic casualties. Traffic accidents, stress related injuries/fatalities, or other kinds of injuries (from broken glass, downed power lines, wind-driven objects) are still possible, but the level of risk is more acceptable. Further, an injured person can probably be reached by emergency teams. A vertical evacuation shelter which collapses in the middle of a storm surge is beyond assistance. Horizontal evacuation entails great inconvenience, but risk of catastrophic failure is low if the plan is implemented in time. Vertical evacuation is far more convenient and swift—but catastrophic failure is possible (Salmon 1984, 294).

Other legal and political problems also exist for the use of vertical evacuation. One problem is uncertainty concerning the legal liability of the public and the owners of such structures. Should a building collapse during a hurricane, must the building's owners assume any legal liability for this event? Also, Salmon (1984) predicts that a heavy reliance on vertical evacuation will tend to defuse support for limiting development in high-hazard areas. He recommends leaving vertical evacuation out of hurricane preparedness plans in areas where horizontal evacuation remains possible. In areas where evacuation times are already long and continue to climb, vertical evacuation might be best used in collaboration with short-trip horizontal evacuation.

Development Management

Many state and local governments have adopted specific policies for managing urban development. These *development management* policies seek to influence the amount, type, location, rate, public cost, and/or quality of development and redevelopment in order to achieve public interest objectives. Sometimes called "growth management" or "land use" policies, these policies are implemented through plans, police power regulations, public spending, taxation, and land acquisition programs. Because they deal with widely recognized, day-to-day public needs, development management policies tend to have broad political and administrative support (Godschalk, Brower, et al. 1979; Godschalk 1985).

A smaller number of state and local governments have adopted specific *hazard mitigation* policies. These policies seek to reduce human injuries and property losses from natural hazards by anticipatory growth-guidance actions. Traditionally structured around single types of hazards, such as floods or earthquakes, such policies recently have started to become more generic in order to deal with multiple hazards (National Research Council 1983; Mushkatel and Weschler 1985). Because they deal with less widely recognized policy problems, however, such anticipatory hazard mitigation policies previously have not enjoyed broad political or administrative support (Rossi, Wright, and Weber-Burdin 1982).

Both development management and hazard mitigation policies typically use the same types of implementation tools to carry out their goals. Land use plans, zoning ordinances, subdivision regulations, public health regulations, public facility programs, land acquisition, and taxation are employed by both.

State *coastal management* programs, enacted under the impetus of the Coastal Zone Management Act of 1972, offer an opportunity to combine coastal hazard mitigation and growth management, increasing the effectiveness and political feasibility of hazard mitigation by linking it to federally supported coastal management and to publicly accepted development management activities (Brower and Carol 1984; Healy and Zinn 1985; Godschalk and Cousins 1985).

Linking Hazard Mitigation and Development Management

Hazard mitigation and development management should be closely linked. To illustrate the conceptual linkage, a hazard reduction strategy for each growth characteristic dealt with by development management is outlined below.

Location. A mitigation strategy defines two types of locations: high- and low-hazard areas. In high-hazard areas, increased development is discouraged by limiting density and intensity of use, reconstruction after damage occurs, and further extension of public facilities and services; buildings are strengthened and made more hazard-resistant; public open space acquisition and natural system conservation are encouraged; and incentives are provided to property owners to transfer their development rights or density allowances to low-hazard areas.

Rate. A mitigation strategy explicitly considers the timing of development relative to hazard threats. It defines the carrying capacity of evacuation and shelter systems, as well as the carrying capacity of natural and man-made protective systems, and calculates the demands on those systems from emergencies occurring under various levels of growth and land use. It sets up a process for ensuring that system capacities are not exceeded by system demands in emergency situations, regulating the growth rate when necessary to prevent overloads.

Type. In high-hazard areas, a mitigation strategy requires high-occupancy structures to be engineered for safety and sheltering under disaster stresses. It encourages clustering of buildings on least-hazardous site areas, the placement of low-intensity uses in higher-hazard areas, and the consideration of building and lot designs that permit moving threatened buildings away from hazard locations. Public facilities such as schools and hospitals would be directed into low-hazard areas.

Amount. Population size, like growth rate, is balanced with the capacity of evacuation, shelter, and protective systems. A mitigation strategy seeks to ensure that the emergency demands on these systems do not exceed their capacity by either limiting the size of the population at risk or by increasing the systems' capacity through public investment, planning, and regulation.

Public Cost. Past public subsidies to development in hazard areas have increased exposure of people and property to risk. A mitigation strategy systematically identifies the risk-increasing effects of public expenditures, especially for infrastructure, and withdraws or reduces those expenditures that increase risk exposure. It transfers the cost of development and storm protection in hazard areas from the public sector to the private sector.

Quality. A mitigation strategy demands high-quality design, construction, and conservation practices for all projects located in or near high-hazard areas. Buildings and structures at risk are required to withstand probable hazard stresses, not only to protect their occupants but also to minimize the danger of missile and battering damage to adjacent buildings. Environmental systems providing hazard protection are required to be maintained or enhanced for optimum performance during disasters.

Implementation Tools

As table 2.1 indicates, there are six major categories of tools and techniques available for managing growth and development: (1) plans, (2) development regulations, (3) land and property acquisition, (4) taxation, fiscal, and other incentives, (5) capital facilities policy, and (6) information dissemination. Each of these approaches, and the specific hazard mitigation measures subsumed within them, are discussed and assessed in greater detail in chapter 6 under local mitigation tools and techniques. Because these measures are the ones mainly used to carry out hazard mitigation at the local level, their detailed coverage is reserved for this later chapter and only a general treatment of benefits and limitations is presented here.

Benefits and Limitations of Development Management

Most hazard analysts agree that development management programs based on land use plans are among the most promising approaches to effective hazard mitigation. A comprehensive assessment of research on natural hazards noted: "A recurrent theme in dealing with all of the natural hazards is the potential of land use management to promote socially desirable uses of vulnerable areas in the United States" (White and Haas 1975, 193). An in-depth review of hurricane impacts stated: "For effective reduction of the impact of a hurricane and the risks of living in a hurricane-prone area, coordinated action at several levels of government is needed, beginning with some form of land-use planning and regulation" (Simpson and Riehl 1981, 23).

On the other hand, many analysts are skeptical about the political feasibility of convincing governments to adopt and implement hazard mitigation strategies based on land use controls (Rossi, Wright, and Weber-Burdin 1982). The main problem they identify is one of the low political salience of hazard mitigation. Another often cited problem is the increased cost of housing attributed to more rigorous land use controls, along with the opposition of development interests to government intervention into the land development market (Porter 1986).

Integrating hazard mitigation into accepted development management tools offers a way of overcoming the low-salience problem. It is less difficult to add a hazard mitigation section to an existing plan, regulation, or program than to adopt a totally new set of tools. Such a multiple objective approach also makes sense in terms of the coordination of government actions. As White and Haas (1975, 198–199) state: "What is needed is an integration of multiple use and multiple means principles of management affecting hazard areas to insure that the consideration of hazard is only one aspect of a *coordinated* approach. In some instances hazard may turn out to be the lead aspect, in others it may be incidental to purposes such as open space preservation or wildlife management."

Increased support for adopting hazard mitigation tools also may come from state or federal government policies. Intergovernmental programs such as the coastal management program, discussed in the chapters on federal and state mitigation activities, play critical roles in directing the attention of local decisionmakers to the need for mitigation, in defining planning and regulatory frameworks, in providing technical assistance to local programs, and in providing financial assistance for mitigation activities.

Development management's negative impacts on housing costs and development interests have been widely debated. While there is little doubt that safe and environment-conserving development costs more initially, the long-term savings to society may well counterbalance these initial costs. Many communities with vigorous development management plans have instituted subsidized housing programs and density bonuses for provision of affordable housing to offset increased housing costs. And many developers who initially opposed development management have become advocates of it as they profited from its increases in growth quality and reductions in uncertainty.

Mitigation Alternatives

This chapter has reviewed the major types of approaches to coastal storm hazard mitigation, and the benefits and limitations of each type. Historically, these approaches began with a focus on engineering techniques to protect property through alteration of the coastal environment and through strengthening buildings and facilities, supplemented by evacuation techniques to move exposed populations from storm paths. More recently, the focus has shifted to the use of development management techniques to change land use patterns so as to reduce the exposure of people and property to storm damage.

Each approach has its proponents. A vigorous debate has been mounted over the advantages of structural or engineering approaches versus non-structural or growth management approaches. We do not believe that this is an "either or" question. Rather, we see the need for employing various techniques of all types, depending on the specifics of the local situation. Our preference is to bring together a kit of mitigation tools, as part of an overall planning and hazard mitigation effort. While the emphasis in this book is primarily on the hazard mitigation aspects of development management, we recognize that in most situations the tool kit should include environmental alteration, building strengthening, and evacuation, as well. It is in this area of *comprehensive* hazard mitigation that opportunities for improvement exist.

Notes

1. Recent evacuation studies by the Corps of Engineers depart from traditional "time-to-landfall" measures, substituting a "decision arc" method. In the Eastern North Carolina Hurricane Evacuation Study (U.S. Army Corps of Engineers 1987, 201–250), decision-makers use two tools: (1) a Decision Arc Map showing a series of twenty-nautical-mile arcs spreading seaward from the southernmost boundary of their county and (2) a transparent STORM plot showing the distance that gale force (34 knot) winds reach outward from the hurricane eye at the center. Clearance time is calculated, based on the hurricane category, expected evacuee response rate, and degree of tourist occupancy. This is plotted at the decision point (arc) which provides enough time to safely evacuate, located by multiplying clearance time in hours by the forward speed of the hurricane in knots. The STORM plot is overlaid on the Decision Arc Map, tracking the hurricane's movement, and evacuation must be ordered prior to the time when its gale force winds reach the decision point.

References

Allenstein, Karen. 1985. *Land Use Applications of the SLOSH Model*. Chapel Hill, N.C.: University of North Carolina, Department of City and Regional Planning.

Beatley, Timothy. 1985. *Development Management to Reduce Coastal Storm Hazards: Policies and Processes*. Chapel Hill, N.C.: University of North Carolina, Center for Urban and Regional Studies.

Beatley, Timothy, and David J. Brower. 1986. "Public Perception of Hurricane Hazards: Examining the Differential Effects of Hurricane Diana." *Coastal Zone Management Journal*

14, no. 3: 241–269.

Berke, Philip. 1987. "Vertical Shelter from Hurricanes: Risk Perceptions and Politics." In *Coastal Zone '87*, edited by Orville T. Magoon et al., 4: 3819–3829. New York, N.Y.: American Society of Civil Engineers.

Brower, David J., and Daniel S. Carol. 1984. *Coastal Zone Management as Land Planning*. Washington, D.C.: National Planning Association.

Burby, Raymond J., and Steven P. French. 1981. "Coping with Floods: The Land Use Management Paradox." *Journal of the American Planning Association* 47, no. 3 (July): 289–300.

Cheatham, Leo R. 1979. *An Assessment of Some Economic Effects of FIA Land Use Requirements on Urban Coastal Zone Development*. Mississippi State, Miss.: Mississippi State University, Water Resources Research Institute.

Coastal Resources Collaborative. 1985. *Attitudes about Growth and Development in Southern Shores: Results of a Mail Survey*. Chapel Hill, N.C.

Department of City and Regional Planning, University of North Carolina, Chapel Hill. 1984. *A Carrying Capacity Study of Hatteras Island*. Chapel Hill, N.C.: University of North Carolina.

———. 1983. *Currituck County Outer Banks Carrying Capacity Study*. Chapel Hill, N.C.: University of North Carolina.

Federal Emergency Management Agency. 1986. *Coastal Construction Manual*. Washington, D.C.: U.S. Government Printing Office.

French, Steven, Todd L. Miller, Raymond J. Burby, and David A. Moreau. 1980. *Managing Flood Hazard Areas: A Field Evaluation of Local Experience*. Chapel Hill, N.C.: University of North Carolina, Center for Urban and Regional Studies.

Godschalk, David R. 1985. "Urban Development Policies and Strategies." In *The Practice of State and Regional Planning*, edited by Frank So, Irving Hand, and Bruce McDowell. Chicago, Ill.: Planners Press.

Godschalk, David R., and Kathryn Cousins. 1985. "Coastal Management: Planning on the Edge." *Journal of the American Planning Association* 51, no. 3 (Summer): 263–265.

Godschalk, David R., and David J. Brower. 1985. "Mitigation Strategies and Integrated Emergency Management." *Public Administration Review* 45 (January): 64–71.

Godschalk, David R., David J. Brower, et al. 1979. *Constitutional Issues of Growth Management*. Chicago: Planners Press.

Healy, Robert G., and Jeffrey A. Zinn. 1985. "Environment and Development Conflicts in Coastal Zone Management." *Journal of the American Planning Association* 51, no. 3 (Summer): 299–311.

Humphries, Stanley M., and Larry R. Johnston. 1984. *Reducing the Flood Damage Potential in Ocean City, Maryland*. Prepared for the Department of Natural Resources, State of Maryland.

Kusler, Jon A. 1982. *Innovative Local Floodplain Management: A Summary of Local Experience*. Boulder, Colo.: Institute of Behavioral Science, University of Colorado.

Lesso, William G. 1979. "The Effect on Building Cost Due to Improved Wind Resistant Building Standards." Austin, Tex.: Texas Coastal and Marine Council.

Long Island Regional Planning Board. 1984. *Hurricane Damage Mitigation Plan for the South Shore—Nassau and Suffolk Counties, N.Y.* Hauppauge, N.Y.

Mushkatel, Alvin H., and Louis F. Weschler. 1985. "Emergency Management and the Intergovernmental System." *Public Administration Review* 45 (January): 49–56.

National Research Council. 1983. *Multiple Hazard Mitigation*. Washington, D.C.: National Academy Press.

New Hanover County, North Carolina. 1982. *County Involvement in Beach Erosion*. Wilmington, N.C.

Pilkey, Orrin H., Jr., William J. Neal, Orrin H. Pilkey, Sr., and Stanley R. Riggs. 1980. *From Currituck to Calabash: Living with North Carolina's Barrier Islands*. Durham, N.C.: Duke University Press.

Pilkey, Orrin H., Sr., et al. 1983. *Coastal Design: A Guide for Builders, Planners, and Home Owners*. New York, N.Y.: Van Nostrand Reinhold.

Porter, Douglas R., ed. 1986. *Growth Management: Keeping on Target?* Washington, D.C.: Urban Land Institute.

Post, Buckley, Schuh, and Jernigan. 1983. *Lower Southeast Florida Hurricane Evacuation Study*. Technical Data Report. Tallahassee, Fla.

Rogers, Golden and Halpern. 1981. *Hurricane Evacuation and Hazard Mitigation Study for Sanibel, Florida*. Philadelphia, Pa.

Rossi, Peter, James Wright, and Eleanor Weber-Burdin. 1982. *Natural Hazards and Public Choice: The State and Local Politics of Hazard Mitigation*. New York, N.Y.: Academic Press.

Ruch, Carlton. 1981. *Hurricane Relocation Planning for Brazoria, Galveston, Harris, Fort Bend, and Chambers Counties*. College Station, Tex.: Texas A&M University, Sea Grant College Program.

Salmon, Jack D. 1984. "Vertical Evacuation in Hurricanes: An Urgent Policy Problem for Coastal Managers." *Coastal Zone Management Journal* 12, no. 2/3: 287–300.

Sheaffer and Roland. 1981. *Evaluation of the Economic, Social and Environmental Effects of Floodplain Regulations*. Washington, D.C.: Federal Emergency Management Agency.

Simpson, Robert H., and Herbert Riehl. 1981. *The Hurricane and Its Impact*. Baton Rouge, La.: Louisiana State University Press.

South Carolina Water Resources Commission. 1982. *Floodplain Management Program Newsletter*, June–July, pp. 1–5.

Southwest Florida Regional Planning Council. 1981. *Regional Hurricane Evacuation Plan*. Fort Myers, Fla.

————. 1983. *Hurricane Evacuation Plan Update.* Fort Myers, Fla.

Tampa Bay Regional Planning Council. 1981. *Tampa Bay Region Hurricane Evacuation Plan.* St. Petersburg, Fla.

————. 1984. *Tampa Bay Region Hurricane Evacuation Plan: Technical Data Report Update.* St. Petersburg, Fla.

Texas Coastal and Marine Council. 1981. *Model Minimum Hurricane Resistant Building Standards for the Texas Gulf Coast.* Austin, Tex.

Texas Department of Public Safety. 1984. *Hazard Mitigation Plan for the Counties on the Upper Texas Coast Affected by Hurricane Alicia.* Austin, Tex.

U.S. Army Corps of Engineers. 1980. "Lake Pontchartrain, Louisiana and Vicinity, Hurricane Protection, Description and Diagram." Galveston District.

————. 1981. *Low Cost Shore Protection ... A Guide for Local Government Officials.* Washington, D.C.

————. 1987. *Eastern North Carolina Hurricane Evacuation Study: Technical Data Report.* Wilmington District.

Walton, Todd L., and William Sensabaugh. 1983. *Seawall Design on the Open Coast.* Gainesville, Fla.: Sea Grant College, University of Florida.

White, Gilbert F., and J. Eugene Haas. 1975. *Assessment of Research on Natural Hazards.* Cambridge, Mass.: MIT Press.

White, Gilbert F., et al. 1976. *Natural Hazard Management in Coastal Areas.* Washington, D.C.: National Oceanic and Atmospheric Administration.

Yasso, Warren E., and Elliott M. Hartman. 1976. *Beach Forms and Coastal Processes.* Albany, N.Y.: New York Sea Grant Institute.

3 Mitigation after Camille, Frederic, and Alicia

The importance of mitigation policy has slowly emerged from our experience in coping with the aftereffects of major hurricanes striking built-up coastal areas during the last two decades. The learning curve has not been smooth or consistent, but the idea that foresighted development management can mitigate or avoid some of the destruction spawned by hurricanes has gradually been accepted in theory if not yet completely in practice.

This chapter tracks the evolution of mitigation policy and practice through a review of posthurricane experience in three coastal jurisdictions: Harrison County, Mississippi, struck by Hurricane Camille in 1969; Gulf Shores, Alabama, struck by Hurricane Frederic in 1979; and Galveston, Texas, struck by Hurricane Alicia in 1983.[1]

By looking at the two decades of posthurricane recovery and reconstruction experience spanned by these three cases, we can see the effects of changes in public policy for dealing with disasters, the obstacles to implementing rational mitigation plans, and the possibilities for increased future integration of hazard mitigation and growth management. Before describing the cases, a brief overview of the evolution of national disaster mitigation policy is presented to show when each case occurred relative to the changing policy context. More detailed discussions of this context are provided in chapter 4.

Disaster Policy Evolution

Early national policy focused on *structural* solutions to flood disasters. The Flood Control Act of 1936 established the U.S. Army Corps of

Engineers' structural flood control program, which was the primary approach for a long period. The Corps built seawalls and other structures to stabilize shorelines where wave action was the principal cause of erosion. These structures were sometimes criticized for causing adverse environmental effects and creating a false sense of security from storms.

Thirty years later, *nonstructural* solutions began to be seriously considered. The problem of uneconomic use and development of floodplains was recognized in President Johnson's Executive Order 11296, issued in 1966. This order directed federal agencies to mitigate flood hazards through reducing federal expenditures and actions that contributed to floodplain development. However, implementation of the order was slow and ineffective. According to a recent government handbook (FEMA 1986, 14):

> Prior to 1966, the Federal role in addressing natural hazards consisted principally of providing assistance to disaster victims through low interest loans, grants and other forms of emergency aid, and building or financing major structural works, such as dams and levees to protect populations and development at risk. The year 1966 marked a turning point, with growing national policy emphasis on nonstructural measures in addition to major engineering works, in order to reduce the impacts of natural hazards.

The recent era of *disaster mitigation* policy in the United States began with the passage of the National Flood Insurance Act in 1968. The national *floodplain management* policy of requiring floodproofing through building codes and elevated structures in flood hazard areas in return for federally subsidized flood insurance was initiated by that act, which was based on voluntary community participation in the flood insurance program. The policy was greatly strengthened in 1973 with the passage of the Flood Disaster Protection Act, whose prohibition of federally insured loans to property owners in flood-prone areas of communities not participating in the flood insurance program, in effect made community participation mandatory and extended floodplain management nationwide.

A critical concept, the *hazard mitigation plan*, was established in Section 406 of the Disaster Relief Act of 1974, which required public recipients of disaster relief funds to evaluate natural hazards and take action to mitigate them (Clary 1985). That act also set up grants to states to conduct *Hurricane Preparedness Studies* based on storm surge models, with population preparedness as first priority and property protection as second priority.

Related actions included the passage of the 1972 Coastal Zone Management Act, which initiated widespread coastal planning. Under this act participating states were required to designate areas of particular concern, including hazard-prone areas. This was followed by the 1982 Coastal Barrier Resources Act, which sought to reduce federal expenditures subsidizing development on hazardous coastal barriers. This act withdrew federal flood insurance and financial assistance to new development projects on undeveloped coastal barriers.

In 1977 President Carter issued Executive Order 11988, requiring federal agencies to avoid public investment in floodplains if practicable alternatives exist, and Executive Order 11990, requiring similar action to reduce destruction of wetlands. In 1979 President Carter issued Executive Order 12127, consolidating all federal emergency functions in a new agency, the Federal Emergency Management Agency (FEMA).

FEMA brought other federal agencies together in an interagency agreement in 1980 establishing Interagency Regional Hazard Mitigation Teams that assess desirable mitigation actions after each presidentially declared national disaster. Also in 1980 FEMA began requiring state and local governments to assume 25 percent of public assistance costs for restoring public facilities following a national disaster. In 1983 FEMA introduced the concept of "integrated emergency management," bringing together programs for dealing with all natural, man-made, and technological hazards. Also in 1983 the National Weather Service modified its system of hurricane warnings to include the probability of a strike.

The three cases described here both influenced and were influenced by evolving national hazard policy. As table 3.1 shows, the cases span the critical recent period of national mitigation policy development, running from the late 1960s to the present. By putting these three selected local cases of hurricane recovery into the context of the evolution of national policy toward an emphasis on mitigation, it is possible to illustrate the opportunities for increasing the effectiveness of coastal storm hazard mitigation, as well as the difficulty and complexity of changing old patterns.

Table 3.1   Contemporary Hazard Mitigation Policy
and Hurricane Experience

1966	Presidential Executive Order 11296 required federal agencies to reduce floodplain development
1968	National Flood Insurance Act required floodplain management in exchange for national flood insurance coverage eligibility
1969	*Hurricane Camille* (Harrison County not yet under federal flood insurance program)
1970	Federal Disaster Assistance Act included additional disaster assistance funds to Mississippi coast
1972	Coastal Zone Management Act encouraged coastal planning, including hazards identification
1973	Flood Disaster Protection Act prohibited federally insured loans to floodplain property in communities not under NFIP
1974	Disaster Relief Act required state and local mitigation plan in order to receive federal aid (Section 406) and authorized Hurricane Preparedness Planning Program
1977	Presidential Executive Orders 11988 and 11990 mandated federal agencies to refrain from financing or permitting development in floodplains and wetlands unless no practicable alternatives exist
1979	Presidential Executive Order 12127 created FEMA to coordinate federal disaster management
1979	*Hurricane Frederic* (Gulf Shores previously enrolled under National Flood Insurance Program)
1980	Interagency Regional Hazard Mitigation Teams established through interagency agreement
1980	FEMA required state and local governments to assume 25 percent of public assistance program costs
1982	Coastal Barrier Resources Act withdrew federal flood insurance and financial assistance from undeveloped coastal barriers
1983	National Weather Service began including probabilities in hurricane advisories
1983	FEMA initiated Integrated Emergency Management System
1983	*Hurricane Alicia* (Galveston under NFIP and Hazard Mitigation Team requirements)

Harrison County Recovers from Hurricane Camille

Hurricane Camille

Hurricane Camille struck the Mississippi Gulf coast shortly after midnight on August 18, 1969. No ordinary storm, Camille was one of the two most severe recorded hurricanes ever to strike the United States. Rated as category five on the Saffir-Simpson scale, the highest rating, Camille brought winds of over 200 miles per hour, a seven-mile-wide storm center, and a storm surge of up to twenty-three feet (Leyden 1985; U.S. Army Corps of Engineers 1970).

Camille pounded the coast for four hours, causing 144 deaths on the Mississippi shore, most by drowning. It then proceeded northeast, causing flash floods and additional casualties in Virginia and West Virginia. Nationwide, damages ran over one billion dollars. The state of Mississippi suffered over $500 million in damages, with over $300 million of this in coastal Harrison County. Some 3000 homes were destroyed in the county, another 27,500 damaged, and 200 businesses were destroyed or damaged.

About 10 percent of Harrison County's land area was flooded. Parts of its waterfront communities of Long Beach, Gulfport, and Biloxi, and all of Pass Christian, were inundated by floodwaters (see figure 3.1). The storm surge proceeded inland and then rebounded back across the developed coastal peninsulas. Storm waters rose to 22.6 feet at Pass Christian, 21.6 feet at Long Beach, 21 feet at Gulfport, and 19.5 feet at Biloxi. Some eighty hurricane-generated tornadoes added to the destruction. Within three to four blocks of the coastline, devastation was complete. Coastal Highway 90 was flooded, two bridges were washed out, and public utilities and hospitals were knocked out of service.

Prestorm Institutional Context

Despite the passage of the National Flood Insurance Program in the year before Camille, no Mississippi communities were yet participating in the program. The lack of the stronger construction standards required under the program had a major impact on the ability of the Harrison County communities to withstand the hurricane. Buildings subject to wave action had not been required to be elevated or to be designed or built to resist hurricane wave and wind forces. Even a house designed by a local archi-

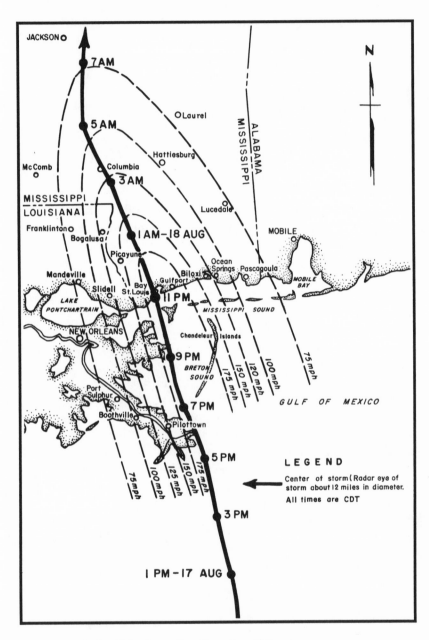

Figure 3.1 Path of Hurricane Camille at Landfall

tect to be "hurricane proof" was destroyed, killing the owner and others who had taken shelter there.

The lack of flood insurance also had a major impact on the ability of the communities to recover and rebuild. Federally subsidized flood insurance was not yet available and few homeowners carried private flood insurance policies. Insurance payments covered only 20 percent of the total damages.

The Mississippi coast has been the repeated target of hurricanes. Over the past century the frequency of hurricane landfall within 100 miles of Biloxi is once every ten to fifteen years. Prior to Camille, Harrison County suffered major hurricane damage in 1893, 1906, 1915, 1916, 1947, and 1965. Hurricane Betsy caused $400 million in damage in 1965.

Various mitigation actions have been attempted following hurricane strikes. Building strengthening through adoption of minimum construction standards was an early response. Biloxi began enforcement of a local building code after a severe 1911 hurricane, and Gulfport also administered a local building code for many years. After Hurricane Betsy in 1965 the stricter Southern Standard Building Code was adopted by Biloxi, Gulfport, and Long Beach. However, neither Pass Christian nor Harrison County had adopted construction standards prior to Camille.

Structural reinforcement of the coastal environment also was an early response. After the 1915 hurricane partially destroyed coastal Highway 90, a twenty-six-mile, ten-foot-high seawall was built seaward of the highway to act as a storm barrier. The $3.5 million project was funded through two local bond issues, financed by a share of the gasoline taxes collected in the county. This seawall was breached in several places during a 1947 hurricane, and an artificial beach was pumped up in 1951 to protect the seawall and highway. Harrison County financed the new beach with two-thirds local funds and one-third federal funds, under a contract mandating that the new beach be dedicated to public use.

A waterfront landowner brought suit in 1962, claiming ownership of the filled beach in front of his property. The Mississippi Supreme Court ruled in his favor (*Harrison County* v. *Guice*, 140 S.2d 838). However, in an appeal of a 1968 challenge brought by the federal government to require that the beach be maintained for public use, the U.S. Court of Appeals overruled the 1962 decision and upheld the county's obligation to keep the beach open for public use (*United States* v. *Harrison County,*

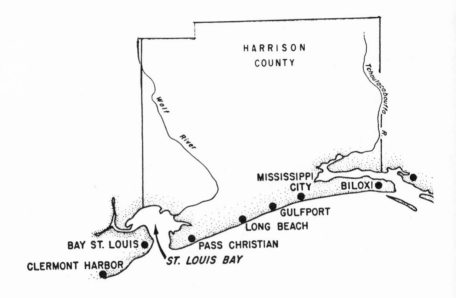

Figure 3.2   Coastal Harrison County, Mississippi

Mississippi, 399 F.2d 485). This "open beaches" decision has largely prevented development of the area south of the seawall, where only public recreational facilities are permitted.

Some planning and zoning were in place prior to Camille, but there was no attempt at integrating hazard mitigation and development management (MetaSystems 1970). The Gulf Regional Planning Commission, established in 1965, offered technical assistance to the local governments and had nearly completed work on a regional land use plan in 1969. Long Beach, Biloxi, and Gulfport had prepared comprehensive plans and consultant studies, but they did not address storm hazard mitigation. Each of the four municipalities administered a zoning ordinance without floodplain designations or regulations. The county had no zoning or planning.

The economic base of Harrison County depended on tourism, seafood production, and federal payrolls. Since the nineteenth century tourists have come from Louisiana, Alabama, and northern Mississippi to enjoy the coastal beaches. More recently, the area has been a vacation spot and locale for real estate investments for New Orleans oil interests. Harrison County also has been an important seafood market since the last century. Federal activities include Keesler Airforce Base in Biloxi, the Navy Seabee base in Gulfport, Veterans Administration hospitals, a military retirement home, and federally owned forests. The NASA test facility and Ingall's Shipbuilding Company in neighboring counties also influence the local economy.

Population in the county in 1970, just after the hurricane, was about 135,000. Biloxi and Gulfport were near 50,000 each, while Long Beach was about 6,000 and Pass Christian about 3,000. During the ten years before Camille, the population of the Mississippi coast grew by 27 percent while the rest of the state either lost population or remained stable. Despite a continuation of the long trend of building back after coastal storms with an increase in the amount and value of property at risk, population growth in the coastal communities has not increased substantially during the fifteen years it has taken to recover from Camille.

Poststorm Recovery

In rebuilding after Camille, opportunities for hazard mitigation were largely ignored, with the exception of the limitations of a stricter building code and the elevation requirements of the National Flood Insurance Program. Recovery was guided by a determination to build back bigger and stronger than before. Larger hotels and restaurants were built, and many residential areas were rezoned for commercial use.

Despite the view of many local residents that the recovery was successful, lingering effects of Camille are visible fifteen years after the storm. Vacant lots and old concrete slabs mark unreconstructed properties. The site of the Richileau Apartments, where twenty-seven people were killed during a "hurricane party," remained vacant for some fifteen years, at least partly due to the stigma of disaster associated with the site.

Two distinct stages were observed in intergovernmental relationships during the recovery process (Leyden personal interviews 1984). First, a spirit of cooperation dominated; federal, state, regional, and local officials worked together to channel disaster assistance funds to devastated areas. The localities accepted state and federal planning assistance because reconstruction funds were tied to adoption of land use regulations. Within a year, the second stage began, in which individualism and local autonomy were reasserted and the emphasis on regional planning and cooperation collapsed.

Intergovernmental Relationships

Immediately after the storm the Governor's Emergency Council was established by executive order to oversee cleanup, reconstruction, redevelopment, and long-range regional planning. The council also took on the role of coordinating federal disaster relief when President Nixon designated it as the contact point for all federal aid. Under threat that federal funds would be cut off and the area declared ineligible for the National Flood Insurance Program unless a stricter building code and formal elevation requirements were adopted, the council was given broad authority to set priorities for state and federal expenditures. It imposed a moratorium on new coastal construction, drafted a revised building code, created a nonprofit coastal building inspection agency, and hired a consultant to analyze regional economic development needs.

The Governor's Emergency Council was established because of a belief that "local governments would not or could not institute, maintain, and enforce regulations necessary to protect life and property against disasters through adequate construction requirements and land use regulations" (Coast Code Administration 1969). However, local government officials resented the bureaucratic procedures of the council, which they saw as a group of outsiders interfering in reconstruction. A special legislative act requiring the local governments to adopt the council's uniform building code was abandoned due to perceived lack of support among coastal legislators. Instead, the municipalities individually adopted the new code, and within a year all Harrison County municipalities had adopted it. Regional code enforcement also proved unpopular, and both Biloxi and Gulfport maintained their own building inspectors. By 1971 inspections were being done by the county and the municipalities, a situation that has resulted in problems of code violations, particularly on illegal habitation and lack of breakaway walls in first floor areas below the base flood elevation.

Financial Assistance

Camille devastated the tax base of Harrison County (Williams 1979). In the two years after the storm municipal revenues fell behind operating expenses by $3.7 million. Long Beach lost 30 percent of its taxable property; Pass Christian lost 70 percent.

The federal government made sections of the Disaster Relief Act of 1970 (Public Law 91-606) retroactive to August 1969 in order to provide Camille relief funds. These included assistance to individuals, businesses, and local governments. Local governments could get grants to replace lost property tax revenues and to reconstruct damaged public facilities. Including relief organizations and nonfederal agencies, an estimated $50 million in Camille disaster aid was expended in the Corps of Engineers Mobile District (Mobile to New Orleans).

The larger municipalities were better equipped to secure federal funds. The small city of Pass Christian only received enough funding to return to the point where it was "just surviving." Throughout Harrison County, however, there was dissatisfaction with the amount and process of disaster funding. In a 1977 assessment of local development needs many infrastructure improvements and repairs were identified which local officials believed were leftover from inadequately repaired Camille damages.

Redevelopment

Confusion immediately following the storm allowed unregulated repairs and rebuilding. First the building permit requirement was waived throughout the county. Then the council's moratorium was imposed, but it was not uniformly enforced. Finally the moratorium was lifted before the revised building code was adopted in final form. Fortunately there was a lag in reconstruction due to lack of insurance loss payments (most policies did not cover flood losses) and shortage of rebuilding funds.

Commercial and residential building records indicate a shift in development to the northern, nonhazard areas of the county following Camille. Between 1960 and 1968 Gulfport and Biloxi accounted for 69 percent of the county building permit value. Between 1969 and 1974 this fell to 26 percent. Land prices for vacant lots and damaged properties also fell after Camille and remained depressed for some time.

During recent years coastal development and land values have risen. Condominium projects are increasingly seen, and land values are considered to be at an all time high. Despite the problems of a shallow bay with sometimes questionable water quality (which makes it hard to compete with the Alabama coastal resorts), the lingering disaster stigma, and the scarcity of available coastal property without elevation problems, the development market has strengthened again.

Hazard Perceptions

Since Camille, local residents have been extremely hurricane conscious. While 50,000 people refused to evacuate during Camille, the county's coastal area was 100 percent evacuated during Hurricane Frederic in 1979. The slowness to rebuild after Camille and the trend toward building in the nonwaterfront, upland areas of the county point to a clear impact on development patterns.

A contrary result also has taken place. Due to the severity of Camille, it is perceived as a once in a lifetime event which cannot be planned for or mitigated (Leyden 1984). Residents believe that nothing can survive another storm of this same force, leading them toward an anti-hazard-mitigation attitude.

Another perception concerns the positive side of the impacts of Camille on the county. Residents point to the removal of substandard buildings, the increased awareness of the importance of building standards, and the influx of federal money to the local economy as benefits of the storm.

Development Management

Harrison County's poststorm mitigation efforts were motivated by the need to qualify for the NFIP, federally guaranteed mortgages, and other federal funds. Private insurance companies had threatened to discontinue coverage in the coastal counties. The first step was adoption of the new coastal building code, with its designated hurricane critical exposure zone and required first-floor elevation.

Many zoning changes were counter to good mitigation practice. Land in the hazard area was rezoned from low-density residential to commercial and then to multifamily residential when commercial development failed to materialize. Another counterexample is the 1984 construction of a sixty-nine-unit condominium project, the Villages at Henderson Point, on a five-acre site south of Highway 90 on a peninsula that was leveled by Camille. Currently, few zoning provisions address hazard mitigation.

Since 1972 all four municipalities and the county have adopted flood-plain ordinances. These require all construction to comply with the minimum elevation and floodproofing requirements of the National Flood Insurance Program. Elevation requirements vary from eleven to eighteen feet above mean sea level.

Land acquisition after Camille was limited to forty-five parcels of beachfront property designated as part of Biloxi's urban renewal area prior to the storm. In a clash of redevelopment and mitigation priorities Biloxi approved a thirteen-story, low-income apartment complex on the waterfront, adjacent to the urban renewal area.

Mitigation Assessment

Despite local opinion about a successful recovery, mitigation actions taken since Camille are clearly inadequate (Leyden 1985). Instead of taking the lessons to heart, none of the municipalities has squarely addressed the need for reconstruction and mitigation policies following the next disaster.

Such policies should include:

1. Limits on allowable densities in high hazard areas, including downzoning of multi-family areas.
2. Limiting new waterfront construction to water dependent uses.
3. Designating existing uses on the Gulf side of Highway 90 as nonconforming, so as to bring about their eventual elimination.
4. Acquiring additional land for conservation and recreation, especially in low-lying hazard areas.
5. Strengthening the building code, especially standards for pilings.
6. Coordinating wastewater extensions with the County Wastewater District to limit development in hazard areas.
7. Maintaining current infrastructure inventories to facilitate disaster claims and replacement.

In the meantime, development on the Mississippi coast has been kept to a moderate level by several factors: low water quality in the Mississippi Sound; court-imposed development restrictions on the waterfront side of Highway 90; the memory of Hurricane Camille's fury; and decreasing availability of adequate drinking water supplies due to surface water pollution, overpumping of groundwater wells leading to drawdown and salt water intrusion, and inadequate water supply infrastructure. Whether these factors will limit development in hazard areas sufficiently to protect life and property is uncertain, especially in the face of another market rise. Given current negative attitudes toward active development management, however, such factors may be the main source of additional hazard mitigation in Harrison County.

Gulf Shores Recovers from Hurricane Frederic

Hurricane Frederic

Hurricane Frederic roared across the Gulf coast of Alabama at 10:00 P.M., September 12, 1979 (see figure 3.3). With winds gusting up to 145 miles per hour and a storm surge of up to fifteen feet above mean sea level, it devastated the beachfront development in its path. Classified as a category three storm, it had one of the widest centers ever recorded —extending fifty miles across. Its rain, winds, and tornadoes left a path of destruction some 250 miles wide and 150 miles deep (Godschalk 1987; Hegenbarth 1985).

Fortunately, Frederic struck after Labor Day had marked the end of the tourist season, and the bulk of the summer visitors had left the oceanfront tourist areas. Even so, some 250,000 persons were evacuated. Only five deaths were directly attributable to Frederic, but it was one of the most physically destructive storms ever to hit the upper Gulf coast, resulting in losses of $2.2 billion. Thirty counties in Alabama, Mississippi, and Florida were declared by President Carter as disaster areas eligible for federal assistance under Public Law 93-288 (U.S. Army Corps of Engineers 1981).

The most severe damage was received by Baldwin County, Alabama, where a thirty-two mile stretch of coastal barrier known as Pleasure Island took the brunt of the storm (see figure 3.4). High-water elevations ranged up to fifteen feet above mean sea level there. Some 565 Pleasure Island structures were destroyed, and another 250 were severely damaged. In Gulf Shores, the only incorporated municipality on Pleasure Island, 90 percent of the first two tiers of development were either totally destroyed or so badly damaged that they could not be rebuilt, public utilities were

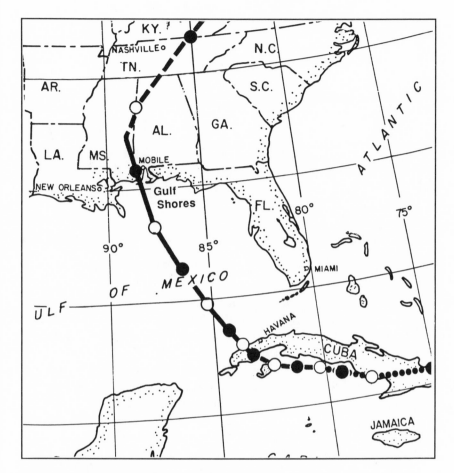

Figure 3.3   Path of Hurricane Frederic at Landfall

knocked out, the main coast highway was breached in numerous places, and the tourist-based economy was wiped away. Claims were received from some 90 percent of the 800 federal flood insurance policyholders in Gulf Shores, amounting to over $16 million in damages. Losses in Baldwin County totaled over $254 million.

Natural environmental systems were severely disrupted. The coastal dunes were flattened or badly eroded. The storm surge broke a new inlet

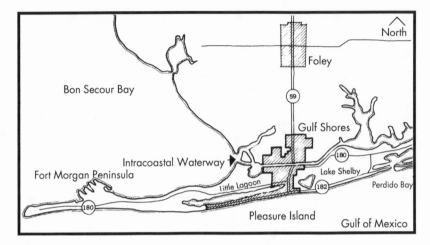

Figure 3.4   Southern Baldwin County and Pleasure Island

through from the Gulf into the freshwater Lake Shelby, east of Gulf Shores. The shoreline eroded as much as 100 feet, and sand was pushed back into the salt marshes.

Hurricane aftershocks also disrupted the Gulf Shores governmental system (Godschalk 1987). Disagreements arose among elected and appointed officials and citizens. Within a week the head of Civil Defense resigned; within a year the mayor and all council members but one were voted out in the next municipal elections; and within two years the town clerk, a post similar to that of a town manager, and the head building inspector were replaced. The trauma of the hurricane extended well into the postdisaster period.

Prestorm Institutional Context

Gulf Shores was not unprepared to meet the physical force of a hurricane, according to prevailing hazard policies. It had entered the regular phase of the National Flood Insurance Program in 1971 and adopted the Southern Standard Building Code at that time. It revised its 1963 zoning ordinance in 1972 with assistance from the Office of State Planning in the Alabama Development Office (although serious loopholes remained in this zoning, including no side-yard or coastal setbacks). A flood control ordinance requiring all new development in flood hazard zones to comply with federal flood insurance regulations was passed in 1978.

Yet much of the existing beachfront development in Gulf Shores had been built before the adoption of building, electrical, or mechanical codes. Many of the houses were wooden vacation cottages, located on low-lying lots bounded on the south by the Gulf of Mexico and on the north by the beach highway, State Road 182. While most of them were elevated eight or nine feet above mean sea level, they were unprotected from twelve- to fifteen-foot hurricane storm surges. A number of beachfront structures had been built in front of the protective dunes.

Two years before Frederic, Alabama's Coastal Area Act established the Coastal Area Board to carry out coastal management programs. One week before Frederic, this board voted to require a forty-foot building setback behind the primary dune crest on all beachfront lots in order to protect the primary dune system from development so that it could serve as a buffer and stabilizer for the shore. After Frederic flattened the dunes, this requirement became controversial and ultimately a variance was granted, exempting the densest area of Gulf Shores from the setback. The controversy has continued.

Baldwin County had not had a direct hit from a hurricane of Frederic's force since 1926. It was seventy-five miles east of the Camille storm center in 1969 and received winds of only seventy-five miles per hour and a high-water mark of nine feet in that storm. Still, there was flood damage and dune erosion, and Baldwin County was designated a disaster area after Camille.

At the time of Camille, Gulf Shores had only 900 permanent residents. Between 1970 and 1980 its population went up 48 percent to 1349 permanent residents. These figures do not include the seasonal population; this is better illustrated by the increase in housing units, from 130 in 1970 to 1567 in 1980. Baldwin County's population increased 32 percent between 1970 and 1980, from 59,382 to 78,556.

Baldwin County, part of the Mobile metropolitan area, has an economic base dominated by agriculture. The Pleasure Island economy is primarily dependent on resort residential income, with the permanent population employed in tourism or fishing. Alabama's Gulf State Park is a popular tourist destination, along with the beachfront motels and condominiums. By the late 1970s high-density resort condominiums were being built in the adjacent Florida beachfront areas, and development pressures were moving toward Pleasure Island, ready to replace the modest beach cottages of the place some called the "Redneck Riviera."

Poststorm Recovery

Following Frederic, there were strong economic and psychological pressures to rebuild as quickly as possible. The town's source of livelihood, its tourist-oriented beachfront, was wiped out. Its residents and business people were anxious to return their property and their community to normal. There was an overriding sense of sympathy for the disaster stricken homeowners; there was little sympathy for rules, regulations, and bureaucratic procedures. Public officials were under pressure to be lenient in the application of building codes and zoning ordinances. The prevailing attitude of elected officials was to facilitate a quick reconstruction and to reduce burdens on storm victims.

The recovery was fueled by a coastal development boom which came on the heels of Frederic. Before the storm tourist and rental properties were primarily small, single-family wooden cottages, with only two motels and one condominium in operation. In the year following the storm building permits were issued for 435 new condominium units valued at almost $11 million. That boom has continued into the mid 1980s, dramatically changing the face of Gulf Shores.

Recovery processes generally follow two stages. The first stage, just after the disaster, involves immediate decisions about rebuilding damaged homes, businesses, streets, and public utilities. The concern is to restore basic lifeline facilities, protect public health and safety, and return to more or less normal community and personal operations patterns. The second stage involves decisions about redevelopment and future hazard mitigation. The concern is to rewrite plans, policies, and regulations affecting development in hazard areas. In Gulf Shores the first stage extended roughly from the hurricane in September 1979 into 1980. It included actions on imposing a building moratorium, rebuilding damaged utilities and roads, determining the extent of damage to individual structures, and acquiring hazard area property. The second stage, extending from 1980 into 1985, included decisions about adopting a new zoning ordinance and building code supplement, requiring a side setback for new buildings, and locating a coastal construction setback line (Godschalk 1987).

Intergovernmental Relationships

The newly created Federal Emergency Management Agency (FEMA) played a major role in the Gulf Shores recovery process as overall coordinator of national disaster recovery programs. They reviewed the damage survey reports prepared by the Mobile District Corps of Engineers and determined the amount of funds needed to repair public facilities. They coordinated the activities of other agencies providing loans or grants to disaster victims. They made available funds to acquire damaged property for public use and to hire a structural engineer and a planning consultant to provide technical assistance to the town. In a sense Hurricane Frederic was a testing ground for the new FEMA and its disaster response procedures.

Gulf Shores' ability to recover swiftly from the hurricane's impact was clearly related to the high level of financial and technical assistance provided by FEMA. However, local officials found it frustrating to work with cumbersome federal regulations and communications procedures. Alabama local government norms traditionally expect political leaders to play conservative and custodial roles and to resist pressures for change and innovation. These expectations conflicted with federal demands for more aggressive hazard mitigation.

Conflict also arose with the Alabama Coastal Area Board over application of the new Coastal Construction Setback Line. Because the benchmark for the adopted forty-foot setback was the primary dune crestline which had been obliterated by Frederic, it took eighteen months for the Coastal Area Board staff to map the new setback line. The mapping process relied on tracing the former dune crestline from aerial photographs taken before the storm onto new, poststorm aerials, a long and often subjective process (see figure 3.5). In the Gulf Shores central business district shorefront there was no existing dune system because businesses on the shallow lots had flattened and built over the primary dune. When it became clear that requiring a forty-foot setback from the theoretical dune line in this central tourist business area could preclude development on some beachfront properties, a compromise was reached that granted a variance reducing the setback to five feet in this area. Thus,

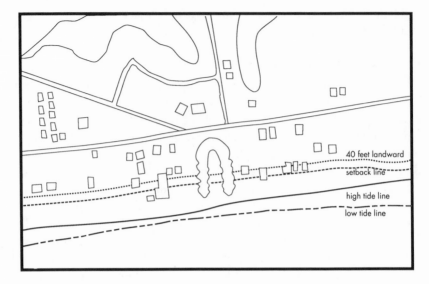

Figure 3.5   Example of the Mapped Coastal Construction Setback Line

Gulf Shores has the paradoxical requirement that high-rise condominiums in the central tourist business area may build thirty-five feet closer to
the water's edge than one-story, single-family houses in the residential
area. This is just the opposite of coastal setback regulations in North
Carolina, which require major structures to be set back twice as far as
single-family houses.

Controversy over the coastal setback has continued. The federal Office
of Ocean and Coastal Resource Management, which administers the
national coastal management program, raised issues about the variance
and the legitimacy of the permitting authority of Gulf Shores, the only
town in Alabama that elected to assume administration of the coastal
construction setback certification from the state. Eventually, these issues
were worked out with the variance remaining. Meanwhile, outside of
Gulf Shores in the rapidly developing part of the Baldwin County waterfront to the east near the Florida line, the Alabama Department of Environmental Management (which has taken over the Coastal Area Board's
responsibilities) has allowed a high-rise condominium to be built in front
of the setback just 100 feet from the waterline in return for the construc-

Table 3.2   Estimate of Total Damages in Gulf Shores Vicinity

State Highways 182 and 59	$ 8,000,000
Damage to Gulf Shores State Park	3,000,000
FEMA Special Revenue Fund Assistance	1,028,644[a]
FEMA Disaster Loan (later repaid)	255,100
NFIP Policy Payments (719 claims)	16,143,007
Total	$28,426,751

a. Eligible expenses.

tion of an "artificial" dune in front of the building. An environmental coalition challenged this weakened setback policy in court, but the building was completed in 1984.

As development pressures increase, another potential intergovernmental conflict has surfaced between Gulf Shores and Baldwin County. Although modest by comparison with active growth management localities, the Gulf Shores development regulations and enforcement actions are much stricter than those of the county. Should developers opt for less-regulated, county locations for their projects, then much Pleasure Island growth could occur under minimum controls. As growth places increasing demands on limited resources, such as water supply and transportation facilities, the need for cooperation and joint planning between these two jurisdictions will grow.

Financial Assistance

Federal disaster payments for public and private property damage in the Gulf Shores area was estimated as some $28 million (see table 3.2). This included $11 million in federal loans and grants to the state of Alabama to repair its two highways and state park, $16 million in flood insurance policy claims, and $1 million in assistance to the town. The Corps of Engineers estimated the total of all public and private losses in Baldwin County at $254 million and the total of federal disaster assistance to the county at $95 million.

As a community dependent on tourist revenues, Gulf Shores relied on sales and use tax revenues. With its tourist facilities in shambles the town was without income. FEMA provided $255,100 in Community Disaster Loans to replace the cash-flow losses. The town also was eligible for over $1 million from FEMA's Special Revenue Fund, which provided 100 percent reimbursement for restoring damaged municipal infrastructure to its prestorm condition (this funding was later reduced to 75 percent federal reimbursement; see chapter 4). It ultimately received payment for some $854,000 of eligible expenses. A critical condition in the Special Revenue Fund stipulated that repairs could only be made to restore public facilities to their prestorm condition and that no "betterment" of public facilities could take place unless strong planning justification was provided.

FEMA also provided $1 million from its newly funded Section 1362 Acquisition Program to acquire five parcels of damaged property in the hurricane hazard zone. These 3.5 acres, located in the center of the tourist business district adjacent to the existing public beach, were deeded to the town. They were added to the public beach and recreation area. Three other damaged properties also were acquired by the town for $211,000, with matching funds from the U.S. Department of Interior. Additional damaged properties were qualified for public acquisition, but without the power of condemnation the program depended on voluntary purchase, which limited its application in Gulf Shores since many property owners were unwilling to sell to the government in the highly speculative real estate market that existed after the storm.

Unlike the communities hit by Camille, Gulf Shores recovered its fiscal balance within two years of its disaster due to a development boom. FEMA Community Disaster Loans can be canceled if the local government revenues during the three years after the disaster are insufficient to meet the operating budget. Gulf Shores disaster loans matured in 1982, and by 1983 they had been paid in full, the first time that a community had reached sufficient fiscal stability within the three-year period to be able to repay the federal loans.

Evidence of the economic recovery is found in the town's fiscal records. From 1979 to 1981 the real property taxes increased from $66,638 to $167,716. Its sales and use tax revenues for that period went from $445,900 to $721,614. In just two years the fiscal disaster was over.

Redevelopment

Immediately after the storm emergency actions were taken to restrict access to the island in order to keep out sightseers and looters and to protect residents from health hazards posed by broken sewer lines, exposed septic tanks, and rotting food. No fresh water was available in the beach area, and most of the water mains were contaminated. The beach highway was covered with tons of sand and debris and was breached in many places. Restoration of utilities and debris cleanup were the first priorities.

Among the first public actions after the hurricane passed was the imposition of a temporary moratorium on redevelopment, preventing reconstruction and repair of damaged buildings. This moratorium was lifted as soon as the beach water and sewer systems were repaired. When rebuilding began, building inspectors were lenient in applying the 50 percent damage assessment that would have required conformance with elevation and floodproofing requirements, and many variances were granted, especially when the homeowner had not been insured (Hegenbarth 1985). Thus, lax enforcement of the building code allowed many older, nonconforming structures to be rebuilt without meeting the flood ordinance and building code standards that new construction had to meet. Some newer nonconforming structures also were allowed to rebuild. The Beachhouse, Gulf Shore's first condominium, was rebuilt in its former location seaward of the dune crest line despite complete destruction of over half of its units and major damage to the rest (see horseshoe shaped building in figure 3.5).

Many other opportunities for long-range hazard mitigation were missed in the push to rebuild as quickly as possible. Rather than simply repairing the damaged sewer lines, which ran along the beach highway close to the Gulf front, the town engineer recommended relocating the main trunk line well back from the highway with feeder lines running down to the beachfront. His plan, while more costly, would have better protected the main sewer lines from future storm damage. But the town could not afford to replace the lines without federal assistance, and they were prevented from "betterment" of the sewer service system without strong planning justification. Without the time or technical resources to prepare the necessary planning justification, the town was forced to replace the sewer lines in their original location.

Relocation of the damaged beach highway, State Road 182, farther
north away from the Gulf waterfront was also proposed. Not only would
this better protect this critical access and evacuation route from future
storm damage, but it would also increase the limited depth of the lots
fronting on the beach. These lots had gotten shallower as hurricane and
annual winter storm erosion ate into the shoreline, and their inability to
be deepened would pose a problem in enforcing the coastal construction
setback line. But the state highway department made the decision to
restore the highway in its original location.

A third missed opportunity concerned replacement of overhead utility
wires with underground cables. Prior to the hurricane the utility companies had agreed to gradually move to underground service, but after the
storm they did not believe they had the time or money to move the main
cables underground, so the utilities were replaced on poles.

The new town council elected in 1980 faced several hazard mitigation
issues. One of the first concerned the adoption of a side setback requirement. Gulf Shores zoning regulations allowed building from lot line to lot
line. In the high density development boom, the community found itself
with three-story condominiums creating a solid wall along the beachfront.
They not only constituted a fire hazard, but they also blocked the view of
the Gulf from the coastal highway. In most U.S. localities side setbacks are
commonly accepted, but in Gulf Shores they became a major issue. Heated
debates pitted developers who said setbacks would make it too expensive
for them to build against citizens who said the town's livelihood would be
endangered without such setbacks. The new council agreed with the
citizens and in 1981 passed ten-foot-minimum, side-yard setbacks, which
increased two feet for each additional story over the first two stories up to
a maximum setback of thirty feet.

Less controversial was the new building code supplement, drafted by a
structural engineer paid with FEMA funds. This Supplemental Building
Code for Coastal Construction in High Hazard Areas sets voluntary
guidelines to strengthen wood-frame, one- and two-family structures.
(Larger structures are covered under the Southern Standard Building Code.)
It was adopted in 1981 with little opposition due to the obvious damage
suffered by older buildings during the hurricane. Other changes to the
building code were enacted to require fire-resistant first-floor construction for buildings over two stories.

A new zoning ordinance, prepared by a planning consultant with a FEMA grant, was adopted in 1982 and amended in 1984. Besides the usual zoning district designations and density regulations, it includes the side setback and coastal construction setback provisions, does not allow dune alteration without a variance, gives density bonuses for reductions in lot coverage, and encourages transfer of density from beachfront to second-tier lots across Highway 182.

One further action taken by the community was a tour of other southern coastal resort areas in order to assess potential development styles and approaches. In 1981 a number of public officials, business people, and citizens spent a week visiting other areas. They agreed that Myrtle Beach was too commercial and Hilton Head too exclusive and that Gulf Shores would need to plan its future rather than simply responding to development proposals.

Hazard Perceptions

Gulf Shores leaders admit that they are not completely prepared for the next hurricane (Hegenbarth 1985). While they point to the stronger and safer new buildings as a result of their improved construction standards and elevation requirements, they concede that their 1984 evacuation plan is inadequate and that flooded approaches and limited capacity could result in bottlenecks at their highway bridges. They are concerned that an outside expert, Dr. Neil Frank, director of the National Hurricane Center, has termed Pleasure Island a "deathtrap," since its evacuation routes will have to deal with over 30,000 peak-season residents, up to six times as many as in 1979.

Meanwhile, they have not adopted a rebuilding strategy to deal with the mitigation opportunities lost during the Frederic recovery. They have not yet planned for the new problems likely to result from the less-regulated development outside the town or from the new more-complicated ownership patterns resulting from widespread time-sharing and condominium ownership.

However, the community is generally pleased with its recovery. With the aid of "hurricane renewal," the town has been transformed from a collection of weekend cottages to a modern, high-density beach resort. It has changed its leadership to a more progressive group of civic-minded citizens. It is fiscally well off, with a 1985 budget of $6.2 million, including an unbudgeted surplus of $1.23 million. As the mayor elected during the recovery sees it: "There was a silver lining to this cloud. We did lose an awful lot of substandard junk that we would never have gotten rid of any other way. People were for the most part not financially hurt. The values of properties began to rise and those substandard junks became valuable pieces of property. Most people have come out of it quite well financially. We also got a lot of publicity. People heard about Gulf Shores all over the country who would never have heard about us otherwise. Property values did not drop. There was practically no panic selling. People had confidence that we were going to come back" (Norton 1982).

Development Management

Following Frederic, Gulf Shores directed its mitigation efforts toward strengthening buildings through its building code and toward an orderly pattern of development through improving its zoning ordinance. It also used federal funds to acquire damaged properties in its central area to extend its public beach.

As growth pressures continue on Pleasure Island, Gulf Shores is increasingly looking to infrastructure-related development management measures. In 1984 its Water Works Board enacted substantial impact fees for water and sewer tap-ons in order to pay for new lines to serve higher-density development on the west beach and to expand water supply facilities.

Waste treatment facilities are inadequate in Pleasure Island areas outside Gulf Shores, as well. Uncoordinated waste treatment facilities, including package treatment plants, have resulted in unacceptably high levels of pollution in the Intracoastal Waterway. In response the Alabama Department of Environmental Management set a 1988 deadline for lowering BOD (biological oxygen demand) levels in the waterway. Gulf Shores initiated a study of ocean outfalls as an alternative to discharging effluent into the waterway.

Finally, community leaders sought to increase evacuation capacity through seeking funds for additional bridge routes off the island. In the summer of 1984 Gulf Shores officials began discussions with state highway planners about this need.

Mitigation Assessment

Gulf Shores believes that it had a successful recovery after Frederic. However, its leaders admit that the storm caught them unprepared to cope with the pressures of recovery and rebuilding (Godschalk 1987). According to the mayor elected after the storm, they were not prepared, and they made mistakes. His advice to coastal local governments is to keep their zoning ordinances and building codes in shape, go underground with their utilities, prepare themselves financially, and elect and appoint officials with the intestinal fortitude to make the right decisions (Norton 1982).

Are they prepared for the next hurricane? In many ways they are not, despite a number of advances. As of 1984 the evacuation plan was inadequate, and the capacity of the escape route bridges was below that needed for peak-season evacuation. The town still had no land use plan. No rebuilding strategy had been prepared to deal with storm-related problems, such as the increasingly narrow lots on the beach side of the coastal highway, prevention of rebuilding damaged structures in obvious high-hazard zones, placing utility lines underground, or managing the booming development of Pleasure Island as a whole to balance it with public protection in time of another major hurricane.

The high-density development following Frederic has drastically increased the scope of the hazard mitigation problem. The next hurricane will strike a totally different Pleasure Island, with three to six times as many peak-season residents as were there in 1979. The mitigation actions taken for a beach of small, family cottages after Frederic will no longer suffice for a barrier island crowded with high-rise condominiums growing almost indiscriminately and with little regard for maintaining the capacity of its natural ecological systems.

Galveston Recovers from Hurricane Alicia

Hurricane Alicia

Hurricane Alicia crossed the western tip of Galveston Island during the predawn hours of August 18, 1983. It was the first tropical cyclone of full hurricane intensity to strike the U.S. mainland after a lull of over three years. Although only a mild Category 3 storm, it caused the most dollar damage of any storm ever striking Texas and was second in total U.S.

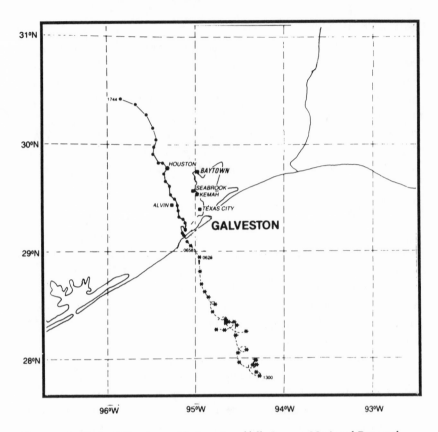

Figure 3.6   Path of Hurricane Alicia at Landfall. *Source*: National Research Council 1984, 5.

coastal property damage only to Hurricane Frederic (Texas Department of Public Safety 1984; National Research Council 1984).

Alicia demonstrated the vulnerability of developed coastal metropolitan areas to major storm forces. Though not a strong hurricane, Alicia's northeast quadrant—its area of maximum winds—buffeted the large, built-up urban area around Houston and Galveston (see figure 3.6). Wind damage was extensive throughout this area, with rain and storm surges causing flooding in locations bordering the Gulf of Mexico and Galveston Bay. Damage was magnified by the amount of high-density urban development in the storm's path. Glass was blown out of a number of skyscrapers in downtown Houston, beachfront houses were flattened on the western end of Galveston Island, and an entire low-lying bay-front subdivision was flooded out in Baytown, an adjoining city on the eastern shore of Galveston Bay.

At landfall Alicia's winds reached 115 miles per hour; they diminished rapidly as the storm moved inland. Hurricane tides rose over nine feet on the Gulf side of Galveston Island, eroding away some 75 to 100 feet of beach near its west end. Because of the funneling effect, tides along the upper Galveston Bay area rose to ten to twelve feet. Alicia's rains were not heavy; the six to nine inches of rainfall in the low-lying Houston-Galveston corridor caused less flooding than expected (Texas Department of Public Safety 1984).

Nine Texas counties were declared national disaster areas. Estimated total damage from Alicia was over $1.5 billion. As a result of Alicia, 21 deaths and 7200 injuries were recorded; some 2300 dwelling units were destroyed and another 3500 received major damage; over 18,600 families were affected by storm damage. Total privately insured losses were estimated at $675.5 million, with another $119 million in losses under the National Flood Insurance Program. FEMA approved 135 projects under its public assistance program to communities at a total cost of $43.26 million, 75 percent of which was paid by federal funds.

Several unique features of Alicia influenced the emergency response. First, it had been a slow moving tropical storm headed toward the coast well south of Galveston until 5:00 P.M. on August 16, when it was declared a hurricane less than a day and a half before it struck. It strengthened rapidly in the twelve to eighteen hours prior to landfall and turned sharply north-northwest toward Galveston during the afternoon of August 17. Second, it was the first hurricane since precautionary evacuation warnings had been issued during Hurricane Allen in 1980. Although Allen came ashore well south of Galveston, 65 percent of Galveston's residents evacuated and city officials were criticized for issuing an "unnecessary" evacuation notice. Third, it was the first storm for which the National Weather Service's new probability system of predicting hurricane landfall was used.

Prestorm Institutional Context

Hurricanes are no strangers to the Texas coast, striking an average of every two and a half years. During this century fourteen hurricanes have

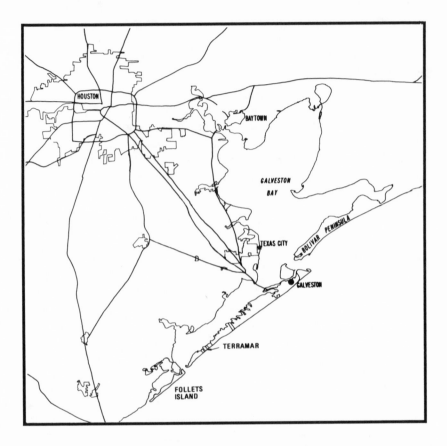

Figure 3.7   Galveston Island, Texas. *Source*: National Research Council 1984, 2.

crossed the Gulf coast in the vicinity of Galveston. Prior to Alicia the most recent severe hurricane flooding on Galveston Island was caused by Hurricane Carla in 1961. The most destructive was the 1900 hurricane which demolished an estimated 3,600 buildings and killed at least 6,000 people in Galveston.

Following the great hurricane of 1900, Galveston built a concrete and granite seawall in front of its developed area (see figure 3.7). With an elevation of some 15.5 feet above mean sea level, this structure extends ten miles from the east end of the island, protecting the older waterfront businesses, hotels, and residences from medium-sized hurricanes with storm surges of less than sixteen feet. The twenty-plus miles of developing beachfront from the end of the seawall to the western tip of the island are unprotected.

Most of the permanent Galveston population is located behind the seawall. It was generally contained there until the 1970s by the unwillingness of the local lending institutions to finance development in the unprotected West Beach area (Miller 1983). However, the risk to owners and lenders was reduced by federal flood insurance, which became available in Galveston County in May 1970, and since then a surge of residential and commercial development has taken place in the West Beach area. At the time of Alicia some $371 million worth of new development for the west end was under consideration.

Two other large structural protection projects have been constructed in the area. The Texas City Hurricane Protection Project consists of sixteen miles of earth levees and gates protecting property along the west shore of Galveston Bay in Galveston County from storm flooding. The Freeport Hurricane Flood Protection Project includes forty miles of levees to control storm tides.

The National Weather Service began to include landfall probabilities with hurricane advisories during the 1983 hurricane season. The forecasts are expressed as percentage probabilities that selected coastal communities will experience hurricane or tropical storm conditions. Under this rather complicated technical forecast system, probabilities given for a twenty-four-hour period must be added to probabilities for preceding time periods in order to derive the total expected probability of a strike in a particular area. These cumulative probabilities do not reach high numbers (the highest Galveston probability reached prior to Alicia was 51 percent), a feature that worries some officials concerned that public reaction will be limited due to the "low" numbers. Hurricane probability workshops were conducted in four Texas communities in early August 1983, just prior to Alicia.

The Texas Coastal Hurricane Preparedness Program utilizes storm surge modeling to aid evacuation decisionmaking during hurricanes. It applies the SLOSH (Sea, Lake, and Overland Surge from Hurricanes) model to determine the distance and height of inland surge penetration in specific segments of the Texas coast. Run by Texas A&M University, the program's first study covering five counties in the Houston-Galveston area was completed and in the hands of government officials in 1981. Its map of "evacuation" zones (areas that can be flooded by storm surge from hurricanes with sustained winds up to 130 mph) and "contingency" zones (for sustained winds over 130 mph) for the Galveston Bay area indicates estimated evacuation times of fourteen hours for evacuation zones and twenty-six hours for all zones in Galveston County, except for the Bolivar Peninsula east of Galveston Island. The map states:

> If you are surprised or suspect that the time recommended for partial or total evacuation of your area is too conservative, just remember that very few new major highways have been added to the Galveston Bay area during the past 25 years, while the number of people and automobiles in this area has increased tremendously. To make matters worse, most of the areas along the bay shore have suffered significant land subsidence, causing evacuation routes to flood more easily as a result of rainwater runoff as well as by storm surge.

Hurricane Carla in 1961 heightened awareness of the seriousness of the flooding hazard posed by the major land subsidence in the area. First noticed in the early 1940s, subsidence of over one foot has occurred in more than 3,000 square miles, with a maximum of about ten feet. Galveston has subsided about a foot, while the Baytown area has subsided as much as nine feet. The primary cause of subsidence is pumping of groundwater for water supply. In 1976 the Texas legislature established the Harris-Galveston Coastal Subsidence District and gave it the power to issue permits controlling the withdrawal of groundwater. Since then, surface water supplies have been replacing wells in eastern Harris County where subsidence has stopped or slowed considerably, but subsidence has been increasing in west Houston where some 60 percent of the water supply is still drawn from wells.

The Texas Open Beaches Act, chapter 61 of the Texas Natural Resources Code, ensures the right of public access to and use of public Gulf beaches and prohibits construction of obstructions or barriers that interfere with such access and use. "Public beaches" are defined as including the area between mean low tide and the natural vegetation line. This definition implies that the public right to use the beach is a "rolling" easement that advances or recedes with the movement of the natural vegetation line, a dynamic border which can move long distances inland when subjected to hurricane forces. Thus houses originally built landward of the vegetation line but ending up on the public beach when that vegetation line receded beneath them could not be repaired or maintained because they would become obstructions to public use and were, as a matter of law, on public land. This became a major issue following Alicia.

Prior to Alicia Galveston had enacted some development regulations aimed at hazard mitigation. A 1980 sand dune ordinance requires dune and vegetation protection and prohibits construction in the dune area west of the seawall and within 500 feet landward of mean high tide without a building permit. In 1983 Local Building Code Amendments added a chapter on Flood Hazard Areas incorporating the most recent FEMA flood elevations to the previously adopted Standard Building Code. Two weeks prior to Alicia Galveston enacted Supplement One to the local amendments, containing stronger building code specifications for all construction seaward or west of the seawall (except for Jamaica Beach which is a separate incorporated jurisdiction).

Galveston also was using relatively new state authority for tax increment financing to support developer-constructed infrastructure (roads, sewers, storm drains, and the like) in the west end. Under tax increment financing agreements the city would freeze tax assessments in the new development area at their predevelopment level and then pay the developer back for the infrastructure from the increase in tax revenues from the more highly developed property. As it paid the developer, it would take title and operational responsibility for the infrastructure. In order to invoke tax increment financing authority the city must first declare the area "blighted." Seven of the nine tax increment finance zones designated in Galveston are in unprotected hurricane hazard zones (five on the west end and two in front of the seawall on the east end).

Galveston annexed the island's west end in 1976 and 1977. It zoned the area for Planned Development, but no comprehensive plan was developed nor were development criteria laid out, despite the vulnerable ecology and extreme hazard exposure of the west end. Basically, the city was in the position of responding to individual private development requests as they were made. At the time of Alicia a development boom was underway on the west beach, with some 5000-7000 dwelling units proposed in four major projects.

Population in Galveston as of 1983 was approximately 62,000, about the same level reported in the 1970 and 1980 census counts. Houston had a 1983 population of about 1.6 million, following major growth periods. Because of its access to the Houston ship channel, Galveston Bay, and the Gulf of Mexico, the area has attracted massive industrial, oil refining, and petrochemical complexes. High-rise offices and hotels are concentrated in downtown Houston. Galveston's economic base includes an active deep-water port, industrial activities, finance, tourism and the University of Texas Medical Branch.

Poststorm Recovery

Rebuilding after Alicia took place throughout the Houston-Galveston metropolitan area. This discussion focuses on Galveston, where most of the Gulf-front damage occurred, and on Baytown, where one bay-front subdivision suffered almost total destruction and was designated for public acquisition.

The Alicia recovery differed from those of the two earlier cases in Mississippi and Alabama because of the use of the Interagency Regional Hazard Mitigation Team. These teams were established by federal interagency agreement in 1980 in order to promote a comprehensive approach to flood hazard mitigation during the postflood recovery process (see chapter 4). They go to the scene of a presidentially declared disaster and prepare a report within fifteen days, emphasizing nonstructural mitigation measures. The authors of this study took part in the Alicia team, whose report was issued September 2, 1983 (FEMA 1983). A ninety-day Post-Flood Recovery Progress Report was issued in December 1983 (FEMA 1983a). The state then issued its required hazard mitigation plan for the counties affected by Alicia in January 1984 (Texas Department of Public Safety 1984).

The Interagency Hazard Mitigation Team concentrated on four problem areas: (1) supporting the city of Baytown's effort to prevent the reoccupation of over 300 damaged houses in the Brownwood Subdivision, including use of federal Section 1362 funds to purchase all insured properties; (2) improving the ability of structures to withstand hurricane forces, including investigation of building failures on Galveston Island and strengthening of codes and enforcement; (3) encouraging area-wide hazard mitigation programs, including development management and postdisaster reconstruction plans; and (4) guiding FEMA and state mitigation recovery efforts.

Intergovernmental Relationships

The key intergovernmental institution in the immediate aftermath of Alicia was the Region 6 Interagency Hazard Mitigation Team. The title page of this team's report lists nine federal agencies, two state agencies, and two local governments:

Federal Agencies
Federal Emergency Management Agency
Department of Agriculture
Department of Army
Department of Commerce
Department of Housing and Urban Development
Department of Interior
Department of Transportation
Environmental Protection Agency
Small Business Administration

State Agencies
Texas Department of Water Resources
Texas Department of Public Safety

Local Governments
City of Baytown
City of Galveston

The same authors are listed on the 90-day Post-Flood Recovery Progress Report. FEMA was the lead agency for the Hazard Mitigation Team work.

As a condition of receiving disaster loans or grants under the Disaster Relief Act (Public Law 93-288) and the Code of Federal Regulations ([CFR], Title 44), a state must agree to evaluate and mitigate natural hazards in the disaster area. The Division of Emergency Management in the Texas Department of Public Safety took the lead in preparing the state's Hazard Mitigation Plan for the area affected by hurricane Alicia.

An indication of the difference in mitigation perspectives between FEMA and Texas government officials shows up in the response to the Hazard Mitigation Team's recommendations concerning development management. Work Element #7 of the team's report recommended preparation of a regionwide hazard mitigation approach for all bay communities. The background statement notes that urban development around the bay "has largely occurred without regard to" the ever present natural and technological (petrochemical) hazards and that the possibility of evacuation "appears to be more of a pipe dream, than a reality, for most residents" due to an overtaxed road network and lack of a detailed regional hazard mitigation approach addressing short and long range multiple hazards and recommending controls.

The Texas Hazard Mitigation Plan for Alicia took exception to this statement, emphasizing the regular meetings of bay area emergency management organizations, the coordination of evacuation planning, the application of SLOSH modeling, and the feasibility studies that have considered using wrong-way flow on Interstate 45 to increase capacity during evacuation of Galveston Island. No mention was made of the possibility of using development controls to prevent future growth from worsening the problem of the admittedly stressed local road system.

Work Element #9 recommended that Galveston be encouraged to prepare a development management system for the west end of the island, which was unprotected by the seawall. In this area, where the land elevation averages five feet, the Alicia surge rolled over most developed areas, damaging some 60 percent of the homes. With development proposals pending for as many as 7000 new dwelling units that could place an estimated 20,000 additional people in the most hazard-prone and environmentally sensitive part of the barrier island, the report called for the city to take a proactive approach in managing development so as to assure safe and efficient use of its resources. It suggested a development management system based on carrying capacity analysis to identify the thresholds beyond which each natural or man-made system cannot tolerate additional loads without danger to public health, safety, or welfare.

The ninety-day report stated that Galveston plans to develop a comprehensive plan for the west end of the island and is exploring funding options. The state plan did not mention development management as a hazard mitigation approach for Galveston. An obvious dilemma for Galveston was that the city was counting on the new growth proposed for the west end to get its economy moving. The city contracted with several outside consultants to prepare the plan. As of 1986 the plan, which now addressed planning for the entire island, had not been adopted but was under review by the city's planning commission. While the plan is conventional in content, its coverage of west end issues does appear to reflect much of the concern expressed by the Interagency Hazard Mitigation Team. For instance, a "holding capacity" analysis (carrying capacity) has been conducted for two study areas on the west end, although the emphasis of these studies appears to be on traffic and public facilities. Reducing storm hazards is prominently mentioned as a goal in the plan, and several more specific objectives and performance standards are identified to implement this goal. (These have largely to do with site and structural designs to minimize flood damage and evacuation.)

The state plan did discuss a project in the coastal community of Kemah on the northwest shore of Galveston Bay. This small community of 1300 is a commercial and sport fishing center. It has been subject to over four feet of subsidence and frequent flooding. The proposed project was to relocate twenty-one structures, many of them low-rent, "blighted" housing, from the flood hazard area and redevelop it as a 365-slip marina and 50,000-square-foot shopping center, using the city's urban renewal authority and industrial development bonds. The city was to acquire the property in the project area, construct parking lots and other facilities, and resell the land to a private developer, who will construct the marina. This proposal was put forward after the fifteen-day hazard report had been submitted; however, technical assistance was provided by FEMA.

In its summary of most important mitigation measures, the Texas plan included implementation of stronger building code standards, increasing public awareness and local enforcement of and participation in the federal flood insurance program, revising outdated emergency management plans, and increasing community involvement in the Texas Coastal Hurricane Preparedness Program. With the exception of the Baytown and Kemah projects, the Texas plan for hazard mitigation did not include emphasis on the relationships between urban growth in hazard areas, land use planning, and development management, despite the efforts of the Hazard Mitigation Team to demonstrate the need for this emphasis, particularly on Galveston Island.

Financial Assistance

FEMA approved a number of projects under its public (community) assistance program totaling some $51.8 million, of which 75 percent was paid by FEMA. Galveston had 142 disaster projects funded by federal agencies totaling $2.32 million (including FEMA, FHWA, USACE, and other federal agencies). Having to pay 25 percent of these costs was difficult for Galveston because of a locally mandated cap on budget increases and the large proportion of tax-exempt property within the city.

Total NFIP claims paid to individuals for Hurricane Alicia were $118.8 million. FEMA 1362 funds in the amount of $551,302 were provided to purchase 177 damaged, federally insured homes in the Brownwood Subdivision in Baytown. The vacated subdivision was to be turned over to Baytown to be used for open space recreational purposes.

The Brownwood Subdivision case has blossomed into one of FEMA's premier examples of the use of 1362 funds and is often cited in discussions concerning coastal relocation. The Brownwood case, however, has provided both a negative and a positive perspective on this program. While FEMA was able to purchase more than 170 structures, it was not able to purchase the 120 remaining structures in the subdivision (either because homeowners did not wish to sell at that time or were not covered by flood insurance). As well, some 200 vacant lots remained in private hands following the hurricane. Recalcitrant property owners wishing to rebuild in the subdivision mounted a substantial political and legal opposition to the buy-out. Some were unhappy with FEMA's assessment of the market value of their homes while others simply wanted to remain living at that location. Several court challenges seeking damages from the city were unsuccessful.

The city has continued its plans to turn the area into a public park and open space. Baytown has acquired a number of additional properties since the initial 1362 purchase, and as of July 1987 only about fifty-five vacant lots and forty structures were not under contract to the city or remain in private ownership (Strong 1987). Voluntary sales of properties in the area continue to take place. Early on the city attempted to acquire properties through its powers of eminent domain, but after an extremely high property value assessment given to a property owner by an eminent domain jury (in which the city withdrew their action), the city has not attempted to further use eminent domain. In this particular case the city's estimate of the property's worth was $4,000, while the jury awarded a value of $84,000. City officials have speculated that such high awards are due at least in part to the belief by jurors that the city has deep pockets and can afford to pay high prices.

Despite these setbacks and the desires of some property owners to continue living in the area, no rebuilding has in fact taken place in the subdivision since Hurricane Alicia. While the city's building moratorium was lifted several weeks after the storm, major disincentives exist to rebuilding. First, the city has refused to rebuild the public sewer and water system in the area. Second, the cost of rebuilding homes to the 100-year base flood elevation (plus wave heights) would be very high. Finally, there is a general perception among the community that this area is an extremely hazardous and vulnerable location.

Redevelopment

Following Alicia, Galveston adopted a moratorium on construction in the damaged areas on the west end seaward of the main beach highway and south of the seawall. The moratorium, which was in effect for several weeks, prohibited the issuance of building permits for new construction or major reconstruction. Despite provisions for fines for violations, a number of violations took place.

Galveston then appointed a Recovery Task Force of citizens and community leaders to review the damage and recommend mitigation actions, ranging from insurance problems to redevelopment actions. Many of their recommendations were in the form of amendments to strengthen the building code and its enforcement. These were accepted and followed by the city council, who enacted building code supplements and hired additional building inspectors. The Task Force had less success in developing recommendations for problems such as redevelopment of the west end of the island.

The Texas attorney general enforced the Open Beaches Act, advising property owners whose houses had wound up seaward of the poststorm vegetation line not to repair or reconstruct without contacting his office. Two court cases resulted from the implementation of the act: a suit brought against the state by a group of west-end property owners and a suit initiated by the attorney general's office against a homeowner who rebuilt seaward of the new line of vegetation. The state won both of these suits. The appellate court in the state's suit upheld the state's concept of the rolling public easement, basing its opinion on the legal theory of custom.

A major problem in the application of this law in Texas was that the attorney general's office was not in a position to assume an aggressive enforcement and monitoring effort. It relied heavily upon individual property owners voluntarily seeking a determination from the attorney general's office as to the legality of rebuilding. It has been estimated by the attorney general's office that of the approximately 300 homes which were seaward of the vegetation line after Alicia, the attorney general's office responded to approximately seventy-five compliance inquiries from property owners. Of these, as many as half were told by the state that they could not rebuild.

The most significant mitigation action taken on Galveston Island was the strengthening of the building code and code enforcement. Construction of an offshore storm protection barrier for the west end was discussed but not pursued.

Hazard Perceptions

Looking back in the year following Alicia, Galveston leaders credited the storm with initiating economic revitalization of the seawall tourist area. Many hotels there had needed remodeling, and convention business had been declining. Although protected from the storm surge by the seawall, most of the hotels and motels were damaged by wind and rain. Insurance payments provided capital for remodeling.

The hurricane did not deter Galveston's plans to develop the hazardous west end of the island. They proceeded with the use of tax increment financing to encourage higher density development there (see table 3.3). They appeared to assume that strengthening the building code was the major step needed to protect against future hurricanes. If not for a substantial downturn in the economy, which stilled much of the planned west-end development, the potential for catastrophe would be much greater.

Hazard perceptions influenced the evacuation decision process in Galveston. The main evacuation route is a single interstate highway crossing a causeway from the island to the mainland. Complete evacuation is estimated to require as much as twenty-six hours prior to landfall. During the "unnecessary" evacuation for Allen, traffic congestion caused extensive delays and some evacuees took fifteen hours to make the trip to Houston. This time, Galveston public officials hesitated to order evacuation until it was too late to do so. At the time for decision the storm was still a weak hurricane and was forecast to strike southwest of Galveston. However, the storm intensified before landfall and turned north toward Galveston. Fortunately, it was not a bad Category 3 or even a Category 4 storm, and there was not a great deal of flooding of Galveston Island from the bay side. Otherwise, as the National Research Council report (1984, 134) states, "the decision not to evacuate the island might have proved tragic."

Development Management

While not all Texas communities are as strongly antigovernment planning and zoning as Houston, there is, nevertheless, a noticeable lack of development management effort in the state. Counties, governed by county judges, have no zoning authority and rarely initiate land use plans. City plans emphasize economic development. Thus, it is not surprising to find that Galveston, which had not grown during the past two decades, welcomed its development surge on the west end and was reluctant to take any steps that might discourage private developers. On the contrary, it was bending a state tax increment financing law aimed at redeveloping blighted areas to concentrate public resources on encouraging development of hazardous areas.

Mitigation Assessment

Galveston public officials believe it had a successful recovery after Alicia. Once the stress and tension of the immediate recovery period were behind them, the community concentrated on the positive economic impacts generated by the hurricane.

Like Harrison County, Mississippi, and Gulf Shores, Alabama, Galveston is a Gulf Coast community with a conservative attitude toward the regulation of private property and a traditional approach to planning. These same attitudes are embedded in the state governments of these localities. If there is to be a strong movement toward restriction of unwise coastal development in hazard areas within these states, it is clear

Table 3.3   Tax Reinvestment Zones in Galveston, Texas

Zone No.	Tax Zone Name	Date Designated	Description
1	Indian Beach Subdivision	12/81	300 Single, Detached Houses
2	Central City Shopping Mall at 61st	12/81	Wal-Mart Shopping Center
3	San Luis Pass Area	07/82	4500 Houses, Condominiums, and Commercial Businesses
4	Pirates Cove Subdivision	12/82	Single, Detached, Multifamily Houses
5	Seven Mile Road Area	12/82	270 Unit Condominium
6	East Beach Area	12/82	Condominiums, Commercial Businesses
7	Isla Del Sol Subdivision	05/83	312 Single, Detached Houses
8	Campeche Cove, Phase II	06/83	Houses, Multifamily Dwellings
9	Central City Beach	07/83	Condominiums, Apartments
10	Downtown Business District	12/84	Central Plaza Revitalization, Festival Marketplace
Totals			

Source: Department of Planning and Transportation, Galveston, Texas, April 1986.

that the impetus must come from the federal government.

Meanwhile the threat of hurricane disaster continues to grow. Alicia was a lesson in the potential for tremendous damage and destruction posed by growing large urban areas lying in the accustomed paths of hurricanes. Whether this lesson will be learned in time to avert disaster is a critical question for policymakers.

Lessons from Camille, Frederic, and Alicia

Experience with three major hurricanes points up the continuing gaps in mitigation policy. Basically, a hurricane does not change the essential character of a locality in terms of its attitudes toward the use of public policy to intervene in the private development market. Conservative communities remain conservative after the storm. Present mitigation carrots

Private Project Cost	Public Improvement Cost	Life of Zone
$ 28,350,000	$ 2,565,000	15 Years
5,000,000	198,000	3 Years
371,375,400	14,112,000	14 Years
60,000,000	4,000,000	15 Years
17,850,000	1,400,000	8 Years
30,000,000	1,705,914	3 Years
35,000,000	1,640,000	8 Years
70,000,000	2,500,000	10 Years
41,990,000	2,027,741	8 Years
39,000,000	5,000,000	8 Years
$798,565,400	$35,148,655	

and sticks can make some difference, and clearly progress has been made during the past two decades toward more enlightened and effective policy. But as long as the federal government is available to bail out a local government and the residents of hazard-prone areas following a hurricane (through disaster assistance and flood insurance), then communities seeking development are not necessarily impressed by the need to limit growth in their hazard areas. If the market is good, as in Gulf Shores and Galveston, then why not rebuild at higher densities even if evacuation capacity may be exceeded? And as long as the Interagency Regional Hazard Mitigation Team reports are advisory, why should state and local governments take their mitigation recommendations seriously? In short, mitigation needs more than the power of a good idea to become fully effective; it needs more teeth if the public is to be protected from future coastal catastrophe.

Notes

1. Material for the three case studies was gathered by the authors and project research assistants, Kathleen Leyden and Jane Hegenbarth, by means of on-site interviews during June 1984 in Gulf Shores (Frederic), July 1984 in Harrison County (Camille), and August–September 1983 (with the Alicia Interagency Hazard Mitigation Team), and December 1984 in the Galveston area.

References

Canis, W. F., et al. 1985. *Living With the Mississippi-Alabama Shore.* Durham, N.C.: Duke University Press.

Clary, Bruce B. 1985. "The Evolution and Structure of Natural Hazard Policies." *Public Administration Review* 45 (January): 20–28.

Coast Code Administration. 1969. *Regional Code Enforcement.* Gulfport, Miss.

Federal Emergency Management Agency. 1983. *Interagency Flood Hazard Mitigation Report for Hurricane Alicia.* Denton, Tex.

———. 1983a. *Interagency Post-Flood Recovery Progress Report.* Denton, Tex.

———. 1986. *Making Mitigation Work: A Handbook for State Officials.* Washington, D.C.: U.S. Government Printing Office.

Godschalk, David R. 1987. "Rebuilding after Hurricane Frederic: Gulf Shores' Struggle with Mitigation." In *Crisis Management: A Casebook*, edited by Michael Charles and John Kim. Springfield, Ill.: Charles C. Thomas.

Hegenbarth, Jane. 1985. *Gulf Shores, Alabama From 1979 to 1984: Its Redevelopment and Growth Following Hurricane Frederic.* Chapel Hill, N.C.: University of North Carolina, Department of City and Regional Planning.

Leyden, Kathleen R. 1985. *Recovery and Reconstruction After Hurricane Camille: Post Storm Hazard Mitigation on the Mississippi Gulf Coast.* Chapel Hill, N.C.: University of North Carolina, Center for Urban and Regional Studies.

———. 1984. Personal interviews with public officials, citizens, and developers in Biloxi, Gulfport, Long Beach, Pass Christian, and Harrison County. July.

MetaSystems, Inc. 1970. *Mississippi Gulf Coast Comprehensive Development after Camille.* Cambridge, Mass.

Miller, H. Crane. 1983. *Hurricane Alicia: Learning From Galveston.* Washington, D.C.: NOAA, Office of Ocean and Coastal Resources Management.

Morton, Robert A., et al. 1983. *Living with the Texas Shore.* Durham, N.C.: Duke University Press.

National Research Council. 1984. *Hurricane Alicia: Galveston and Houston, Texas, August 17–18, 1983.* Washington, D.C.: National Academy Press.

Norton, Thomas B. 1982. "Rebuilding after a Hurricane." *Proceedings of the Oceanfront Development Conference, Wilmington, N.C. December 1982.* Raleigh, N.C.: North Carolina Division of Coastal Management.

Strong, Randall B. 1987. Personal communication with Baytown Texas City Attorney, concerning status of Brownwood relocation. July 31.

Office of Emergency Preparedness. 1970. *A Year of Rebuilding—The Federal Response to Hurricane Camille.* Washington, D.C.

Texas Department of Public Safety. 1984. *The State of Texas Hazard Mitigation Plan for the Counties on the Upper Texas Coast Affected by Hurricane Alicia on August 18, 1983.* Austin, Tex.

U.S. Army Corps of Engineers. 1970. *Report on Hurricane Camille.* Mobile District (Ala.).

———. 1981. *Hurricane Frederic Post Disaster Report.* Mobile District (Ala.).

Williams, D. C. 1979. *Effects of Hurricane Camille on the Economy of Harrison County.* Mississippi/Alabama Sea Grant Consortium.

The Federal Mitigation Role

The major impetus for coastal hazard mitigation has come from federal agencies, even though the mitigation takes place within state and local government jurisdictions. Different federal agencies have taken leading roles, depending on the nature of the mitigation approach. This chapter discusses and analyzes the major federal programs and policies which influence coastal storm hazard mitigation and the pattern of coastal development.

One way to visualize the structure of federal roles is to identify the lead agencies involved with the major mitigation approaches described in chapter 2 (table 2.1).

Mitigation Approach	Lead Agencies
Alteration of Coastal Environment	U.S. Army Corps of Engineers (USACE)
Strengthening Buildings and Facilities	Federal Insurance Administration (FEMA)
Evacuation (and Hurricane Forecasting)	National Weather Service (NOAA) and FEMA
Development Management	FEMA, NOAA, Department of Interior, Corps of Engineers, and Office of the President

Another way to visualize the federal roles is to think of federal hazard mitigation policy as administered by an interlocking directorate of agen-

cies, each with particular resources and interests. Hurricane hazard mitigation programs are primarily the province of FEMA, the Corps of Engineers, and the National Weather Service, often working together.
Management of coastal growth and natural resources involves a broader
slate of agencies, including the Department of Interior, NOAA, the Corps
of Engineers, and, indirectly through Executive Orders, the Office of the
President. The governance system that shapes and operates disaster policy
is shared not only among federal, state, and local governments but also
within the federal establishment.

This chapter starts with the programs focused on the hazard event
—the hurricane. It then reviews structural and nonstructural programs
aimed at reducing hurricane and coastal storm impacts. A concluding
section discusses future directions and needs in federal policy.

Forecasting Hurricanes and Predicting Their Effects

The U.S. Hurricane Warning System

The federal government has had a long history of involvement in the
forecasting and warning of hurricanes and severe coastal storms. The
National Weather Service (under the National Oceanic and Atmospheric
Administration, NOAA) and its National Hurricane Center in Miami track
hurricanes from their initial formation and serve as the primary source of
information concerning local evacuation and preparedness. While the
National Weather Service has historically provided dependable and state-
of-the-art information concerning hurricane location and movement,
experts are in general agreement that advances in hurricane prediction
and forecasting that would radically increase the amount of warning time
are not likely. As Dr. Neil Frank, former director of the National Hurricane Center, has noted on numerous occasions, the great unknown element in hurricane forecasting is the ocean steering currents—for which
weather data is the least available. The hurricane center has stated that
for the average hurricane it can usually only provide from between twelve
and sixteen hours of warning before hurricane landfall occurs. This is not
likely to improve in the near future:

> While there has been some improvement over the last several years in
> the ability of the National Weather Service to predict the paths of

hurricanes, that agency does not expect a breakthrough which would dramatically increase the 12 to 16 hour lead time. Where there is the most potential for improvement, principally in obtaining information on steering currents over a much wider expanse of the oceans, implementation of the technology may not be economically feasible. For the foreseeable future, therefore, those persons responsible for planning for emergency hurricane conditions can confidently depend only on having 12 to 16 hours of warning (Committee on Government Operations [CGO] 1983, 7).

The weather service issues three types of hurricane warning notices. Hurricane "advisories" are issued when a hurricane is within 300 miles of any shore. These are directed primarily at boats and aircraft in the vicinity. Hurricane "watches" indicate that hurricane landfall is a possibility, that individuals should make appropriate preparations and should keep informed about future weather notices. Watches are issued no earlier than thirty-six hours before expected landfall. Finally, a hurricane "warning" indicates that a hurricane landfall is likely enough to justify evacuation of low-lying areas. Warnings are not issued any earlier than twenty-four hours before predicted landfall.

The National Weather Service began issuing in August 1983 hurricane warnings which included the probability of a landfall. This issued value is the probability of a hurricane coming within sixty-five miles of forty-four selected coastal locations (see Carter 1983). The maximum probabilities that will be issued, under strong steering currents, are 30 percent at thirty-six hours before landfall and 50 percent at twenty-four hours. Probabilities will be generated as far as seventy-two hours in advance of landfall.

Simulating Hurricane Effects: SPLASH *and* SLOSH

The National Weather Service and the National Hurricane Center have also been involved in developing computer models which simulate the wind and surge effects of hurricanes. More specifically, two simulation models have been developed and used to predict hurricane forces: SPLASH (Special Program to List the Amplitudes of Surge from Hurricanes) and SLOSH (Sea, Lake and Overland Surge from Hurricanes). SPLASH precedes SLOSH and can only be used for modeling hurricane effects along smooth and relatively unbroken coastlines (see Allenstein 1985). SLOSH was developed to take into consideration the physical effects of bays, sounds, and other deviations in the coastline and has essentially replaced SPLASH as the leading hurricane simulation model.

The SLOSH simulation is conducted in several stages. First, the model must be "fitted" to the particular coastline under study, incorporating specific data about the natural and man-made environment. This is usually referred to as Phase I. In Phase II the model must be "run" for the study area, which usually means an average of 250 simulations are conducted based upon different hurricane scenarios (for example, different hurricane tracks, forward speeds, size, and intensities). The outputs from these runs are the following: (1) surface envelope of the highest surges above mean sea level, (2) time histories of surges at selected grid points, (3) computed windspeeds at selected grid points, (4) computed wind directions at selected grid points.

SLOSH was originally developed as a forecasting tool that would permit National Weather Service personnel to better predict the likely effects, and elevation and warning needs, associated with a specific oncoming hurricane. SLOSH output, however, has become an essential ingredient to overall hurricane preparedness and evacuation planning by local emergency planners. Increasingly, SLOSH data are perceived as important inputs to mitigation and postdisaster reconstruction planning (see Berke and Ruch 1985).

Funding for SLOSH and the evacuation studies and plans that build upon SLOSH data has in the past come from a number of sources. The Office of Sea Grant, within NOAA, has funded response grants for the Galveston/Houston area and in Southwest Florida (CGO 1983). The Office of Ocean and Coastal Resources Management, also within NOAA, has assisted with funding for the Southwest Florida and Tampa Bay evacuation plans.

The U.S. Army Corps of Engineers has also been involved in the funding and technical guidance of SLOSH analysis and evacuation studies (assisting Lee County, Florida, the Tampa Bay region, and the Southeast Florida region). While no plans exist for future Corps of Engineers funding of evacuation studies, it will likely continue to provide technical assistance. For example, it has served this function in the Tri-State hurricane evacuation study (U.S. Army Corps of Engineers [hereinafter USACE] 1986) and property loss and contingency planning study (covering por-

Table 4.1   SLOSH Study Basins

1. Lake Okeechobee, Fla.
2. Lake Pontchartrain, La.
3. Tampa Bay, Fla.
4. Galveston Bay, Tex.
5. Charlotte Harbor, Fla.
6. Florida Bay, Fla.
7. Biscayne Bay, Fla.
8. Corpus Christi, Tex.
9. Mobile Bay, Ala.
10. Sabine Lake, Tex. La.
11. Pensacola, Fla.
12. Charleston Harbor, S.C.
13. Pamlico Sound, N.C.
14. Matagorda Bay, Tex.
15. Lower Laguna Madre, Tex.
16. Delaware Bay, Del.
17. Buzzards Bay, Mass.
Narragansett Bay, R.I.
18. Chesapeake Bay, Md.
19. Long Island Sound, N.Y.
20. Boston Bay, Cape Cod, Mass.
21. Hilton Head, S.C.
22. Brunswick, Ga.

Source: U.S. General Accounting Office 1983.

tions of Mississippi, Alabama, and Florida) and the eastern North Carolina hurricane evacuation study (USACE 1987).

The National Weather Service has provided the largest portion of the funding for SLOSH studies. Twenty-two basins with high hurricane risks and high populations have been identified for SLOSH studies (see table 4.1). An additional fourteen locations were expected to request inclusion on the list (CGO 1983). As of 1983, Phase I had been completed for twelve basins, and Phases I and II had been completed for seven basins. Phase I was completed at an average cost of $131,000 per basin and Phase II at an average cost of $108,000 per basin.

Major funding problems exist for completing SLOSH. The General Accounting Office estimated that it would cost approximately $4.5 million to complete both phases of all twenty-two scheduled basins and the additional requested or anticipated basins.

Armoring the Coast: U.S. Army Corps of Engineers

The U.S. Army Corps of Engineers has historically been very active in the planning and funding of projects designed to structurally reinforce the coastline against hurricanes and storm forces. These projects include such improvements as seawalls, jetties, and flood control channels. The current Lake Pontchartrain Hurricane Protection Project is indicative of the coast-armoring perspective of the Corps of Engineers. This project involves the construction of a wall which will prevent hurricane waters from entering the lake and flooding the New Orleans area.

The USACE has nine additional studies under way or in review on feasibility of hurricane construction projects. An additional four studies have been completed and transmitted to Congress (CGO 1983).

The USACE also exercises an influence over coastal development through its regulatory authority over dredge and construction fill activities in navigable waters, including wetlands (see Hildreth and Johnson 1983). Prior to 1972 the focus of the Corps' navigable waters permitting system was to ensure that navigability was maintained. With the passage of the Federal Water Pollution Control Act Amendments of 1972, the Corps became responsible as well—through the issuance of Section 404 permits —for regulating discharges to wetland areas and the potentially negative effects these discharges might have. The Section 404 permit is an addition to the dredge-and-fill permit required prior to 1972 with an emphasis on water quality (National Resources Defense Council [NRDC] 1977).

Nonstructural Mitigation: Federal Emergency Management Agency

Created in 1979, the Federal Emergency Management Agency (FEMA) has been designated as the primary federal agency concerned with emergency and disaster preparedness, mitigation, and recovery and, under Executive Order 12148, has been given the responsibility of coordinating emergency- and disaster-related activities of other federal agencies and handling emergency-related dealings with state and local governments. FEMA also controls a number of federal grant programs which have a bearing on hurricane hazard planning.

Hurricane Preparedness Planning Program

Perhaps the most significant federal initiative is the Hurricane Preparedness Planning Program, authorized by the Disaster Relief Act of 1974. These are grants made by FEMA to appropriate state agencies for the development of emergency preparedness plans, with the state agencies given the main responsibility for managing these funds and the coordination of state and local functions in this work. The development of these plans usually involves first a vulnerability assessment and then the development of specific plans for evacuation, response, recovery, and mitigation. As of 1983 the anticipated total amount of FEMA grants for these projects was $6,773,500 (CGO 1983).

Quantitative Hurricane Preparedness Studies are made up of two parts: (1) Population Preparedness Projects are aimed at preparing hurricane evacuation plans based on analyses of the vulnerability of the population at risk from hurricanes (and are key tools for management of emergency preparedness and response), and (2) Property Protection Projects are aimed at preparing hurricane recovery and mitigation plans based on analyses of the property at risk from hurricanes (FEMA 1984). For example, in the Tampa Bay Region the hurricane evacuation plan was completed in 1981 and updated in 1984; the 1983 hurricane property loss study provided a recovery plan and long-range hazard mitigation policies (Tampa Bay Regional Planning Council 1983 and 1984). The Tri-State hurricane evacuation study was completed in 1986 and work then began on the property protection study (USACE 1986).

Hurricane Preparedness Studies are scheduled for some twenty-two areas. The Corps of Engineers is the project management agency in sixteen of these areas. Table 4.2 provides a listing of preparedness planning projects, with their management agencies, study start dates, and SLOSH status.

In reviewing federal efforts to assist local and state hurricane preparedness planning, several problems have been identified. One problem has been coordinating FEMA's hurricane preparedness funding with the National Weather Service's funding and application of SLOSH. Lists of priority basins in high-risk locations prepared by each agency were developed independently of each other.

Table 4.2 FEMA Hurricane Preparedness Program

Hurricane Risk Areas	Management Agency	Start Date	SLOSH Phase II
Tampa Bay, Fla.	Tampa Bay RPC	1981	Yes
Georgia Coast	Coast Area PDC & USACE	1981	Yes
Galveston/Houston, Tex.	Texas	1982	Yes
Southeast La.	USACE	1982	Yes
Southeast Fla.	USACE	1982	No
Tri-State: Fla., Miss., Ala.	USACE	1983	Yes
Hawaii	USACE	1983	Under Study
New Jersey	New Jersey & USACE	1983	Yes
Long Island, N.Y.	Long Is. RPB & USACE	1983	Yes
Puerto Rico	USACE	1983	Yes
Virgin Islands	Virgin Islands	1983	Yes
Beaumont/Port Arthur, Tex.	Texas	1983	Yes
South Carolina	South Carolina & USACE	1983	Yes
Corpus Christi, Tex.	Texas	1984	Yes
North Carolina	USACE	1985	Yes
Brownsville, Tex./ Matamoros, Mexico	Texas & Mexico	1986	Yes
Virginia	USACE	1986	Yes
Massachusetts	USACE	1986	Yes
Delaware	USACE	1986	Yes
Maryland	USACE	1986	Yes
Connecticut Coast	USACE	1987	Yes
Rhode Island	USACE	1987	Yes
Guam/Samoa/Trust Territories	—	1987	No

Source: FEMA 1987. Committee on Government Operations 1983.
Note: PDC = Planning and Development Commission; RPB = Regional Planning Board; RPC = Regional Planning Council; USACE = U.S. Army Corps of Engineers.

While there is significant overlap between the FEMA and NWS high-risk locations, five locations on the FEMA list will not benefit from SLOSH models as a result of this initial lack of coordination and initial unawareness of potential SLOSH data use: Hawaii, Puerto Rico/ Virgin Islands, and Guam/Samoa/Trust Territories are not scheduled for SLOSH; the Georgia coast received funding before the SLOSH model was available; and Southeast Florida also started its study before a SLOSH model was available for its coastline. In this last instance, the Corps of Engineers used other available simulation models to estimate surge heights under various hurricane conditions (CGO 1983, 17).

FEMA has recently reorganized its studies schedule in order to take advantage of SLOSH and now stresses the need to utilize the SLOSH results in developing evacuation plans (CGO 1983). Also, SLOSH has since been applied to several of the five locations not initially scheduled for it (FEMA 1987).

FEMA has also been criticized for the manner in which it oversees preparedness studies. Funds are allocated to states, who can either do the studies themselves or can oversee regional or local bodies who may conduct them. In either event, tight supervision by FEMA is not apparent. Moreover, it has been suggested that FEMA lacks the necessary in-house expertise in this area to adequately ensure that states produce workable and usable preparedness plans. In contrast is the USACE's approach to preparedness funding. It prepares a detailed plan of study at the invitation of a state, contracts out much of the work, and directly oversees the plan's development.

A related criticism is that the review by FEMA of preparedness proposals is conducted without sufficient technical criteria. A recent incident concerning funding for the Louisiana preparedness plan is illustrative. Here FEMA provided $400,000 for updating of topographical maps which the National Weather Service later indicated was unnecessary.

FEMA has also been criticized for failing to adequately coordinate the funding and completion of preparedness plans. In the Louisiana case it permitted the state to assume that funding existed from other federal sources without verifying this or involving the relevant agencies. FEMA has also been criticized for not involving local officials and agencies in proposal review.

FEMA officials responded that they will outline more clearly the goals and objectives of the preparedness program, and provide a better basis for review of proposals. As well, they stated that they would convene representatives from relevant federal agencies to review the resulting prepared-

Table 4.3   Maximum Amounts of Coverage under NFIP

| | Emergency Program | | Regular Program— |
	First Layer	Second Layer	Total Amount Available
Single Family Residential			
Except in Hawaii, Alaska, Guam, U.S. Virgin Islands	35,000	150,000	185,000
In Hawaii, Alaska, Guam, U.S. Virgin Islands	50,000	150,000[a]	185,000
Other Residential			
Except in Hawaii, Alaska, Guam, U.S. Virgin Islands	100,000	150,000	250,000
In Hawaii, Alaska, Guam, U.S. Virgin Islands	150,000	150,000[b]	250,000
Small business	100,000	150,000	250,000
Churches, other properties	100,000	100,000	200,000
Contents			
Residential	10,000	50,000	60,000
Small business	100,000	200,000	300,000
Churches, other properties (per unit)	100,000	100,000	200,000

Source: CFR, Title 44, Section 61.6. a. Add to 35,000. b. Add to 100,000.

ness plans with the intent of developing a "unified federal, state, regional approach" (CGO 1983).

National Flood Insurance Program (NFIP)

The National Flood Insurance Program was established by Congress in 1968 under the National Flood Insurance Act. Administered by the Federal Insurance Administration (FIA) within FEMA, the NFIP provides a nationwide system of federal insurance for structures and property located in designated flood hazard areas. The flood insurance process begins with FIA's identification of localities which could be considered flood-prone. The definition of flood-prone is lands which are prone to flooding with a probability of at least 1 percent per year—or, in other words, which

Table 4.4   Explanation of NFIP Zone Designations

Zone	
A	Area of special flood hazards in which no base flood elevations are determined and an estimated BFE is optional.
A1-A30,AE	Area of special flood hazards with base flood elevation determined. Zones are assigned according to flood hazard factors.
AH	Area of special flood hazards that have shallow flood depths (from one to three feet) due to ponding. Base flood depths are shown on the FIRM.
Ao	Area of special flood hazards that have shallow flood depths (from one to three feet) due to sheet flow. Base flood depths are shown on the FIRM.
A99	Area of special flood hazards where enough progress has been made on a protection system, such as dikes, dams, and levees, to consider it complete for insurance rating purposes.
V	Coastal high-hazard area with wave action velocity waters that is inundated by tidal floods. Base flood elevations have not yet been determined.
V1-V30, VE	Coastal high-hazard area with wave action velocity waters that is inundated by tidal floods. Zones are assigned according to flood hazard factors. Base flood elevations are shown on the FIRM.
B, C, and X	These areas have been identified in the community flood insurance study as areas of moderate or minimal hazard from the principal source of flooding in the area. However, buildings in these actuarial rate zones could be flooded by severe, concentrated rainfall. . . . These rate zones indicate flood areas where insurance is not required but can be purchased in a participating community.
D	Area of undetermined, but possible, flood hazards.
M	Area of special mudslide hazards.
N	Area of moderate mudslide hazards.
P	Area of undetermined, but possible, mudslide hazards.

Source: CFR, Title 44, Section 64.3.

contain a 100-year floodplain. Well over 20,000 flood-prone communities have been identified. Next, a locality, if it chooses, can enter the emergency program. Participation here requires that a Flood Hazard Boundary Map (FHBM) be developed, usually by FIA, which designates the general location and boundaries of the 100-year floodplain. Once this map has been agreed upon and adopted, the locality has twelve months in which to join the emergency phase of the program. As table 4.3 indicates, the level of insurance benefits are lower under the emergency phase.

Before a jurisdiction can enter the regular phase, FIA must develop a more detailed and precise flood hazard map—called a Flood Insurance Rate Map or FIRM. While a number of different types of hazard zones will typically be delineated on a FIRM (see table 4.4), the key differentiating feature of these maps is the calculation of the 100-year flood elevation, upon which most of the required building and land use regulations are based. These maps then also become the basis for the flood insurance rates which are charged to floodplain property owners.

Once the FIRM is issued (following an appeal period) the jurisdiction has six months to enter the regular program or it will be suspended from the NFIP (Conservation Foundation 1980). Once in the regular program, the extent of permissible insurance coverage increases.

For a local jurisdiction to obtain flood insurance for its floodplain residents it must agree to regulate new floodplain development in ways which reduce the impacts of subsequent floods. Localities must review proposals for development in floodplains and require that such development be flood-proofed or elevated. For residential construction the first usable floor of a structure must be elevated to a point at or above the 100-year or base flood elevation (BFE). The higher above the BFE the structure is elevated, the lower will be the insurance rates applied to it. Commercial or industrial structures have the option of either elevating or flood-proofing. NFIP regulations also require that proposed subdivisions be modified in ways which reduce flood damages, and mobile homes must contain adequate tie-down and anchoring systems.

Specific, additional requirements pertain to particular types of hazard zones. From the perspective of coastal localities the most important of these special areas are the Coastal High-Hazard Areas or V-zones (Velocity-zones), which are stretches of coasts with characteristics sufficient to sustain a three foot wave (see USACE 1976). During the first few years in which V-zones were designated, BFE was not adjusted to take into consideration the presence of waves. This was for some time generally perceived to be a deficiency in the methodology, and beginning around 1979, a methodology to calculate and add on wave height was developed.

For development occurring within V-zones, special building requirements are imposed. Residential structures must be elevated on pilings and columns as opposed to elevating through the use of fill. New mobile homes are not permitted in V-zones. Areas below the lowest inhabitable floor must not be enclosed or, if they are, must be enclosed only with breakaway materials. New construction must not disturb existing dunes or mangroves if doing so will lead to an increase in flood potential. All structures must be built landward of the mean high tide. To reflect the additional risks of locating in a V-zone, insurance premiums are higher in these locations.

When the insurance program began in 1969, it was completely voluntary, and there were few strong incentives for localities to participate. To further encourage local participation, some relatively strong incentives were incorporated into the program during the early 1970s. These new provisions stipulated that no mortgages could be provided for structures locating in the floodplain without flood insurance if the lending institution was federally insured. This provision was generally viewed as harsh and too restrictive and was repealed by the Eagleton Amendment in 1975. The incentives which remain are still substantial. No federal loans or grants (for example, HUD, VA, FHA mortgage loans) are permitted in designated flood hazard areas without flood insurance.

As well, disaster assistance for nonemergency recovery in the 100-year floodplain (for example, rebuilding of damaged sewer and water lines) is generally intended not to be available to localities which are not participating in the NFIP. It appears, however, that FEMA has not been stringent in withholding disaster assistance to nonparticipating communities. FEMA has informally adopted a one-time forgiveness standard which would provide disaster assistance for a nonparticipating locality after a flood but would make future assistance contingent upon participation. Secondary market purchases of mortgages by either the Federal National Mortgage Association or the Government National Mortgage Association are prohibited if these mortgages are for properties located in the 100-year floodplain.

A controversial aspect of the National Flood Insurance Program has been the subsidy it provides to hazard zone property owners through less-than-actuarial insurance rates. A 1983 U.S. General Accounting Office (GAO) study concluded that since 1978 subsidies of between $20 and $200 per policy have been provided. Less-than-actuarial rates were

originally incorporated into the system to encourage widespread participation and thus indirectly to reduce future federal outlays for disaster
assistance. As the GAO report states: "Using the very general guidance
contained in the National Flood Insurance Act of 1968, previous program administrators set the subsidized rates on the basis of what they
believed was affordable and would encourage wide participation. The
rates were not set on the basis of any identifiable reduction from the rates
the policymakers would have paid without a subsidy. As a result, the
extent to which rates are actually being subsidized cannot easily be determined" (GAO 1983, ii).

Subsidized rates were found to be a result of a number of factors,
including: untested frequency and severity data in the hydrologic model
used to set rates, incorrect assumptions in setting rates in B and C zones,
invalidated enforcement and engineering assumptions, and problems of
underinsurance. To correct the problems the GAO study recommends establishing a reserve to cover catastrophic losses, establishing a plan to correct
data and methodological weaknesses, establishing a rate structure which
reflects variations in risks but which is not unnecessarily complex, and
using a greater reliance on recent loss experiences in setting rates.

More recent data supplied by the Federal Insurance Administration
(1987) for this book indicates that new rate structures may have offset
earlier subsidies. As table 1.3 (chapter 1) shows, over the 1978–1986
period, the hurricane-prone states paid total premiums of $1.99 billion
while receiving loss payments totaling $1.83 billion.

Local implementation and enforcement of minimum NFIP standards
have also been a problem. While FEMA has the authority to suspend
communities for noncompliance, this is viewed as a harsh sanction and
not frequently imposed. Partly in response to this, and the need for an
intermediate sanction, FEMA has recently enacted a rule (January 1, 1986)
which will permit it to place noncomplying communities on probation. A
premium surcharge of $25 will be placed on every policy in the commu-
nity as a result.

Posthurricane Disaster Assistance

The federal government has long been involved in assisting disaster stricken
localities to recover and rebuild. The most important piece of federal
legislation in this area is the Disaster Relief Act of 1974, which specifies a

number of different recovery programs. This act established FEMA as the main agency coordinating the federal response to emergencies and disasters. Federal disaster assistance does not become available until a presidential declaration of an "emergency" or "major disaster" is declared. An "emergency" is declared when federal assistance is deemed necessary to supplement the efforts of state and local agencies to avert property damages and loss of life. For the distribution of disaster assistance and reconstruction monies a major disaster must be declared by the president. Such a major disaster is defined as a catastrophe,

> which in the determination of the President, is or threatens to be of sufficient severity and magnitude to warrant disaster assistance by the Federal Government to supplement the efforts and available resources of states, local governments, and relief organizations in alleviating the damage, loss, hardship, or suffering caused thereby, and with respect to which the Governor of any state in which such catastrophe occurs or threatens to occur certifies the need for Federal disaster assistance . . . and given assurance of the expenditure of a reasonable amount of the funds of such state, its local governments, or other agencies for alleviating the damage, loss, hardship or other suffering resulting from such catastrophe (Part 200, Section 200.2).

When the state governor requests a disaster declaration of the president, estimates of the type and extent of damages incurred and the extent of financial assistance needed are submitted (and usually developed in collaboration with FEMA officials). The request for a disaster declaration is first submitted to and reviewed by FEMA's regional director, who tenders a recommendation to the director of FEMA, who in turn submits a recommendation to the president. Once a declaration is made, a Federal-State Disaster Assistance Agreement is signed by the governor and the regional director of FEMA specifying the extent and use of federal assistance funds. Eligible disaster-stricken jurisdictions are designated by the associate director of Disaster Response and Recovery. A federal coordinating officer (FCO), usually the regional FEMA director, is then designated to oversee and coordinate the distribution of federal assistance.

Two types of disaster assistance are provided by FEMA: (1) individual assistance (assistance for individuals, families, and businesses), and (2) public assistance (assistance for local and state governments) (see Propst

Table 4.5   Categories of Public Assistance from FEMA

Emergency Work	Permanent Work
1. Debris Removal	1. Road or Street Systems
2. Emergency Protection	2. Water Control Facilities
	3. Public Buildings and Related Equipment
	4. Public Utilities
	5. Facilities under Construction
	6. Private Nonprofit Facilities
	7. Publicly Owned Parks and Recreational Facilities
	8. Timber Removal

Source: CFR, Title 44.

1984). Included under individual assistance are grants and loans for temporary housing and disaster unemployment. Within the category of public assistance eligible damages are classified as either "permanent" or "emergency" work. Within the emergency work category are included debris removal and emergency protection, while under the permanent work category are included the repair of road and street systems, water control facilities, public buildings, public utilities, and so on (see table 4.5). Damage Survey Reports (DSR) must be filed for each proposed public assistance project and are prepared by federal-state-local damage assessment teams (see FEMA 1981). These are then used to develop project applications for actuarial funding, which FEMA can change or approve.

The two categories under emergency work can be funded by FEMA under a presidential declaration of an emergency, while funding for permanent work categories requires the declaration of a major disaster. (See Propst 1984 for a more detailed discussion of each of these categories.)

Also available from FEMA are Community Disaster Loans which are provided to help localities replace tax revenues lost as a result of a disaster. These are loans which must not exceed 25 percent of the annual operating budget of the locality in the fiscal year in which the disaster occurred. Repayment of all or a portion of the loan may be canceled if the jurisdiction is unable to meet subsequent local operating budgets as a result of disaster-related expenses and revenue losses. Only one loan to a jurisdiction is permitted.

Several additional recovery and reconstruction programs are administered by other federal agencies and may have important influences on poststorm redevelopment. The Small Business Administration provides low-interest loans for rebuilding and repairing houses and businesses. Funds are available through the Federal Highway Administration to assist states and localities in repairing highways in the federal-aid highway system which have been seriously damaged in a natural disaster. (The creating statute is found in 23 USCA [United States Code Annotated], Section 125, and implementing regulations are found in 23 CFR, Section 668.101 et seq.) The Office of Elementary and Secondary Education in the Department of Education also provides funds in the case of a presidential disaster declaration for the rebuilding of damaged or destroyed school structures and for supplementing local resources so that predisaster levels of education are maintained (for example, to make up for deficiencies created by loss of revenues and increased expenditures).

Between 1970 and 1981, $3.8 billion has been given to individuals and state and local governments from the President's Disaster Relief Fund, including 376 major disasters and 84 emergencies. In recent years postdisaster recovery programs have come under attack as unnecessary subsidies for hazardous development. Moreover, the presidential declaration of a disaster or emergency is often viewed as more of a political act than one based on the financial and other capabilities of the state to adequately deal with the disaster. A report by the GAO concluded that FEMA has difficulty in assessing whether state and local governments are, in fact, capable of dealing with their own disasters (GAO 1981). While FEMA undertakes relatively consistent procedures for assessing the magnitude and severity of disasters, it lacks policies and guidelines for consistently evaluating the capability and commitment of states requesting disaster declarations.

It is true that in many situations where disaster declarations are made the capacity of state and local agencies to deal with these situations is clearly adequate. State and local officials have come to view such assistance as "deserved," regardless of the extent to which it is actually needed. A case in point is the disaster declaration issued for the North Carolina coast following Hurricane Diana in 1983. This was a relatively weak storm and produced a relatively small amount of total damages—some $80 million. The financial and other commitments created by the storm were clearly within the capacity of the state and its local governments.

The GAO has also raised serious questions about FEMA's current cost-sharing arrangements. Since May 1980 FEMA has required state and local governments to assume 25 percent of the cost of public assistance programs. While no such specific cost-sharing standard existed in the past, states and localities were in theory required to document a "reasonable" commitment to disaster assistance. The GAO (1981) observes that the new cost-sharing requirement has created much protest:

> FEMA's cost-sharing policy has created much opposition and concern on the part of Governors, legislators, and organizations of State officials. The Governors who have had to agree to the cost-sharing in order to receive Federal disaster assistance feel the 75/25 percent cost-sharing policy is an arbitrary FEMA decision that should not have been made without consulting with them and the Congress. They contend that State and local governments already bear a major role in disaster relief because of their ineligible public assistance costs. They also contend that FEMA's new policy further burdens the State and local governments by requiring them to pick up, in addition to the above mentioned cost, 25 percent of the eligible public assistance costs (pp. 36–37).

The FEMA 75/25 policy, then, is discretionary in that it can be raised or lowered depending upon unique disaster circumstances. The GAO report recommends that the cost-sharing question be taken to Congress to "reevaluate the present law and clarify the extent to which supplemental Federal assistance should be given in major disasters and emergencies" (p. 38).

> FEMA's apparently strict adherence to the 75/25 cost-sharing ratio is based on a discretionary assessment that this cost-sharing approach results in a reasonable level of State and local government participation in disaster relief costs in almost all cases. It obviates the administrative problems associated with attempting to determine a reasonable commitment for each disaster and also assures compliance with the statutory purpose that the Federal aid be supplemental. Moreover, FEMA has left itself free to recommend providing more or less than 75 percent of the assistance should it be convinced in a particular situation that an exception is warranted. Under these circum-

stances, FEMA's cost-sharing policy is consistent with existing law. However, the policy has created controversy on the part of Governors, legislators, and organizations of State officials (p. 38).

In 1986 FEMA proposed a major overhauling of its disaster assistance regulations, which addressed, among other things, the concerns raised by the GAO report. Although the proposed regulations were not adopted, they indicate potential means of reforming the present system to encourage state and local governments to accept more responsibility for disasters. The proposed system would have incorporated "capability indicators" into the presidential declaration process. These capability indicators would be based on a formula using the population of the state or county and the ratio of the state's or county's per capita personal income to the national average per capita income (Federal Register 1986, 13336). The amount of state and local contribution would be tied to the magnitude of the disaster in relation to state and local capability, under a multitiered system ranging from 0 percent to 90 percent federal monies for public assistance depending on the ability of the applicants to recover on their own.

Section 1362: Flooded Property Purchase Program

Section 1362 of the National Flood Insurance Act of 1968 provides the FIA with the ability to purchase structures insured under the NFIP and which have been seriously damaged by storm flooding. More specifically, the stated objectives of Section 1362—or the Flooded Property Purchase Program—are:

(1) To reduce future flood insurance and disaster assistance costs by removing repetitively and/or substantially damaged structures from flood risk areas;

(2) To provide an opportunity for owners of repetitively and substantially damaged structures to be permanently removed from flood risk areas, and to reduce risk to life from flooding; and

(3) To complement Federal, State and local efforts to restore flood plain values, protect the environment and provide recreational and open space resources. (CFR, Title 44, Sec. 77.2)

These structures would then be moved or destroyed and the remaining open space land deeded to the local jurisdiction. The general objective of this program is to stop the destruction-reconstruction cycle that exists in areas frequented by repetitive disasters and thus to reduce the number of NFIP claims in such areas. To qualify for buy-out under Section 1362, the following conditions must be met:

(1) The property must be located in a flood risk area as determined by the Administrator;

(2) The property must have been covered by a flood insurance policy under the National Flood Insurance Program at the time damage took place.

(3) The building, while covered by flood insurance under the National Flood Insurance Program, must have been damaged substantially beyond repair or must have been damaged not less than three previous times during the preceding five year period, each time the cost of repair equalling 25 percent or more of the structure's value, or must have been damaged from a single casualty of any nature so that a statute, ordinance or regulation precludes its repair or restoration or permits repair or restoration only at significantly increased cost.

(4) A state or local community must enter into an agreement authorized by ordinance or legally binding resolution to take title to and manage the property in a manner consistent with sound land management use as determined by the Administrator.

(5) The community must agree to remove without cost to the Federal Emergency Management Agency (FEMA), by demolition, relocation, donation or sale any damaged structures to which the community accepts title from FEMA, provided the Administrator may, when it is in the public interest to do so, agree to assume a part or all of the cost of such removal. (CFR, Title 44, Sec. 77.2)

Eligible structures must be insured under NFIP, and 1362 funds are used to pay the difference between insurance claims and the replacement cost of the structure. Monies are also used to pay for the cost of purchasing the land on which structures sit.

FIA utilizes eight "community selection factors" for making decisions about how to spend 1362 monies (see table 4.6). Funding for 1362 was not appropriated by Congress until Fiscal Year 1980 and then was only a very small amount—$5.4 million.

Table 4.6   Community Selection Factors for the Section 1362 Program

1. The permanent removal of flood-prone structures will contribute to existing, on-going programs for permanent evacuation of floodplains.
2. In addition to hazard mitigation, acquisition will contribute to the achievement of multiple community development goals (such as environmental protection, open space/recreation, urban renewal, or some other public purpose).
3. The acquisition and relocation of flood-prone structures will have an economic benefit in terms of eliminating future flood insurance claims, avoiding future damage, reducing future disaster relief costs, avoiding business interruption, and reducing loss of life.
4. The distribution of properties to be acquired under Section 1362 (or the distribution of these properties combined with properties that can be acquired through other programs) will result in a logical, usable, and desirable land use pattern.
5. Alternatives to acquisition under Section 1362 have been investigated and found to be less effective than Section 1362 in meeting the community's floodplain management and hazard mitigation goals. These alternatives could include, but are not limited to, floodproofing, structural flood protection, or acquisition and relocation programs of local, state, or other federal agencies.
6. The community has undergone a planning process and found acquisition/relocation to be the most desirable alternative in terms of cost, degree of flood protection achieved, environmental enhancement, and other factors.
7. The community has demonstrated, or agreed to pursue, an active program of sound floodplain management which exceeds the minimum requirements of the National Flood Insurance Program.
8. The community can actively participate in the planning and implementation of the Section 1362 program through the provision of either financial or staff resources.

Source: Propst 1984, p. 36.

A consultant's report to FEMA on alternative ways of implementing Section 1362 estimated that between 1970 and 1979 over 6,000 structures damaged in over 1,000 communities nationwide would have met the statutory eligibility requirements (FEMA, 1981). Projecting into the future, it is estimated that the number of eligible structures by the year 2000 will number approximately 2,000, requiring some $27 million in federal acquisition monies (that is, for administrative costs plus the difference between insurance payments and value of the structure and the cost of land at comparable sites). The assumptions behind these estimates (for example, fewer properties will be at risk because of elevation requirements) suggest that eligible damaged properties may be more extensive. A major ingredient to a successful 1362 program is that of funding. The FEMA report suggests that some sort of cost-sharing arrangement may be appropriate, perhaps requiring localities to bear the administrative costs and, under some circumstances, the cost of demolition and site clearance.

A major problem for the federal insurance program is the extent to which it subsidizes communities and neighborhoods subject to chronic and repetitive flooding. One procedure used by FEMA in the past for addressing this problem is known as "Constructive Total Loss." Under this approach FEMA provided insurance funds beyond the actual extent of damages to property, and up to its total insurance level, if a local ordinance would prevent the repair or reconstruction of such properties. The idea was to encourage a movement away from floodplain sites that would be repeatedly flooded and would require large flood insurance payments in the future. This practice was discontinued by FEMA in 1983, reasoning that Section 1362 was specified by Congress to be used for relocations out of high flood risk areas (Federal Register 1983, 3–4).

An impediment to participation in the program by owners of a damaged structure may occur in situations where prestorm market values are depressed. In these circumstances 1362 payments of the difference between insurance proceeds and market value may not be sufficient to purchase a similar structure elsewhere. Also requiring localities to place purchased land in perpetual open space may appear unattractive to local officials who are concerned about the loss of their tax base and the other revenues which might be generated through use of the coastal floodplain.

The relatively low level of funding which has been made available for Section 1362 also leads one to question the elimination of the Constructive Total Loss Program. A commentator in a recent article in the *Flood Report* raises just this point: "The problem which has not been adequately addressed by FIA, however, is one of simple economics. The Section 1362 program has a limited budget of approximately $5 million. Consequently many insureds will not be able to avail themselves of the statutory benefits for relocation. The argument can be made that the National Flood Insurance Program is providing inadequate coverage to insureds in high risk areas" (1983a, 4).

FEMA has the authority, as well, under Subpart E of its disaster assistance regulations, to require the relocation of public structures and facilities to safer sites in order for a recipient jurisdiction to receive reconstruction funds. The proposed 1986 modifications to FEMA's disaster assistance regulations would have clarified these provisions. Specifically the regional director can decline requests for funds to rebuild public facilities in areas where "the facility is and will be subject to repetitive heavy damage," or where other federal mitigation requirements apply. If an applicant jurisdiction is denied funding, three options exist:

(1) A grant-in-lieu may be requested to apply the eligible repair or replacement costs, as applicable, to the reconstruction of the facility at a non-hazardous site. The purchase of the site and road and utility services to the site are the responsibility of the applicant.

(2) The estimated restoration costs may be included in a flexible funding grant provided that no part of the grant is used on the facility at the disapproved location.

(3) The estimated restoration costs may be included in a small project grant provided that no part of the grant is used on the facility at the disapproved location. (CFR, Title 44, Section 205.75 [a][7])

Poststorm Mitigation: Federal Requirements

Section 406 of the Disaster Assistance Act clearly establishes that federal disaster assistance is contingent upon the efforts of local and state recipients to mitigate future storm damages. More specifically the law states:

As a further condition of any loan or grant made under the provisions of this chapter, the state or local government shall agree that the natural hazards in the areas in which the proceeds of the grants or loans are to be used shall be evaluated and appropriate action shall be taken to mitigate such hazards, including safe land use and construction practices, in accordance with standards prescribed or approved by the President after adequate consultation with the appropriate elected officials of general purpose local governments, and the state shall furnish such evidence of compliance with this section as may be required by regulation (Public Law 93-288, Title IV, Section 406).

Implementing regulations are found in CFR, Title 44, Part 205, Subpart M. The major formal mechanism for ensuring that the above condition is satisfied is for the FEMA regional director to include a mitigation stipulation in the Federal-State Disaster Assistance Agreement. As part of these stipulations, FEMA typically requires the preparation of a Hazard Mitigation Plan for the particular disaster area (called a "406 plan") which identifies natural hazards, potential mitigation opportunities, and specific measures to achieve these opportunities. This plan, which is usually prepared by the state, is to be completed no later than 180 days after the issuance of the presidential declaration.

In theory a number of individuals have a role in the development of the hazard mitigation plan. Initially a joint federal/state/local survey team is established which collects information from site visits, damage survey reports, and other sources and develops specific recommendations concerning appropriate hazard mitigation measures. A joint federal/state/local planning team is then established, perhaps including the same individuals, that evaluates the adequacy of existing mitigation plans and measures, reviews the recommendations of the survey team, and prepares the Section 406 Hazard Mitigation Plan. Ideally, the planning team includes in this plan specific target dates and schedules for the completion of prescribed mitigation measures and activities, and these become conditions for the obtaining of FEMA grants and loans.

An additional mechanism or institution to promote mitigation during reconstruction is the Interagency Regional Hazard Mitigation Team. As a result of an interagency agreement signed by twelve federal agencies in December 1980, an interagency hazard mitigation team is established following a natural disaster to coordinate relevant federal programs and postdisaster assistance and to ensure that such actions reduce the losses from future disasters (see McElyea, Brower, and Godschalk 1982). Representatives from each agency are appointed to serve on the mitigation team—one for each FEMA region. Relevant state and local representatives are also included on the team. Following a disaster the interagency team conducts site visits, assesses the extent and nature of disaster damages, identifies mitigation opportunities, and develops specific recommendations for mitigation actions (see FEMA 1981). The team prepares a hazard mitigation report within fifteen days following the presidential declaration. A progress report must be prepared by the lead agency in ninety days after the issuance of the initial report. Included as well in this report are specific recommendations for how various forms of federal disaster assistance should be coordinated to achieve these mitigation objectives (see FEMA 1981). The connections between the interagency hazard mitigation task force and the Section 406 planning requirements are very close. The interagency team findings are available in a shorter time frame and may generally be used as a framework for beginning the preparation of the 406 mitigation report.

The 406 mitigation requirements have in the past had little relationship to the disaster assistance funding decisions of FEMA. The proposed 1986 modifications to the disaster assistance rules, however, would have substantially reinforced these requirements. They would have required the 406 plan to include an evaluation of severity, extent, and frequency of the natural hazard and an analysis of hazard vulnerability trends and changes; a description and analysis of current state and local hazard mitigation programs and policies (specifically including discussion of land use planning and zoning practices); and a list of proposed hazard mitigation programs, strategies, and recommendations as well as a specific list of proposed actions with agency and jurisdictional responsibilities and completion dates identified. Local jurisdictions would have to be actively involved in the development and implementation of these plans. States and localities would have to identify appropriate actions to reduce hazard impacts, which they agree to undertake as a condition of future disaster assistance. Disaster assistance would be withheld if appropriate actions were not implemented.

FEMA's public assistance regulations have often been criticized because they virtually prevent reconstruction of buildings and facilities in ways which would mitigate future damages. Public assistance funds have generally been restricted to what would be required to rebuild facilities to their predisaster condition. New "disaster proofing" criteria incorporated into the proposed 1986 disaster assistance rules would largely correct this problem. The regional director could "authorize disaster proofing not required by applicable codes, specifications and standards when in the public interest." Such disaster proofing must substantially reduce potential future damages, must be structurally feasible, must be cost-beneficial and cost-effective, and consistent with other applicable federal regulations (for example, the NFIP). These disaster proofing measures would be acceptable even where they are not an integral part of the repairs to the structure or facility. Under existing regulations disaster proofing modifications were limited to 15 percent of the total cost of the project, and states and localities were not permitted to contribute any funds above these costs. Under the proposed rules FEMA's share of the disaster proofing is still "not to exceed a small percentage of the eligible project cost," but the applicant "may contribute any amount necessary to completely fund any disaster proofing measure that meets the other criteria" (Federal Register 1986, 13373).

Subrogation Suits: Shifting the Responsibility for Flood Losses

FEMA has recently been attempting to retrieve some of the funds it pays out in flood insurance claims through the legal practice of subrogation. Once the insurance claims have been paid, this permits the insurer—in this case FEMA—to sue a third party who may be responsible for bringing about the flood damage. While those who are insured relinquish their rights to such action once claims are paid, FEMA can pursue responsible third parties. In effect, FEMA is attempting through subrogation to shift some of the responsibility for flood damages to local governments who contribute to them by permitting development in hazardous locations, by not enforcing flood protection ordinances, and so on.

The first two subrogation suits brought by FEMA were the *United States v. Parish of Jefferson* and the *United States v. St. Bernard Parish* (both in Louisiana). In the Jefferson Parish case FEMA contended that, among other things, the jurisdiction failed to enforce the minimum standards required under NFIP, such as building elevation and requiring the submission of drainage plans for proposed subdivisions (see Flood Report 1983b). It was also contended that the parish did not adequately inspect or maintain the existing drainage system and that it altered this system, contributing to increased flood damages. The parish was accused as well of being negligent in failing to require an adequate program for water retention and detention. The legal issue in these cases centered on the extent to which a community's entrance into the NFIP constitutes a form of contract and the failure to comply with NFIP standards constitutes a breach of this contract. Recent opinions by the U.S. Court of Appeals for the Fifth Circuit found that no contract existed, deciding in favor of the parishes.

Rather than appeal, FEMA settled with the Jefferson Parish in 1987. In return for dismissal of the litigation the parish and its insurors agreed to pay FEMA $1 million and to comply with floodplain management regulations (U.S. District Court for Eastern District of Louisiana, Civil Action Nos. 81-1810 and 83-2077).

Office of the President:
Executive Orders 11988 and 11990

The Floodplain Management Executive Order (No. 11988) was signed by President Carter in 1977. It mandates the consideration by all federal agencies of actions which would encourage development in floodplains. It directs them to refrain from financing or permitting development in these hazard areas unless no "practicable" alternatives exist. If this is determined to be the case, agencies are required to ensure that these projects are carried out in such a way that flood damages are minimal and natural floodplain values are restored or preserved.

Executive Order 11990, also signed in 1977, instructs federal agencies to provide the same measure of protection to wetlands. Wetlands are not to be destroyed unless no other practicable alternatives exist; and where construction in these areas is unavoidable, agencies must insure that damages to wetlands are minimized.

NOAA and the Coastal Zone Management Act

The Coastal Zone Management Act (CZMA) was enacted by Congress in 1972, creating a formal framework for collaborative planning of our nation's coasts by federal, state, and local jurisdictions. States wishing to participate in the program are eligible to receive financial assistance for planning and developing a management program for their coastal areas. Funds are made available on a matching basis, both for program development (Section 305) and program implementation or administration (Section 306). These programs are subject to the guidelines and review of NOAA. While financial assistance has been the major incentive for participation in the CZM (Coastal Zone Management) program, the federal consistency requirement, contained in Section 307 of the act, has also served to encourage involvement (Brower and Carol 1984). This provision requires federal agencies with programs or development projects in coastal areas to conduct them in such a way that they are, to the maximum extent practicable, consistent with approved state management programs. This requirement in effect provides participating states with a major legal mechanism by which to control federal actions in coastal areas. Since its enactment, twenty-eight of the thirty-five eligible coastal states and territories have developed coastal management programs (Godschalk and Cousins 1985). Only two hurricane-prone states do not have approved coastal management plans: Texas and Georgia.

Under the CZMA provisions states must define inland coastal zone boundaries, determine permissible land and water uses, and designate areas of particular concern. Specifically mentioned in the legislation among areas of particular concern are: "areas of significant hazard if developed, due to storms, slides, floods, erosion, settlement, etc." (see NRDC 1977).

In many cases these state programs have provided, and continue to provide, an important legal, administrative, and political framework for local and state programs which mitigate hurricane and coastal storm hazards. This will become more apparent in the subsequent chapter dealing with state programs, and focusing on several key state efforts.

Department of Interior and the Coastal Barrier Resources Act

Enacted in 1982, the Coastal Barrier Resources Act (CBRA) was an attempt by Congress to remove some of the federal subsidies and incentives for private development in hazardous barrier islands. The law finds that barrier islands "serve as natural storm protective buffers and are generally unsuitable for development because they are vulnerable to hurricane and other storm damage and because natural shoreline recession and the movement of unstable sediments undermine manmade structures" (Public Law 97-348, 10/18/82, p. 1653, *U.S. Statutes at Large*).

The law created a Barrier Island Resources System and designated 186 "undeveloped" segments of barrier island to be included within it. These islands are located along the Atlantic and Gulf coasts from Maine to Texas (for a history of CBRA, see Kuehn 1984).

Under the provisions of the law federal expenditures to assist private development in these designated areas is prohibited. These restrictions apply to expenditures for such things as roads and bridges, community development, and disaster relief. General revenue sharing grants were specifically excluded from these restrictions, however. Also, as of October 1, 1983, the Federal Insurance Agency is prohibited from issuing new flood insurance policies for buildings within designated undeveloped barriers. Certain other activities may be exempted after consultation with the secretary of the interior, including expenditures for energy resource development, maintenance of channel improvements and essential public facilities, and expenditures for national defense purposes. In September 1985 FEMA issued its final rules limiting disaster assistance for undeveloped barrier island units. These regulations virtually prohibit disaster assistance. However, the rule does make several exceptions. Disaster assistance can be made available for:

> (1) maintenance, replacement, reconstruction, or repair, but not the expansion of publicly owned or publicly operated roads, structures, or facilities that are essential links in a larger network or system;
>
> (2) repair of any facility necessary for the exploration, extraction, or transportation of energy resources which activity can be carried out only on, in, or adjacent to coastal water areas because the use or facility requires access to the coastal water body; and
>
> (3) maintenance of existing channel improvements and related structures, such as jetties, and including the disposal of dredge materials related to such improvements. (CFR, Title 44, Section 205.506)

The secretary of the interior is required to review the map of the barrier island system at least every five years and to make whatever modifications might be necessary to reflect natural changes in the land. A 1987 report recommended expansion of the CBRA system to include some additional areas along the Atlantic and Gulf coasts.

There has been much debate about the potential effects of the CBRA provisions. Godschalk (1984) conducted a study of the initial impacts of CBRA, focusing on the impacts in three states: North Carolina, South Carolina, and Florida. The two research methods used in this project were case studies (Hutchinson Island, Florida, and Topsail Island, North Carolina) and a mail questionnaire sent to government officials, developers, and conservationists asking their opinions about likely impacts. The results of the questionnaire indicated that while respondents felt it was too early to see the impacts of CBRA, a majority of the respondents believed that the program would not substantially impede future development. On the other hand, findings from the two case studies indicated that development-retarding effects, at least in the short term, were already being felt from the CBRA program. On an island such as Topsail (North Carolina) where a road and bridge network was already in existence, the primary impact was from withdrawal of federal flood insurance. The long-term effects of this withdrawal will depend upon how easily the funds can be replaced by the private sector. The author speculates that this may encourage a shift to multifamily and condominium development and thus encourage even higher-density uses. On Hutchinson Island (Florida) where sufficient infrastructure does not exist, a major impact will be felt in the form of withdrawal of federal infrastructure funds. This had already forced developers to consider the construction of a bridge and road improvement themselves, perhaps paying for them through the use of impact fees.

While CBRA is a relatively recent enactment, it has already been challenged in federal court. In *Bostic et al. v. United States et al.*, plaintiffs argued that their Onslow Beach (North Carolina) location had been erroneously designated as an undeveloped barrier island and that their procedural due process rights had been violated. They also contended that the means used to achieve congressional goals—namely the restrictions in CBRA—were irrational and should be struck down on substantive due process grounds. The court did not find these arguments convincing, however, and upheld the constitutionality of CBRA (see Flood Report 1984).

Strengthening the Federal Programs

Despite the array of federal programs aimed at reducing coastal storm hazards, important gaps still exist. Perhaps the most important need is for stronger incentives for state and local governments to implement serious hazard mitigation programs. If the flood insurance program, for example, gave reduced rates to localities with strong mitigation measures, then citizens could see the benefits of mitigation in their bills for insurance premiums. If federal funds were available to help carry out state and local plans for relocating structures from high-hazard areas, then communities could undertake these necessary but expensive programs. An example of a successful federal program using incentives is the Coastal Zone Management Program illustrated in the next chapter, which deals with state programs.

Coupled with sweeter carrots could be some stronger sticks, as well. If FEMA could withhold disaster assistance from areas that had disregarded previous hazard mitigation requirements, then mitigation would be taken more seriously. If federal flood insurance could be withdrawn from areas that did not require mitigation following a disaster, that also would enhance mitigation efforts.

In addition, the preparation of hurricane preparedness plans needs a stronger financial base. If the funding priority of these plans was raised and a continuing funding source provided, then the necessary technical studies could be completed for the entire hurricane-prone coast on an expedited basis. These potential changes will be covered in more detail in the final chapter.

References

Allenstein, Karen. 1985. *Land Use Applications of the* SLOSH *Model (Sea, Lake and Overland Surges from Hurricanes)*. Chapel Hill, N.C.: University of North Carolina, Department of City and Regional Planning.

Berke, Philip, and Carlton Ruch. 1985. "Application of a Computer System for Hurricane Emergency Response and Land Use Planning." *Journal of Environmental Management* 21: 117–134.

Brower, David J., and Daniel S. Carol. 1984. *Coastal Zone Management as Land Planning*. Washington, D.C.: National Planning Association.

Carter, Michael T. 1983. *Probability of Hurricane/Tropical Storm Conditions: A Users Guide for Local Decision Makers*. Washington, D.C.: NOAA.

Committee on Government Operations. 1983. *Federal Assistance to States and Communities for Hurricane Preparedness Planning*. 98th Congress, 1st Session, House Report No. 98-537, November 17.

Conservation Foundation. 1980. *Flood Hazard Management and Natural Resources Protection*. Washington, D.C.

Federal Emergency Management Agency. 1981. *Federal Disaster Assistance Program Handbook for Applicants*. Washington, D.C.

———. 1984. *A Guide to Hurricane Preparedness Planning for State and Local Officials*. Washington, D.C.

————. 1987. "Hurricane Preparedness Studies." July 23. Washington, D.C.: Earthquake and Natural Hazards Programs Division.

Federal Register. 1986. "Proposed Rules for FEMA Disaster Assistance and Hazard Mitigation." Vol. 51, no. 75 (April 18).

Flood Report. 1983a. "FIA Abandons Use of Constructive Total Loss Theory." Vol. 1, no. 3 (October).

————. 1983b. "Negligence—Are You Guilty." Vol. 1, no. 5 (December).

————. 1984. "Coastal Barrier Challenge Defeated." Vol. 1, no. 7 (February).

Godschalk, David R. 1984. *Impacts of the Coastal Barrier Resources Act: A Pilot Study.* Washington, D.C.: Office of Ocean and Coastal Resource Management, NOAA.

Godschalk, David R., and Kathryn Cousins. 1985. "Coastal Management: Planning on the Edge." *Journal of the American Planning Association* 51, no.3 (Summer): 263–265.

Hildreth, Richard G., and Ralph W. Johnson. 1983. *Ocean and Coastal Law.* Englewood Cliffs, N.J.: Prentice Hall.

Kuehn, Robert R. 1984. "The Coastal Barrier Resources Act and the Expenditures Limitation Approach to Natural Resources Conservation: Wave of the Future or Island unto Itself?" *Ecology Law Quarterly* 11: 583–670.

McElyea, William D., David J. Brower, and David R. Godschalk. 1982. *Before the Storm: Managing Development to Reduce Hurricane Damages.* Chapel Hill, N.C.: University of North Carolina, Center for Urban and Regional Studies.

National Resources Defense Council. 1977. *Land Use Controls in the United States.* New York, N.Y.: Dial Press.

Propst, Luther. 1984. *A Review of Federal Programs Providing Disaster Assistance to Coastal Local Governments Following a Hurricane.* Chapel Hill, N.C.: University of North Carolina, Center for Urban and Regional Studies.

Tampa Bay Regional Planning Council. 1983. *Tampa Bay Region Hurricane Loss and Contingency Planning Study.* Summary Report. St. Petersburg, Fla.

————. 1984. *Tampa Bay Region Hurricane Evacuation Study: Technical Data Report.* Update. St. Petersburg, Fla.

U.S. Army Corps of Engineers. 1986. *Tri-State Hurricane Evacuation Study: Technical Data Report.* Mobile District (Ala.).

————. 1987. *Eastern North Carolina Hurricane Evacuation Study: Technical Data Report.* Wilmington District (N.C.).

U.S. General Accounting Office. 1981. "Requests for Federal Disaster Assistance Need Better Evaluation." Washington, D.C.

————. 1983. "National Flood Insurance Program—Major Changes Needed If It Is to Operate Without a Federal Subsidy." Washington, D.C.

5 State Mitigation Programs and Policies

State Mitigation Roles

States are key actors in coastal storm hazard mitigation, occupying a strategic position between federal hazard agencies and coastal local governments. While all states provide poststorm emergency management programs, however, there is a wide variety of state attitudes toward appropriate prestorm hazard mitigation roles.

Many hurricane-prone states, especially in the South, reflect the "traditionalistic" political culture norms identified by Elazar (1966), where political leaders are expected to play conservative and custodial roles, rather than initiatory roles, unless pressed strongly from the outside. Thus, the newer hazard mitigation policies, based on nonstructural and development management approaches, have been actively initiated by only a limited number of states.

Outside pressures have been mounting, however. Federal programs have been aimed at encouraging state governments to become directly and actively involved in the regulation and management of their coastal areas. The federal Coastal Zone Management Program has effectively used a voluntary planning approach supported by federal funding to develop rapport and peer pressure for successful state participation, involving traditional as well as progressive states (Matuszeski 1985). FEMA has likewise attempted to promote more active state mitigation roles based on Section 406 of the Disaster Relief Act of 1974 and its other programs, especially the National Flood Insurance Program.

There are also increasing nonfederal pressures. As noted in a mitigation guide for state officials (FEMA 1986, 7), "The importance of state-initiated mitigation efforts in the future becomes particularly evident in view of . . . the fact that most damage-causing natural events do not qualify for Federal disaster assistance; the increasingly higher costs of refinancing losses with or without a disaster declaration; the repetitive nature of many hazard events; and the increasing concern about state and local liability." These pressures, federal and nonfederal, are translated into the disaster policies and programs of individual states.

State governments, in turn, shape the policies and programs adopted by their localities. They may do this directly by establishing certain planning and regulatory standards which localities must satisfy and indirectly through maintenance of prevailing legal, administrative, and political frameworks. Direct and indirect influences may not always reinforce each other. For instance, a direct standard mandating preparation of local comprehensive plans is enforced in both Virginia and Florida. Yet the courts of these two states take very different positions on the constitutionality of local growth management programs; it is less difficult to adopt an innovative growth management program in Florida where the courts take into account the full range of growth management benefits than in Virginia where narrower property rights issues typically are the primary concerns (Godschalk et al. 1979).

Individual state roles in hazard mitigation depend on the priority given to disaster prevention by state government leaders and upon the prevailing state attitude toward government management of development in disaster-prone areas. Within the structure of shared governance it is possible to identify three general types of state hazard mitigation roles. Hazard mitigation "innovators" enthusiastically accept the need for hazard mitigation and devise new state planning and development programs to supplement federal efforts. Hazard mitigation "responders" follow federal guidelines but do not propose additional state actions beyond those required for compliance. Hazard mitigation "skeptics" question the need for federal programs and propose only minimal management of private development in hazard areas.

Which role a state plays depends upon both its historic attitudes toward the proper role of governance and its recent hazard experience. Even a skeptical state may go through periods of enthusiastic hazard mitigation and coastal development management following a major hurricane.

Table 5.1 Summary of State Coastal Management Programs

	CZM program	State mandated ocean setback line	Setback line—local option	No state setback line, but state control of development in front of first dune	State dune protection policy
Texas					
Louisiana	X				
Mississippi	X				
Alabama	X	X			X
Florida	X	X			
Georgia		X			
South Carolina	X		X[b]	X	
North Carolina	X	X			X
Virginia					
Maryland	X				
Delaware	X	X			X
New Jersey	X	X			X
New York	X	X[e]			
Connecticut	X				
Rhode Island	X	X			X
Massachusetts	X			X	
New Hampshire	X				
Maine	X	X[g]			X

Source: Bollens, Leyden, and Beatley 1984.

a. Florida (building code)—requires that each coastal county have a building code that addresses hurricane hazards, but it is up to local option as to which specific building code it adopts.

b. South Carolina (setback line)—model setback regulations are being developed by the state and would be locally optional.

c. South Carolina (reconstruction policy)—policies are being developed for four coastal communities; adoption by these communities would be optional.

Dune protection policy— local option	State building code (including hurricane-related measures)	Building code—local option	State reconstruction policy	State capital improvement policy pertaining to coastal/high-hazard areas	State wetlands program
X		X			X
		X			
		X			X
		X			
	X[a]			X	X
		X			X
		X	X[c]	X	
	X		X	X	X
X	X[d]				X
		X			
		X	X	X	X
	X				X
	X[f]		X		
	X				X
	X		X		X
	X			X	X
		X			X
	X[h]		X		X

d. Virginia (building code)—state building code does not include wind loading requirements.
e. New York (setback line)—state setback line not yet implemented.
f. New York (building code)—state building code became mandatory for communities January 1, 1984.
g. Maine (setback line)—a 200-foot setback is included in the "limited residential" zoning category of the Mandatory Shoreland Zoning Program.
h. Maine (building code)—state building code does not include wind loading requirements.

This chapter reviews current state mitigation activities as identified through recent surveys. This review gives a perspective on the state-of-the-art as presently practiced. Then the chapter describes the programs of two of the states more active in initiating innovative coastal development management aimed at hazard mitigation, North Carolina and Florida. This description suggests two models of possible state approaches. Finally, the chapter concludes with thoughts on the potential for extending state mitigation efforts.

Current State Mitigation Practice

State coastal management programs can directly or indirectly assist in hurricane and storm hazard mitigation. Relevant program elements may include:

1. Participation in the Federal Coastal Zone Management Program
2. Ocean setbacks for new buildings
3. Dune protection policies
4. Storm-resistant building code requirements
5. Poststorm reconstruction policies
6. Limitations on capital improvements in hazard areas
7. Wetlands protection programs

To identify what states do to mitigate hurricane and coastal storm hazards, a phone survey of state agencies in all Gulf and Atlantic coast states was conducted in 1983 (Bollens, Leyden, and Beatley 1984). Survey responses illustrate the range of activities undertaken by these coastal states. Activities of each state are shown in table 5.1 and discussed below.

One of the most prevalent activities is *participation in the Federal Coastal Zone Management Program*. Only three of the eighteen Atlantic and Gulf coast states were not participating at the time of the survey: Texas, Georgia, and Virginia. Virginia has since joined the program with an approved plan. As noted earlier, the federal coastal program has done much to strengthen the political, legal, and administrative structure for state coastal zone planning. It has successfully directed the attention of both traditional and innovative coastal states toward environmental protection and hazard mitigation, otherwise often low-salience items on state and local political agendas.

Building codes are the most commonly adopted mitigation programs. They vary in their stringency and the extent to which they explicitly address storm hazards and often represent the adoption of standard building codes (for example, the Southern Standard Building Code). These building codes are either state-adopted (one state code which must be adhered to by all localities) or local-option. Rhode Island, for instance, has adopted a state building code, while Alabama leaves the adoption of building standards up to its localities.

A number of states are implementing *coastal setback provisions*— either state-administered or local-option. For instance, Georgia under its Shore Assistance Act implements a mandatory setback for oceanfront development, while in South Carolina local setbacks are optional, yet guided by model setback regulations. Two states have enacted provisions which control development in front of the first dune—South Carolina and Massachusetts. Massachusetts has adopted regulations which require a resource impact analysis for beach areas and coastal development standards which all but prevent development in areas seaward of the first dune. As a result of the adoption of the South Carolina Coastal Management Act in 1977, the South Carolina Coastal Council has direct permitting authority over development in front of the primary dune line when a dune exists.

Another popular element is *dune protection legislation*. For instance, under Maine's Coastal Sand Dune Rules no new development is permitted on frontal dunes. Under Delaware's Beach Preservation Act (1972) beachfront homeowners are required to sign a "dune maintenance agreement" and to submit a surveyed plat of the lot showing existing dune conditions and the proposed location of buildings to ensure sufficient protection of the dune.

Only six states have adopted policies to guide *reconstruction following hurricanes and coastal storms*. In Delaware, if a structure is destroyed by a storm, the owner must receive a permit from the state before it can be rebuilt. Furthermore, the owner must ensure that it is rebuilt as far landward as possible. The state of South Carolina, through the South Carolina Coastal Council, has been attempting to encourage the adoption of local recovery plans and policies. Massachusetts has also enacted policies which require the acquisition of a permit for reconstruction of substantially damaged structures (damage amounting to 50 percent of appraised value or greater). The structures must either be moved outside of the flood zone or elevated to a level one foot above the 100-year Base Flood Elevation. Seawalls which are destroyed to a level beyond 50 percent of their value are not permitted to be rebuilt.

Five states have adopted policies pertaining to the state *funding of public facilities in hazardous areas*. Florida has perhaps been the most active in this area. It has enacted several new provisions under its recent growth management package which substantially restrict future public investment in high-hazard storm areas. Delaware has promulgated a policy to discourage the location of "growth sewers" in sensitive coastal areas. Massachusetts, under the provisions of MEPA (Massachusetts Environmental Protection Act), discourages the funding of public works where existing hazards would be heightened and where such actions would encourage further growth in sensitive coastal environments; the state actively discourages the location of major capital facilities (for example, sewer treatment plants) on barrier islands.

Thirteen Atlantic and Gulf coast states currently have in place systems for *regulating and managing their wetlands*. Wetlands management can reduce coastal storm hazards, both by keeping people and property away from hazard areas and by preserving natural buffer areas which absorb storm water. Regulations for the state of Virginia are perhaps typical. Virginia's Wetlands Act (Sec. 62.1-13.1 through 82.1-13.20, Code of Virginia) provides coastal jurisdictions and the Virginia Marine Resources Commission with the authority to regulate proposed development in tidal wetlands. These provisions do not stipulate prohibition of development in these areas, but rather provide for the placement of conditions on development, depending upon particular site constraints. Ecological systems are not to be unreasonably disturbed, and development is to be "concentrated in wetlands of lesser ecological significance, in wetlands which have been irreversibly disturbed before July 1, 1972, and areas apart from wetlands" (Kusler 1980, 198).

Another indication of state coastal hazard reduction activities is provided by a survey undertaken by the Coastal States Organization in 1986. This survey covered all coastal states, including Pacific and Great Lakes states as well as Atlantic and Gulf coast states, so it is broader than our telephone survey. Its twenty-three respondents included thirteen of the eighteen Atlantic and Gulf coast states (Coastal States Organization

Table 5.2   Support for New Hazard Mitigation Initiatives

Method	Would Support	May Support	Would Not Support
Mandatory relocation of threatened structures	1	9	12
Mandatory relocation of damaged structures	7	6	10
Financial assistance for relocation of threatened or damaged structures (e.g., through flood insurance)	10	11	2
Limits on disaster relief for threatened structures that do not attempt to minimize damage	8	10	5
Limits on casualty loss deductions for threatened structures that do not attempt to minimize damage	6	11	4
Prohibition of federal flood insurance for structures with a previous flood insurance claim	4	13	5
Density limits in high-hazard areas	6	11	4
Education about relocation feasibility and other mitigation tools	18	4	0

Source: Coastal States Organization 1986.

1986). Twenty-two respondents reported that the threat of future storm and/or erosion damage to existing shoreline development was a serious concern in their state. Nineteen said that their state attempts to manage new development to lessen future damage through direct land use regulations or construction standards, primarily shoreline setbacks and building codes. Eighteen said that they used indirect development management methods, primarily land use plans and limits on public investment. Twenty said that public works and/or public financing were being used to reduce future damage, primarily through shoreline stabilization and beach nourishment.

In terms of new initiatives the coastal states were asked about the likelihood of support for methods to minimize future damage to existing development from storms and/or erosion. As table 5.2 indicates, there was considerable support for a variety of innovative methods, ranging from flood insurance and disaster relief incentives to density limits and mandatory relocation of damaged structures.

While many states appear to be becoming more active in the management and planning of their coastal areas, enacting and implementing strong state hazard mitigation programs is sometimes difficult. For example, the Texas legislature considered the adoption of a set of innovative hurricane building provisions and a hazard disclosure law but due to intense lobbying by the real estate and development industry were unable to pass these new provisions. More recently the Texas legislature has abolished the Texas Marine and Coastal Council, further illustrating the low level of political support for coastal planning in that state. A "dune bill" was recently defeated in the New Jersey legislature. These regulations would have required more stringent coastal setbacks and would have prevented reconstruction in hazard-prone areas if structures incurred damages which amounted to more than 50 percent of their value.

While surveys can identify individual activities by states, they do not provide the full picture of coastal hazard mitigation policy and program "packages." Case study descriptions are better at presenting these packages. To round out the picture of the state of the art in state hazard mitigation, more in-depth descriptions of the coastal hazard management programs of two states with extensive and innovative efforts are presented. These programs can serve as models to be adapted to the unique political, social, and economic circumstances of other coastal states desiring active hazard mitigation programs.

No state program is static; innovative states change even faster than others. The profiles provided here document these two active programs at a particular point in time. Undoubtedly they will undergo further change.

Mitigation in North Carolina

Hurricanes and Coastal Growth

Next to Florida, North Carolina has received more direct hurricane strikes than any other Atlantic coast state. Particularly memorable and devastating storms include Hazel in 1954 and the Ash Wednesday storm of 1962 (Baker 1978; Neumann et al. 1981). Three hurricanes—Ione, Diane, and Connie—struck the North Carolina coast during a two month period in 1955. Hurricane activity in the past twenty years has been light, although the state was hit by Hurricane Diana in September 1984. Despite the threat of major destruction, by the time Diana hit the coast it was a relatively weak hurricane, and its effects were reduced by a number of mitigating factors (for example, landfall during low tide). The media build-up given to Diana and its relatively small actual impact may have had a negative effect on the perceived importance of future storm hazard planning. However, it prompted one commentator to describe the storm as a "warning from nature" and a foreshadowing of more serious things to come (Kaufman 1984).

Historically the North Carolina coast has not faced the growth pressures of New Jersey or Florida, but second home and resort development have flourished recently. Between 1970 and 1980 permanent population in the twenty coastal counties increased by 17 percent (Beatley 1985). Much greater levels of growth have occurred along the barrier islands and in the most hazardous locations (French 1979). For instance, by 1980 the small town of Long Beach on Oak Island had experienced a seventeenfold increase over its 1960 permanent population (Town of Long Beach 1984). Permanent population figures also tend to underestimate the development pressures experienced by such communities, as much of the building in these areas can be attributed to vacationers and nonresidents. For instance, while the Town of Emerald Isle has an official permanent population of 865, its average seasonal population has been estimated to be around 8,500 (Town of Emerald Isle 1984).

North Carolina has approached hazard mitigation as a component of its coastal planning program. According to the director of the Division of Coastal Management, this program has focused on patiently building a "regional consensus" for effective coastal resource management in the politically conservative coastal area, where initially there was widespread opposition to the concept of coastal management (Owens 1985). The North Carolina model could be characterized as a go-slow program oriented toward local involvement, with consistent and effective staff support, which has led over time to progressive hazard mitigation standards integrated into a development management framework (Brower, Beatley, and Blatt 1987).

The North Carolina Coastal Area Management Act

As part of the U.S. Coastal Zone Management Program, the North Carolina Coastal Area Management Act (CAMA) was passed in 1974. At the heart of this program is a cooperative arrangement between coastal localities and the state, in which the state provides (through the federal government) financial and technical assistance to local land use planning and localities agree to adhere to and implement state regulations and guidelines.

The Coastal Management Program has two primary components: (1) the land use plans developed by coastal localities under guidelines provided the state and (2) the delineation and regulation of "Areas of Environmental Concern" (AECs) by the state (jointly implemented with coastal localities). A twelve-member appointed body, the Coastal Resources Commission (CRC), is responsible for overseeing the Coastal Area Management Program. The Division of Coastal Management (DCM), within the State Department of Natural Resources and Community Development, is responsible for the administration of CAMA and serves a staff function for the CRC. A larger advisory body, the Coastal Resources Advisory Council (CRAC), was established to assist the CRC. The requirements of CAMA apply to twenty counties which experience tidal effects (see figure 5.1).

Local Land Use Planning

Local land use planning is a key component of the North Carolina program. While only the twenty coastal counties are required to prepare land use plans, coastal municipalities were given the option of preparing their own plans. Where the county failed to prepare a plan, the CRC could prepare and adopt a plan for it. These plans must be updated every five years. All twenty counties and fifty-five municipalities have adopted updated land use plans as of January 1985 (Owens 1985). Once adopted, state agency decisions must be consistent with them and through the federal consistency provisions so also must federal decisions.

CAMA administrative regulations stipulate the content and format of local plans. In addition to analysis and assessment of current and future conditions (for example, documentation of population and land use trends and estimation of future land use needs), each land use plan is required to provide policy statements on those land use issues which will affect the community during the ten-year planning period. Policy statements must address resource protection, resource production and management, economic and community development, continuing public participation, and storm hazard planning. Local land

Figure 5.1   North Carolina Coastal Zone Counties. *Source*: Final Environmental Impact Statement, North Carolina Coastal Management Program (Department of Commerce 1978).

use plans must be submitted to the CRC for approval in accordance with review standards (N.C. Administrative Code, Subchapter 7B).

State Permitting System

In addition to local land use plans, a second coastal component of CAMA is the state designation of "Areas of Environment Concern" (AECs). These are special areas where development cannot occur without review and approval by an appropriate body of government (CRC in the case of "major" developments and usually local governments in the case of "minor" developments). These proposals are evaluated against a set of performance standards adopted by the state for each type of AEC and for consistency with adopted land use plans. (They apply equally to major and minor types of development.)

Two primary categories of AECs have been designated: estuarine areas and ocean hazard areas. The estuarine category contains several kinds of AEC designations: coastal wetlands (marsh areas subject to regular flooding), estuarine waters, public trust areas (generally, navigable waters), and estuarine shorelines (extending seventy-five feet landward from mean high-water level). Within ocean hazard areas the AECs are ocean erodible zones, high hazard flood areas (V-zones as designated under the National Flood Insurance Program), and inlet hazard areas.

Five of these AECs—the coastal wetlands, estuarine shorelines, ocean erodible, high-hazard flood, and inlet hazard areas—have particular significance for managing development to reduce hurricane and storm hazards. The ocean erodible zone defines a shoreline area in which structures must be built "set back" from the water. More specifically, the administrative standards define the boundaries of the zone as follows:

(a) A distance landward from the first line of stable natural vegetation to the recession line that would be established by multiplying the long-term annual erosion rate which for the purposes of this Section shall be those as set forth in tables entitled "Long Term Annual Erosion Rates Updated Through 1980," approved by the Coastal Resources Commission on March 18, 1983, and available without cost from any local permit officer or the Office of Coastal Management (except as such rate may be varied in individual contested cases, declaratory or interpretive rulings), times 60, provided that where there has been no long-term erosion or the rate is less than two feet per year, this distance shall be set at 120 feet landward from the first line of stable natural vegetation; and

(b) a distance landward from the recession line established in Subparagraph (a) of this Paragraph to the recession line that would be generated by a storm having a one percent chance of being equalled or exceeded in any given year. (N.C. Administrative Code, Subchapter 7H)

Inlet hazard zones are land areas subject to a high degree of erosion because of their closeness to shifting inlets. More specifically these zones extend landward from the mean low water line for the distance within which the inlet is expected to migrate based on statistical analysis. Their definition must consider such factors as previous inlet territory, structurally weak areas near the inlet (such as an unusually narrow barrier island, an unusually long channel feeding the inlet, or an overwash area), and external influences such as jetties and channelization. These areas are identified on inlet hazard area maps approved by the Coastal Resources Commission. In all cases this area is an extension of the adjacent ocean erodible area, and in no case can the width of the inlet hazard area be less than the width of the adjacent ocean erodible area.

Performance or use standards have been developed by the state to guide and control development in the AECs. For example, a general use requirement for ocean hazard areas is a mandatory setback of all development a certain distance from the ocean, based upon average annual rate of erosion and the natural features of the site, as well as the type of development proposed. If a primary or frontal dune does not exist, low-intensity development must be set back from the first line of vegetation a distance of thirty times the average annual rate of erosion or at least sixty feet where the annual erosion rate is less than two feet. Where a primary or frontal dune exists, this setback distance is measured from either the crest of this dune or the first line of vegetation, whichever is farthest. The setback distance is doubled for substantially larger oceanfront uses:

Because large structures located immediately along the Atlantic Ocean present increased risk of loss of life and property, increased potential for eventual loss or damage to the public beach area and other important natural features along the oceanfront, increased potential for higher public costs for federal flood insurance, erosion control, storm protection, disaster relief and provision of public services such as water and sewer, and increased difficulty and expense of relocation in the event of future shoreline loss, a greater oceanfront setback is required for these structures than is the case with smaller structures. Therefore, in addition to meeting the criteria in this rule for setback behind the primary and/or frontal dune, for all multi-family residential structures (including motels, hotels, condominiums and motelominiums) of more than 4 units or 5,000 square feet, the erosion setback line shall be twice the erosion setback described in .0306(a) (1) of this rule, provided that in no case shall this distance be less than 120 feet. In areas where the rate is more than 3.5 feet per year, this setback line shall be set at a distance of 30 times the long-term annual erosion rate plus 105 feet. (N.C. Administrative Code, Subchapter 7H)

No development is permitted in ocean hazard areas which involves significant removal or relocation of sand or vegetation of frontal or primary dunes. The location of public facilities such as roads, bridges, and sewer lines in ocean hazard areas will not be permitted unless these facilities: (1) clearly exhibit overriding factors of national or state interest and public benefit, (2) will not increase existing hazards or damage natural buffers, (3) will be reasonably safe from flood and erosion related damage, (4) will not promote growth and development in ocean hazard areas.

Specific use standards are designated which regulate such activities as erosion control projects, dune stabilization, and structural access ways in ocean hazard areas. Any construction or substantial improvements (constituting 50 percent or more of the market value of a structure) in ocean hazard zones must satisfy an additional set of standards including provisions to increase wind resistance (must comply with "Coastal and Flood Plain Construction Standards" of the N.C. Residential Building Code) and elevation and piling requirements (similar to NFIP requirements). Additional use standards are stipulated for construction in Inlet Hazard Areas. These serve explicitly to limit the potential density of construction in such areas. Permanent structures here are not permitted at a density greater than one unit (residential or commercial) per 15,000 square feet, and structures cannot exceed four units in the case of residential structures or

5,000 square feet total floor area in the case of commercial buildings.

For coastal wetland areas CAMA regulations indicate that only water-related uses will be permitted in these areas (for example, prohibiting such uses as hotels, motels, restaurants, and residences). Water-dependent uses such as docks and boat ramps would be permitted, as well as bulkheads, groins, and drainage ditches, subject to general standards which prohibit the negative impact of these uses on wetlands (for example, must not increase siltation, must not have negative effects on air and water quality, must not result in stagnant water and so on). Specific use standards have been established for such activities as navigational channels and canals, dredging, drainage ditches, nonagricultural drainage, marinas, docks and piers, bulkheads and stabilization measures, beach nourishment, and groins. Development in estuarine shorelands—the dry lands in the estuarine system—is restricted from, among other things, producing impervious surfaces which exceed 30 percent of the AEC land area. Development in these areas must also provide buffer strips, as well as take other actions sufficient to prevent siltation into estuarine waters.

In the spring of 1984 the CRC promulgated innovative rules which prohibit the use of shore-hardening structures, such as seawalls and groins. This action should serve as a further stimulus to increase management of growth to avoid ocean-generated hazards.

The CAMA provisions now require that coastal localities explicitly address hurricane hazard mitigation and postdisaster reconstruction in their local land use plan. Several factors served as the genesis for these new provisions. A Post-Disaster Task Force was established in the spring of 1981 to develop state policies for dealing with coastal storm hazards. Concurrent with this effort the Division of Coastal Management contracted with researchers at the University of North Carolina Center for Urban and Regional Studies to develop a guidebook to assist coastal localities to plan for storm hazards. From this research the center produced a report entitled *Before the Storm: Managing Development to Reduce Hurricane Damages* (McElyea, Brower, and Godschalk 1982).

The *Before the Storm* report served as an influential model for the incorporation of local storm hazard planning requirements into the CAMA land use planning provisions. In May 1983 the CAMA Land Use Planning Guidelines were revised to require that coastal localities incorporate provisions into their local plans for storm hazard mitigation, poststorm reconstruction, and evacuation.

The Land Use Planning Guidelines of the North Carolina Administrative Code (Subchapter 7B) require localities to prepare storm mitigation policies for their land use plans with the following elements:

(i) A composite hazards map and brief narrative description of hazardous areas located within the planning jurisdiction

(ii) An inventory and analysis of the existing uses of the land and structures in hazards areas

(iii) A description of the relative severity and type of risk or risks and an indication of the monetary value of the losses that might be sustained in each of the hazard areas

(iv) Hazard mitigation policies which apply to all hazard areas, including both public and private facilities

In developing these policies, localities are instructed to consider separate policies to deal with the effects of high winds, flooding, wave action, and erosion; means of dealing with structures and uses which do not conform to the hazard mitigation policies; means of encouraging hotels, restaurants, and similar large commercial structures to locate outside of erosion-prone areas; and policies to acquire for public access parcels located in hazard areas or rendered unbuildable.

The guidelines also require the preparation of a postdisaster reconstruction plan which implements the above policies and explicitly distinguishes between immediate cleanup and repair and longer-term recovery issues. Specifically, reconstruction plans must include, among other things, the establishment of poststorm reconstruction guidelines, including the timing and completion of damage assessments; the timing and imposition of temporary development moratoria; and the development standards to which repairs and reconstruction shall conform.

Localities are to establish schedules for staging reconstruction "according to established priorities assigned to the restoration of essential services, minor repairs, major repairs and new development." Localities are also to prepare policies to guide the repair or reconstruction of public facilities and to consider their possible relocation outside of hazard zones. The locality is also required to consider the establishment of a "reconstruction task force" to oversee poststorm recovery and to deal with the policy questions which arise during the reconstruction phase.

Evacuation is also a strong concern in the CAMA guidelines. The locality, in consultation with the county (where relevant) and the State Division of Emergency Management, must consider the adequacy of the local evacuation plan. "If the required evacuation time exceeds the standard warning time as provided by the National Weather Service, the local government should consider adopting policies which would improve the capacity of evacuation routes, or limit the level of development in areas to be evacuated, or otherwise reduce the amount of time needed to safely evacuate."

Other Mitigation Measures

Land acquisition became an important aspect of the North Carolina Coastal Management Program in 1981. In that year the state legislature adopted the state beach access law and appropriated an initial sum of $1 million for its implementation. In 1982 the state also began participation in the national estuarine sanctuary system. The Division of Coastal Management has responsibility for implementing both of these programs (see Owens 1983). Under the beach access legislation the CRC is directed to give priority in acquisition to parcels which are considered unsuitable for "permanent substantial structures."

North Carolina has adopted a state building code which consists of the Southern Standard Building Code with North Carolina amendments. The wind speed used in much of the coastal zone for minimum wind-loading calculations is 120 mph. This applies to construction on the Outer Banks and parts of Carteret, Onslow, Pender, New Hanover, and Brunswick counties east of the Intracoastal Waterway (N.C. Building Code Council 1978) (see figure 5.2). Anchorage, tie-down, and piling requirements are stipulated for construction in high wind or flood hazard areas. Also, under CAMA regulations buildings located in ocean hazard AECs must be in conformance with "Coastal and Flood Plain Construction Standards" of the state building code, which provides certain standards for pilings, foundations, and building elevation.

The state building code is not an optional document but must be adhered to by all localities. Local governments are not permitted to adopt variations to the state code unless they are formally approved by the N.C. Building Code Council—a twelve-member body appointed by the governor (Green 1980). Such approved modifications are rare, and thus coastal localities are prohibited from adopting more stringent storm-resistant construction standards than those in the state building code. An acknowledgment of this, and the need for more stringent coastal standards, led the council in 1985 to adopt substantial new additions to the N.C. Building Code which would apply only to the coastal region (Beatley 1985). Included among these provisions are more stringent piling depth requirements, fire equipment access requirements, standards for flame-resistant roof materials, and standards requiring sprinkler systems, among others.

North Carolina has also undertaken typical emergency management planning steps, including the preparation of evacuation plans at the county and regional level. The Wilmington Office of the Corps of Engineers, in coordination with FEMA and the North Carolina Division of Emergency Management, completed the *Eastern North Carolina Hurricane Evacuation Study* in 1987. This study covered eighteen coastal counties, 300 miles of open coastline, and 1,700 miles of sound/estuary shoreline, including an estimated 1985 population of 622,800. Clearance times, the times required to clear all evacuating vehicles from the roadway network before the arrival of gale force winds, were computed for each

Figure 5.2   Wind Speed Diagram. Basic design wind velocities in mph

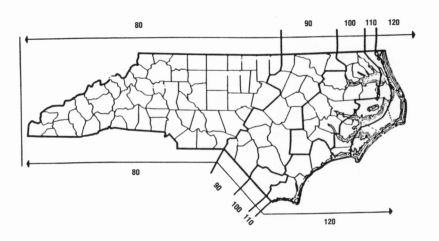

critical roadway segment, based on hurricane severity, degree of seasonal occupancy, and speed of evacuation response. Clearance times ranged from a low of four hours in several locations under moderate conditions to highs of over sixteen hours under worst conditions in Dare County, Bertie County, and Ocracoke Island in Hyde County (U.S. Army Corps of Engineers 1987, 199)

North Carolina Program Evaluation

The North Carolina program has been effective in coastal planning, resource management, and establishing local planning. Heath and Moseley (1980, 34) in their five-year progress report conclude that CAMA led many coastal jurisdictions to establish planning staffs and boards.

> It is too early to tell how many of the new local land-use planning programs in the coastal area could survive if the federal and state incentives that accompanied CAMA were withdrawn .... But this much is clear: the counties, cities, and towns of the coastal area have grasped firmly the planning opportunities offered by CAMA, and the CAMA objective of strengthening local planning programs is very much on target. Notably, this has been accomplished with a minimum of local-state friction or disagreement. Only once did the CRC find it necessary to exercise its statutory option of adopting a land-classification plan for a county that did not adopt its own plan [Carteret County]. The success of CAMA's local planning aspect has helped earn for North Carolina a national reputation for productive state-local collaboration in coastal management.

The political acceptability of CAMA is partly a result of strongly incorporating local officials into CAMA policymaking.

> The strong local flavor of the CRC and CRAC represented compromises that were essential to secure enactment of CAMA in 1974. CAMA's first five years of administration suggest that these compromises were also important to the survival of the program once it was launched. Time and again the knowledge of local conditions and the practical experience of CRC and CRAC members have been of immeasurable value in supplementing staff expertise. And many observers have noted how membership on CRC and CRAC has converted former

opponents and critics of CAMA into valued supporters (Heath and Moseley 1980, 33).

Owens (1985) concurs with this assessment, noting that it is an orientation toward making the land use plans into "people plans" rather than "planner plans" that has increased public acceptance and support of coastal land use planning. This has involved an emphasis on participation and policy rather than technical studies and data.

In the absence of a major hurricane strike it is difficult to assess the effectiveness of the required incorporation of storm hazard mitigation and reconstruction planning into land use plans. A review of the initial fifteen mitigation and reconstruction plans found that only a few propose a significant redirecting of growth and reconstruction in ways which will substantially reduce future damages and loss of life. Most accept the premise that future growth in hazardous areas will continue (Beatley 1985). There is reason to be optimistic, however, because the plans create a new hazard planning framework for mapping of storm hazard areas, quantification of property and people at risk, consideration of local mitigation goals and objectives, and preparation of poststorm procedures and practices (for example, damage assessment teams and reconstruction task forces). These institutional changes set the stage for informed hazard decisionmaking and incorporate consideration of the threat of hurricanes and coastal storms into the long-range planning programs of coastal localities.

Clearly, the regulatory mechanisms of CAMA—particularly the ocean setback—have reduced the extent of people and property at risk. North Carolina took a major step in prohibiting the practice of shoreline hardening, and this will have the effect of moving structures further away from the most hazardous coastal locations. The incorporation of storm hazard mitigation goals and policies into local land use plans should ensure that future regulatory decisions will be even more responsive to hazard reduction. The North Carolina model of first building a regional consensus in favor of coastal management and then working with coastal officials to gradually develop hazard mitigation standards and regulations has proved very effective.

Mitigation in Florida

Hurricanes and Coastal Growth

The state of Florida has been experiencing phenomenal growth pressures in recent years. Over the course of the single decade between 1970 and 1980 its population grew by approximately 3 million. By the year 2010 it is predicted that its population will number almost 17 million, or close to an 80 percent increase from its 1980 level (ELMS [Environmental Land Management Study] Committee 1984). Moreover, Florida is the state most vulnerable to hurricanes and coastal storms, with nearly 40 percent of all landfalling hurricanes since 1899 hitting the Florida coast (Neumann et al. 1981). Florida is one continual coastline, and it is these particularly vulnerable locations which are likely to receive the greatest levels of future growth. It contains approximately 11,000 miles of tidal coastline and some 1160 miles of sandy beaches (O'Connell 1985). These factors have added both to the difficulty of coastal planning in Florida and its urgency and importance.

Florida has included coastal planning within overall state comprehensive planning requirements rather than establishing a special coastal region. Florida went from a skeptical attitude toward growth management in the 1960s to a progressive and innovative attitude during the 1970s and 1980s. In its newfound enthusiasm Florida adopted several of the latest development management techniques from the American Law Institute's *Model Land Development Code*: Developments of Regional Impact and Areas of Critical State Concern. These were combined with a statewide requirement mandating the preparation of local comprehensive plans to be reviewed by the state. Recent legislation has expanded planning requirements and financial support and directed that local plans be consistent with regional and state plans. Unlike the North Carolina model of regional consensus, Florida has devised a model based on mandated compliance with centralized standards.

Developments of Regional Impact

One of the most important components of Florida's growth management system is its procedure for review by regional planning councils of "Developments of Regional Impact" (DRIs). Under the 1972 Environmental Land and Water Act DRIs are identified as development activities which are subject to regional review if they reach a certain size threshold. Included under DRI review are airports, attractions/recreation facilities, hospitals, industrial parks, office parks, schools, shopping centers, and residential uses. Each of these uses can occur without review, as long as its size does not reach the specified threshold. For example, DRI review is required only for new hospitals with a capacity of 600 beds or more. However, an activity which falls below established thresholds still can be identified as a DRI by the Department of Community Affairs if "its character, magnitude or location, would have substantial effect on the health, safety or welfare of citizens of more than one county" (Carraway 1984).

Once a project is determined to be a DRI, a regional planning council assesses its regional impacts and recommends appropriate actions to the local government. The local government in deliberating on the project must consider its consistency with the state land plan, the regional recommendation, and local development regulations (see Hunsberger 1979; Carraway 1984). The regional planning agency's recommendations, however, are only considered advisory.

Development permit decisions can be appealed to the Florida Land and Water Adjudicatory Commission (the governor and the cabinet). Among other parties appeals can be initiated by the regional planning body and the Department of Community Affairs.

While the DRI program has no specific regulations concerning hurricane or coastal storm mitigation, it must assess the impacts of proposed developments on public safety. Approximately five years ago, hurricane hazard reduction began to receive serious attention in the review process and, in particular, evacuation and shelter capacity (Bollens, Leyden, and Beatley 1984; see also Daltry 1980). It is now common for conditions to be attached to DRI approvals requiring project evacuation plans, improvements which facilitate evacuation, or which provide storm shelters.

A recent DRI review process in Monroe County illustrates the extent of this consideration. The review in this case was for the Port Bouganville/Garden Cove development proposed in Key Largo. As a condition of approval for this project, the developers agreed to the construction of low-level hurricane shelter structures (built to certain minimum wind and wave standards), road improvements to improve evacuation capacity, preparation of an evacuation plan and its coordination with county evacuation plans, and procedures for notification and evacuation of hotel/commercial property residents (Wilkerson 1984).

The success of the DRI program is debatable. The ELMS Committee report criticized its inability to address the cumulative effects of smaller projects and the fact that it applied to very few developments. In a cross section of Florida counties the ELMS Committee found that "only in rare cases did the DRI cover as much as 10 percent of the residential development" (ELMS Committee 1984, 40). Developers and representatives of the private sector have, predictably, been quite critical of the DRI process.

> The DRI program was heavily criticized by persons from the private sector who had experience in DRI reviews. They described the DRI as a negative process that evaluates all possible adverse impacts of a development without a balanced consideration of the benefits of the development. Developers complained that this wide-ranging evaluation is unreasonably time-consuming and expensive, and that it often duplicates the reviews conducted by permitting agencies. Other criticisms focused on local governments' practice of using DRI review as a convenient vehicle to require contributions of land or funds from DRI developers to provide needed capital improvements, while other developers in the jurisdiction are not subject to the same requirements. Such exactions are arguably unfair when they fall solely on DRI developments (ELMS Committee 1984, 40).

Among the other criticisms of the DRI regulations are that they are not adequately enforced, that there are not adequate criteria and standards for evaluating DRIS, and that there is great uncertainty and difficulty involved in appealing DRI decisions.

Recent modifications to the DRI process, under the 1985 Growth Management Package, establish "banded" numeric DRI thresholds. When a development is at or more than 80 percent below a numeric threshold it is not a DRI. Developments falling over 120 percent of the threshold must undergo the DRI review process. When a development is between 80 and 100 percent of the threshold it is "presumed" that it is not a DRI, while it is "presumed" that a development is a DRI if it falls between 100 and 120 percent of the threshold. This banded approach reduces the uncertainty of designation.

Areas of Critical State Concern

The second major program created by the Environmental Land and Water Management Act of 1972 is the Areas of Critical State Concern (ACSC) program (Section 380.5, Florida Statutes). Under this program, the Florida Administration Commission (the governor and the cabinet) has the authority to designate an "area of critical state concern." To date, four such areas have been designated: the Big Cypress (800,000 acres of wetlands adjacent to Everglades National Park), the Green Swamp (a central Florida wetlands area), the Florida Keys, and the Apalachicola Bay area in the panhandle (Godschalk 1987). As part of the designation procedure, the Administration Commission also adopts a set of principles for guiding development in the designated area. The Department of Community Affairs is then given the responsibility for directing and overseeing local planning in this area such that it is consistent with these adopted principles. If the localities fail to adopt appropriate development regulations, the state has the authority to prepare and enforce its own development regulations.

As important as the actual designation of areas of critical state concern is the planning process that must precede it. Before an area can be designated under the ACSC program, the state must attempt to gain voluntary enactment by localities of an adequate resource management program. The governor appoints a Resource Planning and Management Committee (RPMC) (see Sec. 380.045, Florida Statutes) which coordinates and oversees this voluntary planning process. As the ELMS Committee reports, this voluntary resource management approach, undoubtedly assisted by the threat of ACSC designation, has in recent years been quite successful.

> In the first three critical areas, local governments were initially uncooperative and even antagonistic when the state adopted regulations for the critical area. Recently, however, cooperative relationships have evolved when state agencies and local governments have worked together on RPMC's. The Charlotte Harbor Committee completed a voluntary resource management plan that has been incorporated into the comprehensive plans of the participating local governments. The Committee is monitoring the implementation of the plan. The Suwannee River Basin Committee drafted a model floodplain ordinance that has been adopted by all eleven affected counties. The

Hutchinson Island Committee was established in 1982 and has recently completed a voluntary resource management plan. Also, an RPMC has recently been formed to study and prepare a report on a growth management program for coastal areas of the Northwest Florida Panhandle (ELMS Committee 1984, 101).

The 1985 Growth Management Package:
Creating a Comprehensive Planning Framework

In 1985 the Florida legislature adopted a growth management package (Growth Management Act of 1985 and act adopting state plan) which substantially revised and reinforced the intergovernmental planning system. Under this new package local, regional, and state comprehensive plans all must be consistent (see figure 5.3).

Consider first the importance of the state plan. The notion of an overall state plan was given a major rejuvenation under passage of the State and Regional Planning Act of 1984. It mandated the preparation and legislative enactment of a state comprehensive plan containing general goals and policies for the state. The act required that within one year of the adoption of the state plan, each state agency develop a specific functional plan which implements and is consistent with the goals and policies in the state plan. The state policy plan was developed during 1984–1985 and

Figure 5.3   New Florida State-Regional-Local Planning Framework

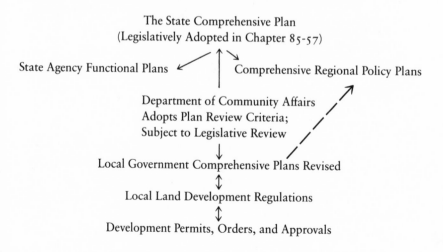

The State Comprehensive Plan
(Legislatively Adopted in Chapter 85-57)

State Agency Functional Plans   Comprehensive Regional Policy Plans

Department of Community Affairs
Adopts Plan Review Criteria;
Subject to Legislative Review

Local Government Comprehensive Plans Revised

Local Land Development Regulations

Development Permits, Orders, and Approvals

was formally adopted by the legislature in the summer of 1985 as part of the growth management package.

The state plan addresses twenty-five substantive areas from education to agriculture. For each of these areas it delineates a general goal and a set of implementation policies. For example, the public safety goal is to protect the public by preventing, discouraging, and punishing criminal behavior, lowering the highway death rate, and protecting lives and property from natural and man-made disasters.

In carrying out the state plan the regional planning councils must adopt comprehensive regional policy plans consistent with state goals and policies. For example, the Southwest Florida Regional Planning Council's (1987) *Regional Goals, Issues, and Policies* contains the same public safety goal as the state plan. It defines the regional disaster issues related to the public safety goal in terms of inadequate hurricane evacuation times and shelters:

> Rapid development in the coastal counties of Southwest Florida is predicted to continue. . . . Dense waterfront developments will likely remain a popular investment. The capacity and location of many existing roadways designated as evacuation routes will become even more inadequate for major evacuation traffic during future hurricanes. . . . Typically, these roadways are at capacity or are over capacity during non-emergency use. This slows evacuation times from coastal areas which can range from 12.5 to 18.5 hours for Category 1 storms up to 22.4 hours for Category 3 storms (Southwest Florida Regional Planning Council 1987, 7-9).
>
> The number of public storm shelters has not kept pace with the growing population and the need for added space. For example, in 1983, there would have been a shortage of 163,000 spaces if everyone needing public shelter had sought it (Southwest Florida Regional Planning Council 1987, 7-12).

The plan then sets regional goals to deal with these defined issues: "By 1995, evacuation times will be restored to 1985 levels, and by 2010, evacuation times will not exceed 18 hours in any part of the region. . . . By 2010, there will be adequate shelter space for citizens who do not wish to evacuate from the region."

Finally, the regional plan sets policies to carry out the goals. For example, two policies drawn from the longer, detailed set of regional disaster mitigation policies illustrate the nature of policy specification: "Residential development should be discouraged from locating in areas most vulnerable to hurricanes" (7-12), and "to reduce public shelter demand, shelter needs should be reduced through stronger building codes for residential areas" (7-14).

Florida's efforts at state-mandated local planning began under the Local Government Comprehensive Planning Act of 1975 (LGCPA) (Sections 163.3161–3211, Florida Statutes). Under this law comprehensive plans were to be prepared by all local governments. If a municipality refused to prepare a plan, the county in which it is located was to prepare it. If the county refused, the state would prepare the plan. Coastal localities were required to include appropriate coastal zone protection elements (Sec. 163.3177[6][g]). While these were to be submitted to the Department of Community Affairs and the Department of Environmental Regulation for review, no final approval was necessary. These local planning requirements did not receive overwhelming support from Florida communities. Many dragged their feet in preparing and implementing these plans.

The 1985 growth management package revises and strengthens earlier mandatory local planning requirements. It sets specific deadlines for local plan adoption or amendment and requires that local plans be consistent with the new state plan and the regional policy plans. The Department of Community Affairs is given responsibility for establishing review rules and criteria and reviewing local plans. Coastal localities must now prepare "coastal management elements" (replacing the previous "coastal zone protection elements"). They must include disaster mitigation and redevelopment components, the designation of high-hazard coastal areas, and beach protection and shoreline use components. Coastal management objectives must include the following disaster-related objectives:

> Limit public expenditures that subsidize development permitted in coastal high-hazard areas subsequent to the element's adoption except for restoration or enhancement of natural resources;
> Direct population concentrations away from known or predicted coastal high-hazard areas;
> Maintain or reduce hurricane evacuation times;

Prepare post-disaster redevelopment plans which will reduce or eliminate the exposure of human life and public and private property to natural hazards.

In addition to these extensive new planning requirements the state legislature also provided substantial funding for localities. If a local plan is found not to be in compliance with these requirements the growth management act provides the Administration Commission with the sanction of cutting off state funds to that jurisdiction (Department of Community Affairs 1986, Rule 9J-5.012[3][b]).

Coastal Construction Regulations

One feature of Florida's program has been the Coastal Construction Control Line (CCCL), first enacted in 1971 and implemented by the state's Department of Natural Resources. Often perceived as a setback line, the CCCL program actually only requires that additional, more stringent building standards be adhered to seaward of the line, which is based on anticipated erosion rates. These standards are very similar to those required in V-zones under the National Flood Insurance Program. Under the new growth management laws the intent of the CCCL is expanded through the creation of a new zone—the "coastal building zone." This new building zone extends the area over which more stringent storm-resistant building standards are required. The building zone is defined to include: (1) all coastal barrier islands (with the exception of 5,000 feet from the CCCL on large barrier islands) and (2) the area between the seasonal high-water line and 1,500 feet landward of a CCCL and for areas without a CCCL, all of the land 3,000 feet landward of the mean high-water line.

Under the new 1985 legislation the state not only requires more stringent building standards in coastal areas but also requires structures to be set back from the ocean. Specifically, the 1985 legislation creates a "Construction Prohibition Zone" in which permits for new construction will not be issued by the Department of Natural Resources. This zone includes the areas which will be seaward of the seasonal high-water line within thirty years (thirty-year erosion line). The zone, however, cannot be any further landward than existing CCCLs, many of which are expected to move further landward as new erosion data are generated. Under the new growth management provision, sellers of property which is partially or totally seaward of a CCCL must inform potential buyers of this fact. Vehicular traffic on the dunes of coastal beaches is also prohibited under the new law.

State Funding Limitations in Hazard Areas

Florida has led coastal states in restricting public investments that encourage private development in vulnerable coastal locations. Executive Order 81-105, issued in 1981, placed limits on the use of state monies to facilitate development on barrier islands where a twelve-hour evacuation time has been or will be exceeded. This order was also intended to restrict the use of state funds to finance reconstruction following a hurricane. The state has found this order somewhat difficult to interpret and enforce, and it does not carry the weight of law. More recently a Memorandum of Understanding between the governor's office and the State Department of Environmental Regulations was entered into to restrict funding for access and transportation systems under the Federal Coastal Barrier Resources Act (CBRA).

Florida's efforts to restrict the use of state funds in these sensitive coastal areas was strengthened substantially as a result of two infrastructure provisions in the 1985 growth management package. First, as of October 1, 1985, no state funds can be used to construct bridges or causeways to barrier islands where such improvements do not already exist. Second, after a locality has adopted an approved coastal management element as part of its comprehensive plan, the state may not issue funds which increase local infrastructure capacity unless such improvements are consistent with it. It is expected that the use of state funds for improvements which are located in, or increase the development of, "high hazard coastal areas," as designated in the local coastal management element, will not be permissible.

Pursuing a similar objective, the Florida Department of Community Affairs, Division of Emergency Management, has recently adopted a state postdisaster redevelopment rule. This rule establishes minimum mitigation requirements that political subdivision and nonpolitical subdivision applicants for federal postdisaster public assistance must satisfy. While the rule is intended to remain in effect for nonpolitical subdivision applicants, if a political subdivision prepares an acceptable plan satisfying the new Florida growth management requirements, their plan then preempts the postdisaster rule. The state will not include local projects on the state's project application to FEMA unless the jurisdiction has adopted hazard mitigation plans before a natural disaster which include certain preventive measures or contractually agrees with the state before a natural disaster to undertake preventive measures. The rule enumerates what these "preventive measures" are to consist of:

1. Building Codes. To comply with Section 161.56(1) Florida Statutes.
2. Flooding. To participate in the National Flood Insurance Program in conformance with the Federal Disaster Relief Act of 1974.
3. Public Infrastructure. To determine the feasibility of eliminating, relocating, or structurally modifying public infrastructure which has suffered natural disaster damage and implement such determinations as deemed cost effective or otherwise appropriate by the political subdivision.
4. Public Information. To establish a public information system, which includes:
   (a) An emergency warning system to notify the public of imminent emergencies;
   (b) A method of notifying the public of the potential dangers and appropriate preparatory measures for natural disasters;
   (c) A method of notifying the public of flood hazard areas; and
   (d) A method of notifying the public of evacuation routes.
5. Preventative Planning Measures. To implement preventative planning measures to include:
   (a) Provisions that sites be designed to utilize and preserve the protective capability of dunes and other natural topographical features and vegetation, where feasible, to ameliorate storm damage; and
   (b) In a coastal area, provisions for post-disaster dwelling unit restrictions designed to, at the maximum, maintain pre-disaster net population densities.
6. To determine on a case by case basis, whether heavy industrial operations, with processes or products potentially dangerous to public safety and the environment; schools; and mobile home parks; can be constructed or reconstructed in a coastal high hazard area and to take action as a result of such determination as deemed appropriate by the political subdivision. In making such a determination, a political sub-

division shall consider the degree of hazard posed by such construction or reconstruction, the potential advantages to the environment by prohibiting such construction or reconstruction, the degree of compliance with local zoning and land development regulations and all appropriate provisions of chapters 161, 163, 187, and 380, Florida Statutes, the availability of alternative sites for the location of such facilities, the impact on public infrastructure of permitting the construction or reconstruction, the costs to the community at large, the effect on residents of the area, and the costs to any affected owners of real property.
Specific Authority: Section 252.35(2), F.S.
Law Implemented: Section 252.35(2), F.S.

For non-political subdivision applicants, the rule states that the state will only consider including eligible damages of such applicants "which have contractually agreed with the department before a natural disaster, to determine the feasibility of eliminating, relocating, or structurally modifying public infrastructure which has suffered natural disaster damage and to implement such determinations where cost effective or otherwise appropriate" (9G-13.004[2]).

Florida Program Evaluation

Florida has gone further than any other Atlantic or Gulf coastal state in building hazard mitigation requirements into its statewide growth management program. Driven by phenomenal population growth concentrated in its low-lying coastal areas and by its extreme vulnerability to hurricanes, Florida has responded with state-of-the-art hazard mitigation policies and programs. Thanks to unrivaled state legislative interest in growth management initiatives, Florida is a model of centrally initiated planning and standards. Its structure of mandatory state, regional, and local plans, all required to be consistent with each other, coupled with its strong environmental protection and hazard mitigation requirements, comprise the most ambitious package of advanced hurricane hazard mitigation/growth management legislation in the country.

If there is a weakness in the Florida approach, it is likely to be found in uneven local implementation of state policies. Given the size of the state and the number of local jurisdictions without strong growth management hazard mitigation capabilities, there are bound to be instances where the state's rational, centralized bureaucratic system is unable to ensure effective implementation. As DeGrove (1984, 122) asserts: "Assessing the implementation effort is complicated by the strongly decentralized nature of the process. Most of the responsibility still lies with the state's some 400 cities, 67 counties, and numerous special districts. These local governments are very uneven in their capacity and political willingness to undertake growth-management initiatives."

Writing before passage of the 1985 growth management legislation, DeGrove (1984, 165) also notes a number of problems with implementation of other parts of the Florida growth management effort: "In the Critical Areas section as well as the DRI section, Florida's land management law has not provided an adequate description of state, regional and/or local responsibilities for assuring that public policies are applied over long periods of time as projects are built out. This is a problem that remains to be addressed more fully." He concludes that Florida's growth management effort is "alive and reasonably well" as of 1984 but suffers from major weaknesses in the monitoring and enforcement area. While the 1985 growth management legislation attempted to deal with these weaknesses, they will likely persist, given the size and complexity of the state.

State Mitigation Models

North Carolina provides a model of state hazard mitigation incorporated into a strong regional coastal management program. Much of the effort in North Carolina has gone toward building a regional consensus that coastal management and hazard mitigation are necessary and toward developing local planning and management capability. At the same time a parallel technical staff effort has developed effective guidelines to undergird the program.

Florida provides a model of state hazard mitigation incorporated into an ambitious statewide growth management program. Much of the effort in Florida has gone toward building a consensus in the state legislature that growth management is necessary. Only recently has a parallel effort been devoted to funding and building up the growth management capabilities of local governments.

Both the regional and the statewide models have their strengths and weaknesses. While neither is perfect, there are no better state hurricane hazard mitigation programs to be found. Other states interested in improving their programs can learn a great deal from the North Carolina and Florida experiences.

References

Baker, Simon. 1978. *Storms, People and Property in Coastal North Carolina.* Raleigh, N.C.: University of North Carolina, Sea Grant College.

Beatley, Timothy. 1985. *Coastal Storm Hazard Planning in North Carolina: A Review and Critique.* Chapel Hill, N.C.: University of North Carolina, Center for Urban and Regional Studies.

Bollens, Scott, Kathleen Leyden, and Timothy Beatley. 1984. *Review of State Programs to Mitigate Storm Hazards.* Chapel Hill, N.C.: University of North Carolina, Center for Urban and Regional Studies.

Brower, David J., and Daniel S. Carol. 1984. *Coastal Zone Management as Land Planning.* Washington, D.C.: National Planning Association.

Brower, David J., Timothy Beatley, and David J. L. Blatt. 1987. *Reducing Hurricane and Coastal Storm Hazards through Growth Management: A Guidebook for North Carolina Coastal Localities.* Chapel Hill, N.C.: University of North Carolina, Center for Urban and Regional Studies.

Carraway, Claire B. 1984. "Florida's DRI Statute: Alternatives to the Standard DRI Review." *Stetson Law Review* 13 (Spring): 619–47.

Coastal States Organization. 1986. "Coastal Hazard Reduction Survey." Raleigh, N.C.: North Carolina Division of Coastal Management.

Daltry, Wayne. 1980. "Practical Approaches to Coastal Storm Protection and Mitigation: The Regional (Substate Agency) Role." *Coastal Zone '80.* New York, N.Y.: American Society of Civil Engineers.

DeGrove, John M. 1984. *Land, Growth & Politics.* Chicago, Ill.: Planners Press.

Department of Community Affairs, Florida. 1986. Chapter 9J-5, Rules. "Minimum Criteria for Review of Local Government Comprehensive Plans and Determination of Compliance." Tallahassee, Fla.: State of Florida, Department of Community Affairs.

Elazar, Daniel J. 1966. *American Federalism: A View from the States.* New York, N.Y.: Thomas Y. Crowell.

ELMS Committee. 1984. *Final Report of the Environmental Land Management Study Committee.* Tallahassee, Fla.

Federal Emergency Management Agency. 1986. *Making Mitigation Work: A Handbook for State Officials.* Washington, D.C.: U.S. Government Printing Office.

Finger, Bill, and Barry Jacobs. 1982. "Coastal Management: A Planning Beachhead in North Carolina." *N.C. Insight* 5, no. 1 (May).

French, Steven. 1979. "The Urbanization of Hazardous Areas: Flood Plains and Barrier Islands in North Carolina." In *Perspectives on Urban Affairs in North Carolina*, edited by Warren Wicker. Chapel Hill, N.C.: Urban Studies Council.

Godschalk, David R. 1987. "Balancing Growth with Critical Area Programs: The Florida and Chesapeake Bay Cases." *Urban Land* 46, no. 3 (March): 16–19.

Godschalk, David R., David J. Brower, et al. 1979. *Constitutional Issues of Growth Management.* Chicago, Ill.: Planners Press.

Green, Philip P. 1980. "North Carolina's Comprehensive Building Regulation System." *Popular Government* (Spring).

Heath, Milton S., and Allen C. Moseley. 1980. "The Coastal Area Management Act." *Popular Government* (Spring).

Hunsberger, Mark D. 1979. "Growth Management Through DRI Review: Learning from the Florida Experience." *Carolina Planning* 5, no. 1 (Spring): 34–41.

Kaufman, Wallace. 1984. "A Hurricane Warning from Nature." *The Independent*, September 28.

Kusler, Jon A. 1980. *Regulating Sensitive Lands.* Washington, D.C.: Environmental Law Institute.

Matuszeski, William. 1985. "Managing the Federal Coastal Program: The Planning Years." *Journal of the American Planning Association* 51, no. 3 (Summer): 266–274.

May, James W. 1985. "Growth Management: A 1984 Update." *Florida Environmental and Urban Issues* 12, no. 2 (January).

McElyea, William D., David J. Brower, and David R. Godschalk. 1982. *Before the Storm: Managing Development to Reduce Hurricane Damages.* Chapel Hill, N.C.: University of North Carolina, Center for Urban and Regional Studies.

Neumann, Charles J., et al. 1981. *Tropical Cyclones of the North Atlantic Ocean, 1871–1980.* Washington, D.C.: NOAA.

O'Connell, David W. 1985. "Florida's Struggle for Approval under the Coastal Zone Management Act." *Natural Resources Journal* 25, no. 1 (January): 61–72.

Owens, David W. 1983. "Land Acquisition and Coastal Resources Management: A Pragmatic Perspective." *William and Mary Law Review* 24, no. 4: 625–667.

———. 1985. "Coastal Management in North Carolina: Building a Regional Consensus." *Journal of the American Planning Association* 51, no. 3 (Summer): 322–329.

Southwest Florida Regional Planning Council. 1987. *Regional Goals, Issues, and Policies.* Part Two of the Regional Comprehensive Policy Plan for Southwest Florida. Fort Myers, Fla.

Town of Atlantic Beach, N.C. 1984. *Storm Hazard Mitigation Plan and Post Disaster Reconstruction Plan*. Prepared by George Eichler and Associates and Satilla Planning.

Town of Emerald Isle, N.C. 1984. *Storm Hazard Mitigation Plan and Post Disaster Reconstruction Plan*. Prepared by George Eichler and Associates and Satilla Planning.

Town of Long Beach, N.C. 1984. *Hurricane Plan*.

U.S. Army Corps of Engineers, 1987. *Eastern North Carolina Hurricane Evacuation Study: Technical Data Report*. Wilmington District.

Wilkerson, Robert S. 1984. "Memorandum: Stipulations for Port Bougainville-Garden Cove." Florida Department of Community Affairs, January 24.

6 Local Mitigation Tools and Techniques

Local Mitigation Roles

Local governments may adopt different roles in coastal storm hazard mitigation, ranging from devising innovative local programs to compliance with federal and state requirements to remaining largely indifferent to mitigation issues. These roles result from a number of factors, including disaster experience, economic growth status, and attitudes toward appropriate governance limits. Like states, many localities in the Atlantic and Gulf hurricane-prone areas have historically favored a limited role for governmental intervention in private affairs. Localities with active local mitigation programs have been relatively rare, though that has begun to change.

Because all mitigation measures are carried out at the local level, where the hurricane strikes and where people and property are exposed and vulnerable in varying degrees depending upon the local mitigation measures taken, positive local government roles are crucial to mitigation effectiveness. In the vernacular this is "where the rubber meets the road." Unless the local government has anticipated the potential destruction of a hurricane strike, its residents must suffer the consequences.

The term "local government" covers a variety of governmental forms. The two most prominent are the incorporated city or town and the unincorporated county. In most of the Atlantic and Gulf coast states, with the exception of the New England states, the territory of cities and towns includes primarily the built-up urban areas of coastal counties, which have been incorporated in order to take advantage of the taxation and governance authority granted by states to municipalities. In New England the entire coastline is subject to municipal governance by incorporated cities or towns (sometimes called townships); there is no unincorporated land. All these forms of local government, under state enabling laws, charters, and home rule provisions, are empowered to plan and regulate development and to carry out disaster planning within their jurisdictions.

This chapter reviews the mitigation tools and techniques available to coastal local governments. It emphasizes the necessity to move emergency management concerns from an isolated public safety position within local government to active coordination with community planning and development management. It identifies potential prestorm and poststorm development management mitigation strategies. It argues that "packaging" hazard mitigation with development management, as discussed in chapter 2, is the most effective approach because it enhances coordination of the relevant tools and techniques that affect the location, rate, type, amount, public cost, and quality of development in hazard areas. Tools and techniques reviewed include those nonstructural approaches listed under growth management in table 2.1: (1) planning, (2) development regulation, (3) land acquisition, (4) taxation and fiscal incentives, (5) capital facilities policies, and (6) programs for information dissemination.

Potential Development Management Mitigation Strategies

Mitigation strategies include preserving and restoring mitigative features of the natural environment, facilitating evacuation of exposed populations, strengthening buildings and facilities to withstand storm forces, and locating new development and relocating threatened existing development out of hazard areas. While development management usually is thought of primarily in terms of influencing new development, a comprehensive development management program can include elements of all these mitigation strategies.

Development management measures can protect and restore existing mitigative features of the natural environment. Barrier island dunes, for instance, act as natural protective systems against hurricane and storm flooding. Dune protection regulations can ensure that these natural systems are not destroyed by development. With dunes in place buildings located behind them are sheltered from the full forces of storm surge and floodwaters. Estuaries and wetlands serve as natural sponges during storms, absorbing and holding storm waters. Wetland protection ordinances can ensure that these valuable holding areas are not filled in to create more upland for development. The destruction of such resources means that floodwaters will be displaced onto other areas, increasing the extent of property and people at risk.

Development management can facilitate evacuation effectiveness. Coordinating the capital facilities programming of new evacuation routes and bridges with land use plans can ensure that evacuation capacity keeps pace with growth in demand. Incorporating shelter provision into new development projects can ensure that new residents can be safely accommodated during hurricane strikes.

Through building codes and other development regulations, exposed structures and public facilities can be strengthened to withstand hurricane winds and waves. Delineation of hazard areas provides a basis for enforcing more rigorous building regulations, as well as for informing builders and residents of the need for additional structural strength.

Locating new development and relocating existing development outside of hazard areas is a primary nonstructural means of protecting both people and property. Nearly all the implementation tools used in development management affect new development location, although relocation of existing development is a more unique and difficult challenge.

Often mitigation strategies are posed in terms of black and white alternatives. For example, "retreat from the shore," including letting existing building fall into the sea as the coastline recedes, is sometimes advocated instead of structural protection measures such as groins and seawalls (Pilkey 1987). This leads to debates about the practicality of retreat when the shore is already built-up and expensive buildings are threatened (Sturza 1987). In fact, local governments may need to adopt strategy "mixes" that may include retreat in some areas, beach renourishment in others, maintenance of natural dunes and wetlands in others, and planned relocation of buildings and roads along with acquisition of property for public open space in others. For example, the mitigation plan for the South Shore of Long Island emphasizes nonstructural measures but also recommends some structural solutions in an effort to recognize variations in development intensity, shoreline conditions, and institutional programs and philosophies (Long Island Regional Planning Board 1984). Such strategies may have both prestorm and poststorm components, with contingent plans that are carried out only after certain types of storm damage.

In the following discussion, each of the major types of implementation tools is discussed. Examples of their use under various mitigation strategies are provided. The unique economic, political, and geographic circumstances of individual localities will determine their feasible blends of protection, retreat, relocation, renourishment, and/or rebuilding.

Planning

Various types of local plans affect mitigation. Most communities have prepared the first type, *land use or comprehensive plans.* Some communities also have prepared the second type, *poststorm reconstruction plans,* either separately or as elements of their emergency management or comprehensive plans. A few local areas may have prepared separate *coastal storm hazard mitigation plans.*

Land use or comprehensive plans can provide a rational basis for land use decisions. A community's land use plan serves as the guiding framework and formulation for orienting growth and development by identifying community goals and objectives, development scenarios, and various strategies and means for their achievement. Typically such plans provide a communitywide picture of desirable patterns of development and growth and appropriate activities and uses to be permitted in particular sectors. A local land use plan may establish, for instance, that high-hazard areas in the community should be reserved for recreational uses or for low-density development. The plan may designate these hazard areas and then provide a set of policies and standards for controlling development in them. Local plans may result in the reduction of storm hazards in their overall effect or they may contain specific hurricane and storm hazard mitigation components. The Development Plan for Sanibel Island, Florida, for example, contains as a central feature the reduction of hurricane and storm hazards (City of Sanibel 1980). The future plans of all coastal localities in Florida and North Carolina must include storm mitigation components (see chapter 5).

Reconstruction plans can serve either as general guidelines for making decisions about redevelopment following a storm or as detailed instructions about which uses and site-specific areas and parcels will be permitted to be rebuilt and in what ways. It has often been suggested that developing such plans in advance of the disaster will provide political and legal support for halting what is typically a very rapid rebuilding of structures in precisely the same hazardous locations (Haas, Kates, and Bowden 1977; Rosenthal 1975). Recovery and reconstruction plans provide deliberate statements of policy and intention concerning what will be acceptable and unacceptable forms of rebuilding. Ideally, such reconstruction plans call for preventing rebuilding, reducing the density of redevelopment, or otherwise protecting development in the most hazardous locations.

Recovery and reconstruction plans also typically establish special procedures for postdisaster decisionmaking. Included in these procedures may be the establishment of a special recovery or reconstruction task force which recommends actions for guiding and managing rebuilding (McElyea, Brower, and Godschalk 1982; Haas, Kates, and Bowden 1977). Depending upon the extent to which detailed reconstruction plans exist, such a body would have the responsibility of identifying or implementing planned actions to reduce the threat of future hurricanes and severe coastal storms (such as the enactment of a redevelopment moratorium while a reconstruction plan was prepared). Special recovery procedures may also include the formation of damage assessment teams which would provide the reconstruction task force, and other decisionmakers, with crucial information concerning the extent and nature of hurricane forces and damages caused by them (Brower, Collins, and Beatley 1984).

Separate coastal storm hazard mitigation plans typically include a vulnerability analysis covering property and people at risk from coastal storms, along with strategies and recommendations for prestorm and poststorm mitigation. For example, the plan for Atlantic County Barrier Islands and Ocean City, New Jersey, discusses people and property at risk and the implementation of storm hazard mitigation strategies in its first section and then provides a section with site specific recommendations for each coastal area (New Jersey Department of Environmental Protection 1985).

Benefits and Limitations of Planning

The cost of preparing plans and instituting new planning processes varies depending upon their scope and composition. Generally the types of plans discussed here can be developed with modest public investment, particularly if assisted by outside planning agencies (for example, a regional planning council, state planning agency). Moreover, these plans—both before and after the storm—can serve as a foundation for rational decisionmaking concerning development and redevelopment in the community. Unless a community has been through the process of analyzing its vulnerability and debating mitigation alternatives, it will be at a loss to cope with these issues in the stressful aftermath of a disaster.

Clearly, however, plans by themselves are not highly effective. It is only when they are put into effect through ordinances, the allocation of public funds, and specific community decisions that they will have an impact on reducing local storm hazards. Plans are necessary, but not sufficient, for an effective storm hazard mitigation program. For this reason, we emphasize the use of plans as one element of an overall development management/ hazard mitigation program.

To continue their effectiveness, plans must be continually updated, monitored, and evaluated. As development patterns or coastal conditions change, plans must be revised in light of these new circumstances. Projections and assumptions must be monitored and adjusted as necessary. Finally policies must be assessed in terms of their relevance and implementation techniques evaluated in light of their actual, as opposed to expected, results.

Development Regulation

The most widely used development management tools are those which regulate the location, amount, density, and type of development in coastal localities. Basic types include zoning and subdivision ordinances and variations of these standard regulations. Conventional zoning ordinances may be used to control the type (for example, residential, commercial, recreational), intensity (for example, bulk, height, floor area ratio, setback provisions), and density of development which occurs in high-hazard areas.

Examples of reduction in densities along high-hazard shorelines are plentiful. Several localities along the highly vulnerable South Shore of Long Island, New York, have reduced permissible densities (Long Island Regional Planning Board 1984). Hollywood, Florida, in an effort to protect a relatively undeveloped segment of its shoreline, and to keep the area's population within existing evacuation capacity, severely down-zoned this area from high-density hotel and multifamily uses to single-family detached residences. In its recent hurricane hazard mitigation and postdisaster reconstruction plan, the town of Emerald Isle, North Carolina, cites its efforts to reduce storm hazards by keeping densities down (see Town of Emerald Isle 1984). The town of Sullivan's Island, South Carolina, permits single-family detached units on half-acre lots, keeping the extent of property at-risk on that island low. The hurricane hazard mitigation and reconstruction plan for Onslow County, North Carolina, recommends that future densities be lowered considerably in West Onslow Beach (Topsail Island) to facilitate evacuation, including more extensive reductions where the hurricane hazard is greatest. The mitigation and reconstruction plan for the town of Nags Head proposes rezoning portions of its beachfront in order to prevent the future location of high-density uses (Brower, Collins, and Beatley 1984).

A relatively common and effective approach is the requirement that new construction be set back a certain distance from the ocean's edge. These requirements can be found both at the state and local levels. In North Carolina, for instance, new multifamily structures locating in Ocean Erodible Zones (oceanfront areas) must be setback a distance of sixty times the average annual rate of erosion for that particular stretch of coast. Numerous individual coastal localities have adopted setback requirements (see Kusler 1982). Glynn County, Georgia, for instance, has enacted restrictions which vary depending upon the nature of the coastline (that is, whether or not an active dune sequence exists). Sullivan's Island, South Carolina, has what amounts to a setback provision through the delineation of a recreation and conservation district in which development is prohibited. The reduction of damages from hurricanes and storm flooding is specifically cited in each of these ordinances as a major reason for the setbacks.

Subdivision ordinances govern the conversion of raw land into developed uses and the type and extent of improvements made in this conversion. Subdivision regulations can control the density, configuration, and layout of development. They operate in ways similar to zoning to control the amount and density of development on a particular site. The requirement of a minimum lot size can reduce the amount of new development exposed to storm hazards. Site plan review and other requirements of subdivision approval can provide the opportunity to orient the location of development sites in ways which minimize storm risks. For instance, subdivision provisions may require that new single-family dwellings on lots in hazard areas be sited in ways which maximize distance from high-hazard oceanfront areas.

Subdivision approval can be made contingent upon mitigative actions, such as the protection of dunes, wetlands, and natural vegetation. For instance, subdivision and site plan provisions may require that structures locate a sufficient distance from protective dunes. Builders may also be required to "cluster" structures on the safest portions of a parcel, to minimize exposure to storm hazards (see Whyte 1968 for a general description of the clustering concept and Urban and Regional Research 1982 for an application to hazard reduction). In Gulf Shores, Alabama, developers are encouraged to cluster the development of new structures on the landward side of the highway paralleling the shore, placing recreational and parking facilities on the waterside. A potentially effective strategy is to require or encourage clustering of structures on safer sites or portions of parcels during reconstruction. This is a primary strategy proposed for Long Island communities by the Long Island Regional Planning Board (see LIRPB 1984).

A promising alternative is to protect the option of moving a structure back from the ocean when the shoreline erodes by requiring lots which are sufficiently deep for this purpose. Such extra-deep lots could be considered analogous to the extra-large lots sometimes required to permit the replacement of a saturated septic tank field, the so-called repair area concept. If necessary, a threatened house could be moved back onto the landward portion of the lot in a safer location. Concomitant with this approach would be the prohibition of immovable structures in such areas. New York has established just such a system for highly eroding areas of Long Island (see chapter 5).

As already noted, many of these techniques may be appropriate to impose following a hurricane or severe storm. A moratorium on reconstruction can give a locality more time to determine how it wishes to redevelop, and to decide on actions it can take which will minimize the impacts of the next storm.

Benefits and Limitations of Development Regulation

The cost of regulation has been the source of much debate among planners and policymakers. The administrative costs involved in imposing hazard regulations would for most localities be relatively small, as all but the smallest of localities are likely to have already adopted and implemented zoning and subdivision ordinances. Reducing coastal storm hazards through such an existing regulatory framework may be relatively costless (administratively). Of course, should a locality wish to develop a regulatory framework from ground zero, public expenses will necessarily be greater, depending upon the complexity of the proposed system.

A more serious concern is usually expressed about the economic side effects from such regulations. A number of interests may be affected. At the most discrete level, landowners and developers whose property has been down-zoned as a result of regulations will often experience severe economic effects. Should regulations reduce the absolute amount of development permitted in a locality, it is possible that the general public may experience the economic effects that sometimes result from a lower tax base. This is highly debatable, however, as reduced development also leads to fewer service demands and fewer negative impacts on the natural and man-made environment. It is also possible that reduced levels of permissible development, particularly those which are commercially oriented, may lead to lower levels of economic activity and may harm local residents who are unemployed or underemployed.

Many of the regulatory options for reducing hurricane and coastal storm hazards do not involve reducing the absolute amount of permissible development but rather its location relative to hazard zones. The coastal setback, for instance, typically permits the same intensity of development but simply in a slightly different location, for example, farther away from the ocean. It is debatable whether such restrictions serve to dampen overall levels of development. This will depend on the substitutability of nonhazardous or less-hazardous land and the availability of similar development sites in other jurisdictions which do not have hazard zone regulations. Analyses of the economic effects of the Florida setback requirements have argued that such an alteration of building location does not have a severe negative economic effect (Florida Department of Natural Resources 1982; Shows et al. 1976).

Recent experiences with this type of siting has indicated that there is little or no impact. The Dorchester Condominium, erected in Pelican Bay in Collier County, is sited some 1,300 feet from the water line. Elevated walkovers are being constructed to the beach to provide access and view is unimpeded from the living floors. The price and absorption of this condominium would indicate that the market treated it as a gulf front structure. For smaller units the view would be impeded and thus there might be some negative impact on price. However, the rule imposes no height restriction and therefore the unit could be elevated to obtain the desired view. Such elevations, however, would have a cost (Florida Department of Natural Resources 1982, 14).

The effectiveness of development regulations depends both upon the stringency of the measures enacted and the resources and political will invested in enforcing and implementing these regulations. Land use regulations can be circumvented through such things as zoning amendments, special exceptions, and so on. Consequently an effective form of development regulation must entail provisions which substantially restrict hazard area development (for example, a setback of more than a few feet) and these provisions must be diligently enforced and implemented.

Relocation and Land Acquisition

A highly effective approach to reducing coastal storm damage is to prevent the development of hazardous lands through their public acquisition. Several types of land acquisition are possible. Fee-simple acquisition involves obtaining the full "bundle of rights" associated with a parcel of land. Undeveloped lands could then be maintained for open space or other public recreational uses which would not involve exposing people or houses to storm threats (Field Associates 1981; Kusler 1979).

An alternative to fee-simple acquisition is the purchase of less-than-fee-simple interests in land, in which the public buys only the development rights. Under this arrangement a jurisdiction would pay the landowner the fair market value of this right in exchange for agreeing to leave the land in an undeveloped state for some specified period of time or in perpetuity. This is usually accomplished through a restrictive covenant which runs with the deed.

Also included in this category of development management measures are relocation programs. Relocation can take at least two forms: (1) relocation of a threatened structure to another site and (2) relocation of the contents of a structure while demolishing or putting to a new use the remaining structure(s) (see Johnson 1978). Relocation of the structure to a hazard-free or less hazardous site, while physically possible, often may be economically infeasible. This will depend on the type of structure involved and the distance over which it must be moved. Relocation of families and their belongings to new housing outside the hazard or high-hazard area may generally be a more feasible approach. This is particularly true following extensive storm damage, where demolition of damaged properties (rather than extensive reconstruction) involves fewer opportunity costs. The recent efforts in Baytown, Texas, to purchase properties in the Brownwood subdivision—an area devastated by Hurricane Alicia—are illustrative of the technique (see chapter 3). Through the use of federal monies, an entire subdivision of destroyed or heavily damaged single-family homes which had been subjected to repeated flooding was prevented from rebuilding in its extremely hazardous location (see FEMA 1983a and 1983b).

Benefits and Limitations of Relocation and Acquisition

There is perhaps no more certain way to ensure that future development does not occur in hazardous locations than for the public to purchase such areas. The use of acquisition poses a number of practical problems, however. The most significant perhaps for most coastal localities have to do with cost and how such acquisitions are to be financed. Fee-simple acquisition of undeveloped land in coastal areas experiencing moderate to high levels of market demand will tend to be very expensive —prohibitively expensive for many communities. The purchase of already-improved land will be even more expensive, although damaged properties purchased in the aftermath of a storm may reduce these expenses substantially.

Where "preemption" or "right of first refusal" is legally possible, this technique can make public acquisition more feasible. Such a mechanism would essentially permit the locality to insert itself in the place of a property buyer in any local land transaction involving hazard areas. This would, then, allow a local government to oversee all land transactions in those areas and to expend its limited funds in acquiring only those lands which are truly threatened by development (that is, are in fact in the process of being sold for development uses). Another approach to cost reduction is reselling fee-simple acquisitions with certain deed restrictions limiting future development in hazardous areas. Proceeds from these sales could then be used on a revolving fund basis to fund additional acquisitions.

A locality may also be able to more efficiently use its available acquisition funds by coordinating its acquisition decisions with those of private environmental conservation organizations, such as the Nature Conservancy and the Trust for Public Land. These organizations are often able to move more quickly in land and open space acquisition than are local governments. Although their acquisition decisions are typically based on nonhazard objectives, a community may be able to influence these private purchase decisions, for instance by sharing the costs of their acquisition or in some way facilitating them.

The acquisition of development rights may also be more feasible. However, while a leading reason for preferring development rights acquisition over fee-simple acquisition is that public expense will be less, this will still be very expensive. In areas where market demand is high, the purchasing of a development right will constitute the major portion of the parcel's fair market value (Coughlin and Plaut 1978). Because of this fact, this approach may be no more financially feasible than fee-simple acquisition.

Taxation and Fiscal Incentives

Development management may also include attempts to indirectly influence patterns of development and growth through the use of taxation and other fiscal incentives. The use of differential assessment of certain types of land for tax purposes is based on the theory that by reducing the property tax burden on undeveloped parcels of land holding costs will be decreased, in turn prolonging the time to which they are devoted to undeveloped uses. Almost every state now has a provision for some form of differential assessment (Coughlin and Keene 1981; Keene et al. 1976). The uses typically eligible for such reductions are farm and forestland, open space, and recreational uses. These are uses which do occur in coastal high-hazard areas and whose maintenance in an undeveloped state could reduce the amount of property and people exposed to the storm threat.

Another set of fiscal approaches includes the use of special assessments and impact fees. Building in and inhabiting high-hazard areas often involves substantially greater public costs than in similar less-hazardous sites. These costs are seen when a hurricane or coastal storm strikes, or even threatens, a locality. There are, for instance, public costs of evacuation, search and rescue, temporary housing, the reconstruction of public facilities such as roads, utilities, water and sewer lines, and so on. Public policy can acknowledge that such additional public expenses will exist as a result of permitting this development to occur and assess the additional costs to those who will ultimately benefit from these expenditures. This can be accomplished through several means.

One approach is to attempt to tie more closely benefits received and costs incurred through the use of special benefit assessments. This would be similar to the special assessment charged to property owners benefiting from the public installation of roads, drainage, and sewer and water services. Such assessments are applied within a district in which property owners are determined to receive a distinct and substantial benefit in excess of the general benefits received by the public at large (Hagman and Misczynski 1978). Applying this concept to storm hazard management, a locality would thus be required to delineate an area in which "special storm services" are provided and in which residents would be subject to the special assessment.

A variation on this theme is the impact fee. Here the levy may be designed to recoup and mitigate the overall "impacts" of a project or development on the community at large—impacts that may extend beyond the immediate environs and requirements of a project or development (Hagman and Misczynski 1978; Snyder and Stegman 1987). For instance, while a special assessment may be levied to cover the immediate costs associated with the floodproofing of sewer and water service, an impact fee might be used to pay for mitigation of the broader impacts on the locality created by the development. For example, the jurisdiction might levy an impact fee according to the extent to which a new project reduces the overall ability of the locality to evacuate in the event of a hurricane. While it may not be designed to cover the costs of an onsite improvement for the particular development's benefit, the impact fee is designed to compensate the community for the costs of adding evacuation capacity.

One potentially effective incentive to reducing the amount of property-at-risk is to permit the transfer of development rights (TDR) from a high-hazard "sending" zone to a low-hazard "receiving" zone in another part of the jurisdiction (Carmichael 1974; Costonis 1973; Rose 1975). Such a system could either be voluntary or mandatory. Under the latter a locality would simply zone the storm hazard area so that fewer units of development are allowed (or prohibit new development entirely), and the owner of land within this zone would then be permitted to transfer all or some of this unused development density to parcels in designated low-hazard areas or to sell these on the open market to others who own land in areas designated for development. The locality would then permit increased levels of development in the low-hazard zone as a result of possessing extra development rights; thus a natural market for the transfer of these rights is created. A voluntary approach would simply present this transfer as an additional option for the landowner—a way of maintaining the land in its undeveloped use if the landowner wishes. The landowner in this case would still have the option of developing his land or selling it for development purposes.

Benefits and Limitations of Taxation and Fiscal Incentives

Differential assessment is widely used, but its effectiveness at retaining land in undeveloped uses is generally found to be low where the market price of land is high (Keene et al. 1976; Coughlin et al. 1977; Coughlin and Keene 1981). Consequently, differential assessment is likely to be most successful in circumstances (perhaps specific locations in the jurisdiction) where development pressures are slight-to-moderate and where landowners are actively interested in maintaining the present undeveloped use of the land. This suggests that differential assessment will not be an appropriate tool for managing development in oceanfront and barrier island areas where market demand is extremely great. Differential assessment will tend to be a more appropriate tool for discouraging development in bay and riverine areas subject to hurricane and storm forces.

Differential assessment will also be a more effective tool at reducing development of hazardous sites when used in collaboration with other approaches, such as the regulation of new development, the fee-simple purchase of land, and the transfer of development rights. For instance, reducing the permissible development density in a hazard location together with preferential assessment may reduce opportunity costs to the landowner enough to reduce actual conversion of hazard lands to developed uses.

It is important to understand, also, that differential assessment is not costless. As a result of reduced or preferential assessment for hazard parcels, local tax rates must be increased (assuming the same level of local services is maintained). This effect is commonly referred to as the "tax shift" and will be greatest in situations where the value of undeveloped preferentially treated land is highest.

The effectiveness of impact fees and special hazard area assessments will depend on their intended public objectives. They are most useful in recouping the areawide costs associated with development projects. They will not prevent growth in high-hazard areas, though they can indirectly discourage development there. Their effects on discouraging new development will depend on the availability of substitute parcels of land not subject to such fees or assessments and the elasticity of demand for hazard area development. The greater the ease of land substitutability (that is, ability to find similar hazardous parcels in a neighboring jurisdiction or similar nonhazardous parcels in the same jurisdiction), the greater will be the effect of discouraging development in those areas where the fees or assessments apply. The greater the elasticity of demand for oceanfront or hazard zone development (that is, the greater the sensitivity of demand to changes in price), the greater will be the relocation or displacement effect. One economic side effect of this may be a reduction in the local tax base, if development chooses to locate in other jurisdictions that do not have such fees or assessments. Ideally, this would not result if these additional charges applied only to hazard area development while displaced development could be accommodated in other less hazardous sites within the same jurisdiction.

It is difficult to predict in advance who will actually bear the costs of impact fees or assessments. Depending upon actual market conditions, it is likely that these costs will be shared by new homeowners, owners of developable land, and developers.

A transfer of development rights (TDR) program avoids many of these problems and uncertainties but presents many of its own. For instance, a large-scale TDR program requires extensive information and knowledge about local market conditions and land development trends. How large, for example, should the receiving zone be (by how much should the locality raise permissible densities?) to ensure an adequate demand for development rights? How readily will landowners in sending zones sell their development rights and when? As experience in the Pinelands (Carol 1987) and in Montgomery County, Maryland (Banach and Canavan 1987), has shown, these are critical questions. Development of a TDR program usually requires the services of a development rights specialist or an economist to devise a system that will operate effectively in the market.

The transfer of development rights can also be viewed as a form of compensation when restrictions are placed on development in storm hazard areas. For instance, although an oceanfront landowner may be prevented from developing his land (that is, it is now zoned for open space or recreational uses), he may be able to realize a portion of this development potential by selling his allocated development rights to developers of areas of the jurisdiction less susceptible to storm hazards. Viewing TDR primarily as a form of compensation raises several questions; key among them is the extent of compensation deemed to be desirable or equitable. At what point will the market value of a development right be unacceptably low as a form of compensation? If full or substantial compensation is a goal, this may require a more active role for government in the development rights market, say, by entering the market to buy rights at times when demand is low.

Capital Facilities Policy

Coastal development—its type, location, density, and timing—is highly influenced by capital facilities such as roads and sewer and water service. Such public investments have been aptly called the "growth shapers." Two primary dimensions to capital facilities policy have implications for local storm hazard mitigation: one is geographical (where capital facilities are placed) and the other temporal (when they are placed) (Roberts 1986; Nugent 1975). With respect to the first dimension, a locality can develop an explicit set of capital facilities extension policies designed to avoid high-hazard areas, thus reducing the amount of development and property which is placed at risk and reducing the potential threats to personal safety.

Redirecting capital facilities, and thus the development which accompanies them, into "safer" areas of the locality can be facilitated through several means. One is the clear delineation in the land use plan of urban service areas or districts in which the jurisdiction agrees to provide certain facilities and services (for example, see the 1985 Lee County, Florida Plan, which is based on an urban service district concept). This district would also likely entail a temporal dimension, for example, including sufficient land to accommodate further growth under certain assumptions about evacuation capacity and public facilities. Such a practice has several advantages. It provides a long-term perspective on growth and development and permits developers, residents and the locality generally to visualize where and when such facilities will become available in the future (and in turn where they cannot be expected). This, in effect, modifies long-term expectations about where future development will and will not be acceptable to the community. Development pressures may tend to shift naturally as a result of this public designation, as developers, landowners and others realize that certain facilities will not become available outside of these designated areas. The provision and availability of facilities may determine the amount of overall development that can take place in a locality, and suspicions of "no growth" objectives are often held. Designation of a service area in "safer" parts of the locality and a good faith effort to satisfy growth demands will tend to enhance the political and legal acceptability of such an approach.

In addition to delineating urban service areas in the plan, the locality needs a policy instrument by which to implement the plan through systematically identifying, financing, and sequencing specific capital improvements. This is accomplished by adopting a capital improvements program (CIP). Ideally, the CIP follows closely designated service boundaries, as well as the comprehensive plan, zoning, and other regulatory and planning provisions. The CIP provides a five- to six-year framework for making short-term decisions about which improvements to make and where. Avoidance of storm hazard areas can be incorporated into this instrument as a specific CIP policy.

A close connection between the designation of service areas, the capital improvement program and the overall planning process in a jurisdiction (including the local comprehensive plan) is essential. This is recognized under current planning and growth management requirements in Florida, for example, where the connection is legislatively mandated (Roberts 1986). From a practical standpoint the concept of guiding growth through capital facilities should be closely linked to the objective of reducing the public costs of such facilities and the extent of public investment at risk in high-hazard areas. The latter is, by itself, a legitimate argument for denying facility extension. This is a facility-related reason which is likely to enhance the legal standing of hazard-sensitive capital facilities extension policy.

Opportunities may also exist after a storm has occurred to implement these capital facilities objectives. If facilities such as roads and sewers are sufficiently damaged, they may be rebuilt in areas which are less susceptible to damage from the next storm. Even if such facilities are not relocated, they may be repaired and reconstructed in ways which make them stronger or less susceptible to storm forces. Roads can be elevated, for instance, and sewer and water lines can be floodproofed.

Poststorm reconstruction may be used not only to reduce the possibility of future facility damage but also to reduce other storm-related hazards. If facility repairs are not permitted to occur after a storm, this may preclude or discourage private development. This technique was used subtly in the Baytown, Texas, case. The option of selling-out and leaving the Brownwood Subdivision was made much more attractive to home-owners because they were uncertain that sewers and roads would be restored and maintained. As a further example, placing power and telephone lines underground after the storm will ensure safer evacuation when the next storm threatens.

A similar approach might be taken to the rebuilding or reconstruction of damaged public buildings such as town halls and fire stations. If sufficiently damaged, it may be logical to move these structures to safer sites in the locality. After Hurricane Camille, for instance, the Pass Christian Town Hall was rebuilt on higher ground and, consequently, was much better protected from future storm damages than if rebuilt in the same location. When structures are not relocated, it may be possible to repair or rebuild them in ways that reduce their susceptibility to future storm damages (for example, through elevation). It may be desirable, as well, to rebuild these structures in ways which permit their usage as storm shelters.

Benefits and Limitations of Capital Facilities Policy

Reducing direct public investment—such as construction of public buildings and roads in hazard areas—is highly effective at reducing future public storm damages. Such a policy makes sense in terms of net social efficiency. Moreover, these are investments which the public has a firm handle on and can control directly.

However, the effectiveness of public investment decisions at discouraging hazardous private development depends upon local conditions and market demand. Limiting public investment will only be an effective deterrent if development in high-hazard areas is dependent upon these public facilities. For instance, if coastal development is able to obtain water through individual site wells and dispose of wastewater through septic tanks, limiting provision of public sewer and water facilities by the locality will do little to impede growth in hazardous zones. It may be necessary for the locality to foreclose other service/facility options available to development by restricting the issuance of septic tank permits, for example. Without valid health reasons, however, foreclosing such alternative options for development may be legally difficult. It is advisable that the jurisdiction closely coordinate its environmental protection, health, and other community objectives with those of reducing storm hazards. Restricting the depletion of coastal groundwater supplies, for instance, may also serve to advance the effectiveness of capital facilities policy at reducing the number of people and property at risk in high-hazard areas. However, if restricting the provision of public services and facilities leads to a greater assumption of their costs by the private sector, then housing prices will increase.

Information Dissemination

Classical economic theory holds that the more informed consumers are, the more rational and allocatively efficient their market decisions will be. This implies an additional set of mitigation strategies which aim primarily at supplementing and enlightening individual market decisions regarding the hurricane and storm threat. Several approaches can be taken in this vein.

The first approach is to seek mechanisms and processes which facilitate the effective informing of potential consumers of homes and other buildings of the actual risks associated with their location (for example, in a high-hazard district). This can be done in several ways. It might be required that real estate agents and those selling homes inform prospective buyers about the potential dangers from storm forces. Exactly this approach was proposed in Texas but was not enacted due to opposition from real estate and development interests (Texas Coastal and Marine Council 1981). This approach has been used in California in an attempt to inform prospective homebuyers of the risks of living near earthquake fault lines (Palm 1981). Under the Alquist-Priolo Special Studies Zone Act a real estate agent or individual selling property must disclose to the prospective buyer the fact that the property lies in a "special studies zone" (earthquake fault zone).

Another approach is to attempt to reduce storm hazards by increasing information on the "supply side." This might take the form of construction practice seminars for coastal builders and developers, introducing hazard-reducing methods for building and designing structures, as well as for siting and planning the orientation of buildings in vulnerable locations. This approach was proposed as a primary mitigation strategy following Hurricane Alicia in 1983 (FEMA 1983a).

Benefits and Limitations of Information Dissemination

The administrative costs of a hazard disclosure requirement are likely to be relatively small, particularly if it is attached to an already existing development review process. But its effectiveness at reducing development in hazardous areas is also likely to be marginal. A recent study of the effects of the Alquist-Priolo earthquake hazard zone disclosure requirement (Palm 1981) indicates that it has had little measurable effect on the market behavior of housing consumers. Among the problems identified are the tendency for homeowners to place a low priority on the earthquake threat, the issuance of the disclosure in the latter stages of a home purchase after the decision and commitment to buy are made, a downplaying of the importance of the earthquake hazard zones, and a disclosure vehicle (for example, a line that simply says "in Alquist-Priolo zone") that conveys little or no real information about the earthquake risk. As Palm (1981, 102) observes, "At present, real estate agents are disclosing at the least sensitive time in the sales transaction, and are using methods which convey the least amount of information about special studies zones."

Consequently, if a similar disclosure approach is to be applied to hurricane and storm hazards in an effective way it must learn from the California experience. Namely the disclosure must be provided early in the sales transaction, preferably during the initial agent-purchaser meeting, and this disclosure must convey real and accurate information about the location and nature of the hazard. Not only should the disclosure form or procedure be "labeled" in a meaningful way (for example, the home is in a "storm hazard zone" as opposed to an ambiguous "special studies zone"), it must provide a full description of the nature of storm-related risks. Strong resistance from the real estate industry in coastal areas can be expected, and efforts to convince them of the utility of such a procedure will be essential to its success. More "passive" types of hazard disclosure might also be used. Included in this category would be requirements that hazard zone designations be recorded on deeds and subdivision plats and that public signs be erected indicating the boundaries of storm hazard areas (and perhaps the location of past storm damages).

Similar reservations about effectiveness apply to construction practice seminars. The success of such seminars depends essentially on the commitment and willingness to change of builders and developers. Perhaps the most significant impediment to this type of private sector mitigation is that real estate development is a competitive industry in coastal regions and the incurring of substantial mitigation costs by one developer may place him at a competitive disadvantage. This is a major reason, for example, why building codes, subdivision restrictions, zoning ordinances, and other jurisdictionwide requirements are to be preferred to voluntary changes in construction practice. The jurisdictionwide requirements set general rules and create a common set of expectations which do not require any one developer to be placed at a competitive disadvantage.

Promising Local Mitigation Approaches

This chapter has reviewed the primary development management tools and techniques, the "nonstructural" approaches which can be used to mitigate hurricane and coastal storm hazards. In the past these approaches have been overlooked in favor of more traditional approaches such as seawalls or building construction standards. Future hurricane and storm hazard mitigation must be integrated into the broader planning and development framework at the local level.

Effective mitigation strategies in the future will be "packaged" into multiple-objective growth management policies. Localities will consider the reduction of storm hazards in their land use and comprehensive planning, just as they now consider such issues as water quality, traffic congestion, and the need for open space. Fortunately many of these other local goals overlap with and support storm hazard reduction, making an integrated program possible.

Future hazard mitigation will use a variety of tools and strategies. During the prestorm period in growing coastal communities new growth can be directed toward less hazardous locations. In already built-up communities, such as Miami Beach, beach nourishment, strengthening, relocation, and other approaches which protect massive existing investments will be needed. In communities with both developed and undeveloped shorelines, such as Long Island, some combination of techniques will be called for. In all these situations, development management can be used after the storm to redirect reconstruction to areas less susceptible to future storm forces.

As this chapter shows, the power of development management as a disaster mitigation approach stems from its broad array of tools and techniques, its centrality as a function of local government, and its ability to influence the placement and form of buildings and facilities. Early attempts at local disaster planning, typically separated from development management in a civil defense or emergency response agency, were limited to a smaller kit of tools, a narrower role in governance, and a reactive stance to the existing urban form and infrastructure.

References

Banach, Melissa, and Denis Canavan. 1987. "Montgomery County Agricultural Preservation Program." In *Managing Land-Use Conflicts*, edited by David J. Brower and Daniel S. Carol. Durham, N.C.: Duke University Press.

Beatley, Timothy, and David J. Brower. 1985. "Development Management as a Means of Mitigating the Impacts of Coastal Storms." Presented to the Fourth Symposium on Coastal and Ocean Management, July 30–August 2, Baltimore, Maryland.

Beatley, Timothy. 1985a. *Development Management to Reduce Coastal Storm Hazards: Policies and Processes.* Chapel Hill, N.C.: University of North Carolina, Center for Urban and Regional Studies.

————. 1985b. *Coastal Storm Hazard Planning in North Carolina: A Review and Critique.* Chapel Hill, N.C.: University of North Carolina, Center for Urban and Regional Studies.

Brower, David J., William Collins, and Timothy Beatley. 1984. *Hurricane Hazard Mitigation and Post-Storm Reconstruction Plan, Nags Head, North Carolina.* Chapel Hill, N.C.: Coastal Resources Collaborative.

Carmichael, O. M. 1974. "Transferable Development Rights as a Basis for Land Use Control." *Florida State University Law Review* 2:35–107.

Carol, Daniel S. 1987. "New Jersey Pinelands Commission." In *Managing Land-Use Conflicts,* edited by David J. Brower and Daniel S. Carol. Durham, N.C.: Duke University Press.

City of Sanibel, Florida. 1980. *Comprehensive Land Use Plan.*

Costonis, John. 1973. "Development Rights Transfer: An Exploratory Essay," *Yale Law Review* 83.

Coughlin, Robert E., and Thomas Plaut. 1978. "Less-than-fee Acquisition for the Preservation of Open Space: Does It Work?" *Journal of the American Planning Association* 44, no. 4 (October): 452–462.

Coughlin, Robert E., et al. 1977. *Saving the Garden: The Preservation of Farmland and Other Environmentally Valuable Landscape.* Philadelphia, Pa.: Regional Science Research Institute.

Coughlin, Robert E., and John Keene, eds. 1981. *The Protection of Farmland: A Reference Guidebook for State and Local Governments.* Washington, D.C.: U.S. Government Printing Office.

Downing, Donald. 1975. "Sewer and Water Pricing and Investment Policies to Implement Urban Growth Policy." *Water Resources Bulletin* 2, no. 2 (April).

Federal Emergency Management Agency. 1983a. *Interagency Hazard Mitigation Report Covering Brazoria, Chambers, Fort Bend, Galveston, Harris, and Matagorda Counties.* Denton, Tex. September.

————. 1983b. *Interagency Post-Storm Recovery Progress Report.* Denton, Tex. December.

Field Associates. 1981. *State and Local Acquisition of Floodplains and Wetlands: A Handbook on the Use of Acquisition in Floodplain Management.* Washington, D.C.: U.S. Water Resources Council.

Florida Department of Natural Resources. 1982. *Economic Impact Statement: Walton County Coastal Construction Control Line.* Tallahassee, Fla.: Division of Beaches and Shores. September.

Godschalk, David R., David J. Brower, et al. 1979. *Constitutional Issues of Growth*

Management. Chicago, Ill.: Planners Press.

Godschalk, David R., and David J. Brower. 1985. "Mitigation Strategies and Integrated Emergency Management." *Public Administration Review* 45 (January): 64–71.

Haas, J. Eugene, Robert W. Kates, and Martyn J. Bowden. 1977. *Reconstruction Following Disaster*. Cambridge, Mass.: MIT Press.

Hagman, Donald, and Dean Misczynski. 1978. *Windfalls for Wipeouts: Land Value Capture and Compensation*. Chicago, Ill.: ASPO Press.

Johnson, William K. 1978. *Physical and Economic Feasibility of Nonstructural Flood Plain Management Measures*. Ft. Belvoir, Va.: Institute of Water Resources.

Keene, John, et al. 1976 *Untaxing Open Space*. Washington, D.C.: Council on Environmental Quality.

Kusler, Jon A. 1979. *Floodplain Acquisition: Issues and Options in Strengthening Federal Policy*. Washington, D.C.: U.S. Water Resources Council.

———. 1982. *Innovation in Local Floodplain Management: A Summary of Community Experience*. Boulder, Colo.: University of Colorado, Institute of Behavioral Science.

Lee County, Fla. 1985. *The Lee Plan*. Fort Myers, Fla.

Long Island Regional Planning Board. 1984. *Hurricane Damage Mitigation Plan for the South Shore—Nassau and Suffolk Counties, N.Y.* Hauppauge, N.Y.

McElyea, William, David J. Brower, and David R. Godschalk. 1982. *Before the Storm: Managing Development to Reduce Hurricane Damages*. Chapel Hill, N.C.: University of North Carolina, Center for Urban and Regional Studies.

New Jersey Department of Environmental Protection. 1985. *Coastal Storm Hazard Mitigation: Atlantic County Barrier Islands and Ocean City, New Jersey*. Trenton, N.J.

Nugent, Michael. 1975. "Water and Sewer Extension Policies as a Technique for Guiding Development." *Carolina Planning* 1, no. 1 (Winter): 4–11.

Palm, Risa. 1981. *Real Estate Agents and Special Studies Zones Disclosure: The Response of California Homebuyers to Earthquake Hazards Information*. Boulder, Colo.: Institute of Behavioral Science, University of Colorado.

Pilkey, Orrin H. 1987. "A Time for Retreat." In *Cities on the Beach: Management Issues of Developed Coastal Barriers*, edited by Rutherford Platt, Sheila Pelczarski, and Barbara Burbank. Chicago, Ill.: University of Chicago, Department of Geography.

Roberts, Thomas H. 1986. "Capital Improvements Programming After the Growth Management Act: A Planner's Perspective." In *Perspectives on Florida's Growth Management Act of 1985*, edited by John DeGrove and Julian Juergensmeyer. Cambridge, Mass.: Lincoln Institute of Land Policy.

Rose, Jerome. 1975. *Transfer of Development Rights*. New Brunswick N.J.: Center for Urban Policy Research, Rutgers University.

Rosenthal, John C. 1975. "Reconstruction After a Natural Disaster—A Need for Rapid Planning and Development." Paper presented to a conference of the American Institute of

Planners, San Antonio, Texas.

Shows, E. Warren, et al. 1976. *The Economic Impact of Florida's Coastal Setback Line: A Study of Bay County, Florida.* Tampa, Fla.: University of South Florida.

Snyder, Thomas, and Michael Stegman. 1987. *Paying for Growth.* Washington, D.C.: Urban Land Institute.

Stroud, Nancy. 1978. "Impact Taxes: The Opportunity in North Carolina." *Carolina Planning* 4, no.2 (Fall): 20–27.

Sturza, R. P., II. 1987. "The Retreat Alternative in the Real World: The Kill Devil Hills Land-Use Plan of 1980." In *Cities on the Beach: Management Issues of Developed Coastal Barriers*, edited by Rutherford Platt, Sheila Pelczarski, and Barbara Burbank. Chicago, Ill.: University of Chicago, Department of Geography.

Texas Coastal and Marine Council. 1981. *Model Minimum Hurricane Resistant Building Standards for the Texas Gulf Coast.* Austin, Tex.

Town of Emerald Isle, N.C. 1984. *Storm Hazard Mitigation Plan and Postdisaster Reconstruction Plan.* Prepared by George Eichler and Associates and Satilla Planning.

Urban and Regional Research. 1982. *Land Management in Tsunami Hazard Areas.* Seattle, Wash.

Whyte, William. 1968. *The Last Landscape.* Garden City, N.Y.: Doubleday Books.

7 Mitigation Practice in High-Hazard Coastal Localities

Survey of Practice

Aside from individual case studies, little systematic knowledge has been available in the past concerning the extent to which coastal localities are addressing hurricane and severe coastal storm hazards, the types of approaches used, and the extent to which they are effective at reducing these hazards. Without such a comprehensive understanding of local mitigation practice, policymakers have had to rely upon partial evidence in attempting to formulate improved mitigation approaches.

In 1984 a comprehensive survey of localities vulnerable to hurricanes and severe coastal storms was undertaken to obtain a better and more complete understanding of the nature of current local mitigation practice. This survey employed a mail questionnaire, administered to high-hazard coastal localities along the Gulf and Atlantic coasts. This chapter presents the basic descriptive findings from this survey. The following chapter analyzes the influence of community variables and background characteristics on the adoption and effectiveness of mitigation measures.

The survey questionnaire was designed to document and evaluate mitigation efforts of those coastal localities which are most susceptible to hurricane and coastal storm forces. Our survey defined these localities as ones which contained "Velocity-zone" or "V-zone" areas. V-zones are coastal waterfront areas where significant waves are anticipated in addition to rising floodwaters during severe storms. Under the National Flood Insurance Program, FEMA provides maps to participating localities showing the location of their V-zones. Technically V-zones are those areas of sufficient fetch to support a minimum three-foot wave (U.S. Army Corps of Engineers 1975). Within these areas, higher actuarial flood insurance rates apply and special building strengthening provisions are required.

Our survey population included 598 localities with V-zones in eighteen Gulf and Atlantic coast states (Alabama, Connecticut, Delaware, Florida, Georgia, Louisiana, Maine, Maryland, Massachusetts, Mississippi, New Hampshire, New Jersey, New York, North Carolina, Rhode Island, South Carolina, Texas, Virginia).[1] In addition four counties in Hawaii were included for a total of 602 localities surveyed. Because coastal localities of very small population were unlikely to have staff resources for extensive development management programs, and in an attempt to keep the survey size to a manageable level, jurisdictions of less than 1,000 in population (as of the 1980 census) were not surveyed.

These high-hazard coastal jurisdictions were asked which techniques they were currently using for: (1) structural alteration of the coastal environment, (2) strengthening buildings and facilities to better withstand storm forces, and (3) guiding and managing development. They were asked to estimate the effectiveness of their current measures in reducing storm hazards and to identify problems or obstacles that they faced in implementing mitigation programs. In addition, they were requested to provide information about their coastal floodplains, recent storm experience, relationships with state and regional agencies, staff resources, and community characteristics. (The questionnaire is included in the Appendix.)

Where possible, the questionnaire was sent to a local planning director. If there was no local planner, it was sent to a city manager or county administrator. Where these officials were not available, the recipients were building inspectors, mayors, planning board members, and civil defense officials. Almost two-thirds of the responses were received from planners: planning directors or assistant directors (26 percent), staff planners or engineers (24 percent), and planning board chairmen (13 percent). The remainder of the responses came from building inspectors (9 percent), city managers or county administrators (8 percent), emergency management or civil defense officials (5 percent), town clerks (4 percent), mayors (3 percent), and various others (8 percent). The results thus embody primarily the views of professional, appointed officials, rather than elected officials. They also tend to be weighted toward the views of local planners.

Table 7.1 Distribution of Survey Respondents
by Geographical Region and State

Region/State	Adjusted Survey Population	Survey Responses	Percentage of Total Respondents	Response Rate
New England	135	81	20.1	60.0
Connecticut	19	10	2.4	52.6
Maine	24	19	4.7	79.2
Massachusetts	70	39	9.6	55.7
New Hampshire	4	0	0	0
Rhode Island	18	13	3.2	72.2
Mid-Atlantic	151	90	23.3	59.6
Delaware	6	6	1.5	100.0
Maryland	20	17	4.2	85.0
New Jersey	60	35	8.8	58.3
New York	65	32	8.1	49.2
Southeast	71	57	14.2	80.3
Georgia	17	10	2.4	58.8
North Carolina	22	18	4.4	81.8
South Carolina	21	20	5.2	95.2
Virginia	11	9	2.2	81.8
Gulf	240	171	42.3	71.2
Alabama	8	4	1.0	50.0
Florida	153	119	29.2	77.7
Louisiana	22	14	3.4	63.6
Mississippi	11	6	1.5	54.5
Texas	47	28	7.1	59.6
Pacific	4	4	1.0	100.0
Hawaii	4	4	1.0	100.0
Total	602	403	100.0	66.9

Table 7.1 shows the distribution of the survey population and responses. The final response rate was 66.9 percent, with responses from 403 of the 602 localities surveyed.[2] Pacific, Gulf, and Southeastern localities had the highest response rates, with over a quarter of the responses coming from Florida respondents.

Table 7.2   Priority of Storm Hazard to Elected Governing Body
in Comparison with Other Local Issues

	Frequency	Percentage
Very high priority	66	16.5
High priority	120	30.0
Medium priority	105	26.3
Low priority	81	26.3
Very low priority	28	7.0
(N = 400)		

Priority of Storm Threat

Current literature analyzing the politics of natural hazards suggests that storm threats are of relatively low importance to public officials (Rossi, Wright, and Weber-Burdin 1982; Drabek, Mushkatel, and Kilijanel 1983). We expected similar results from our questionnaire. Approximately 73 percent of the respondents, however, indicated that their jurisdiction's governing body considered the threat of severe coastal storms of at least medium priority in comparison with other local issues (see table 7.2). Close to half of the respondents (46.5 percent) indicated storm threats to be of either high or very high priority. A partial explanation for this is that these coastal localities would feel the full force of a coastal storm and have the most to lose (that is, the risk to people and property is greatest here) should a hurricane or severe storm occur.

Mitigation Programs and Perceived Effectiveness

Explicit Storm Hazard Reduction Strategies

Respondents were first asked if their locality had an explicit storm hazard reduction strategy in addition to their participation in the National Flood Insurance Program. Surprisingly, given the literature statements about the low saliency of natural hazard mitigation to local governments, half (50.7 percent) of the respondents indicated that such an explicit strategy did exist.

Those who indicated that their locality had such a strategy were asked to indicate its specific objectives. Ten objectives were listed in the ques-

Table 7.3   Objectives of Storm Hazard Reduction Strategy

Rank	Frequency	Percentage
1. Increasing ability of private structures and facilities in hazardous areas to withstand storm forces	122	60.1
2. Conserving protective features of the natural environment (e.g., dune protection)	119	58.6
3. Increasing evacuation capacity	98	48.3
4. Increasing ability of public structures and facilities in hazardous areas to withstand storm forces	96	47.3
5. Locating new public structures and facilities in areas less susceptible to storm hazards	93	45.8
6. Guiding new private development into areas less susceptible to storm hazards	92	45.3
7. Provision of adequate storm shelters	82	40.4
8. Structurally altering and/or reinforcing the coastal environment (e.g., seawalls, bulkheads)	70	34.5
9. Relocation of existing public facilities and structures into less hazardous areas	12	5.9
10. Relocation of existing private development into less hazardous areas	9	4.4

(N = 203)

Note: Respondents were asked to check all relevant categories. Only those with explicit storm hazard reduction strategies were asked to respond, hence N is smaller for this question.

tionnaire with respondents permitted to circle as many objectives as were applicable. Table 7.3 lists the ten storm hazard reduction objectives in order of the frequency of their selection. The two most frequently selected objectives (by about 60 percent of the respondents in each case) were: (1) increasing the ability of private structures and facilities to withstand storms and (2) conserving the protective features of the natural environment. The two objectives most closely related to development management also received a relatively high percentage of responses (45 percent): (5) locating public facilities in less susceptible areas and (6) guiding new development into less hazardous areas. On the other hand relocation, either of private or public structures

Table 7.4   Programs Which Structurally Alter the Coastal Environment

	Currently in Use	Percentage	Average Effectiveness Rating[a]	Standard Deviation
1. Shoreline protection works	281	69.7	3.20	1.00
2. Flood control works	136	33.7	3.48	1.02
3. Sand-trapping structures	136	33.7	2.72	.98
4. Sand-moving programs	126	31.3	2.76	1.21

(N = 403)
a. On a five-point scale.

and facilities, was not an objective frequently pursued by these high-hazard coastal localities.

Programs Which Structurally Alter the Coastal Environment

Three questions on the survey dealt with the specific programs and measures which localities had in place which, either by design or by effect, served to reduce storm hazards. Each question pertained to a particular category of storm reduction programs. The first related to actions or desires which served to structurally modify or alter the coastal environment. Included in this category are sand-trapping structures (groins and jetties), sand-moving programs (beach nourishment and beach scraping), shoreline protection works (bulkheads, seawalls, and revetments), and flood control works (dikes, channels, and retaining ponds).

As shown in table 7.4, substantial use of each of these approaches was found, although shoreline protection works was a clear leader with more than two-thirds of the responding communities indicating that such measures were in use (70 percent). The use of sand-trapping, sand-moving, and flood control works was about even, with approximately one-third of the responding communities using these. Note that respondents could select multiple categories on their response.

Respondents were also asked to evaluate the extent to which these programs tended to reduce local storm hazards. Comparing the average effectiveness score for each type of approach indicates which are believed to be most successful in reducing storm hazards.[3] Flood control works and shoreline protection received the highest effectiveness ratings, with the

Table 7.5   Programs and Policies Which Strengthen Buildings and Facilities

	Frequency	Percentage	Average Effectiveness Rating[a]	Standard Deviation
1. Minimum elevation and floodproofing required by NFIP	378	93.8	3.86	.89
2. Building code	362	89.8	3.62	1.00
3. Special storm-resistant standards construction	190	47.1	3.82	.87
4. Floodproofing of public facilities and structures	162	40.2	3.47	.85
5. More extensive elevation and floodproofing	60	14.9	3.98	.90

(N = 403)
a. On a five-point scale.

remaining two categories falling considerably behind. Sand-trapping structures received the lowest rating even though they were used by almost as many localities as flood control works.

Programs Which Strengthen Buildings and Facilities

The second category of programs asked about were those designed to strengthen buildings and the private and public facilities that accompany them (see table 7.5). As expected, almost all responding localities had a building code in place (90 percent) and had met the minimum elevation and floodproofing standards required by FEMA under the provisions of the National Flood Insurance Program (94 percent). About 47 percent of the respondents indicated that they had special storm-resistant building standards in place, and well over one-third were floodproofing public facilities and structures. Only 15 percent of the responding localities, however, had adopted elevation and floodproofing standards which were more stringent than those required under NFIP.

Of those strengthening measures in use, more extensive elevation and floodproofing were considered the most effective. These were followed closely, however, by the minimum NFIP standards and special storm-resistant standards. Building codes were rated fourth in terms of effective-

Table 7.6   Number of Development Management Measures in Use

Number of DM Measures	Frequency	Percentage
0−5	117	29.0
6−10	223	55.3
11−15	56	13.9
Over 15	7	1.7

(N = 403)

ness, and finally floodproofing of public structures and facilities received the lowest effectiveness rating in this category. It is important to recognize that overall the building and facility strengthening measures were considered much more effective at reducing coastal storm hazards than the structural environment reinforcement measures.

Development Management Measures

The concept of "development management" is defined for the respondent in the beginning of the survey to include "programs and policies which control or influence the location, density, timing and type of development which occurs in a jurisdiction." Respondents were asked to indicate which development management tools and measures were currently used in their jurisdiction and the extent to which they serve to reduce local storm hazards. Respondents were asked to answer this question even if a program or policy was not specifically designed to reduce storm hazards.

The development management measures were organized under six headings: (1) planning, (2) development regulation, (3) public facilities policy, (4) taxation, financial, and other incentives, (5) public acquisition, and (6) information dissemination. Overall, twenty-one different measures were listed in this question, ranging from zoning and subdivision provisions to below-market property taxes.

An initial way to understand the extent of use of these techniques is to see how many localities used how many different techniques. Table 7.6 separates localities according to the number of measures currently in use. Most localities were using some form of development management as we defined it. Approximately 29 percent of the localities were using five techniques or fewer. Consequently, more than 70 percent of the respon-

Table 7.7   Planning Measures

	Number of Localities Currently in Use	Percentage	Average Effectiveness Rating[a]	Standard Deviation
1. Comprehensive/land use plan	340	84.4	2.94	1.04
2. Evacuation plan	272	67.5	3.53	.99
3. Capital Improvement Program	216	53.6	2.53	1.09
4. Recovery/reconstruction plan or policies	87	21.6	2.98	1.02
5. Hurricane/storm component of comprehensive plan	80	19.9	3.33	1.04

(N = 403)   a. On a five-point scale.

dents have six or more techniques currently in use. About 16 percent have eleven or more of these measures in use. The majority of localities, roughly 55 percent, fall within the six to ten range.

Following is a more detailed look at the specific development management measures contained within each subcategory. It should be remembered that respondents were asked to indicate the use and effectiveness of these measures regardless of whether they are explicitly designed to reduce storm hazards.

Planning

Under planning instruments, as shown in table 7.7, the comprehensive or land use plan was the most frequently used with some 84 percent of the respondents indicating that they had such a plan. Evacuation plans ranked second in frequency with 68 percent of the localities having such a plan, while the capital improvement program ranked third with about half the respondents indicating its use. Not surprisingly plans and policy documents dealing specifically with the reduction of storm hazards were considerably fewer in number. About 22 percent had recovery/reconstruction plans or policies and 20 percent had hurricane/storm components of their comprehensive plans.

Table 7.8   Development Regulation

	Number of Localities Currently in Use	Percentage	Average Effectiveness Rating[a]	Standard Deviation
1. Zoning ordinance	354	87.8	3.16	1.06
2. Subdivision ordinance	347	86.1	3.06	1.16
3. Shoreline setback	218	54.1	3.59	1.01
4. Dune protection	152	37.7	3.69	1.04
5. Special hazard area ordinance	109	27.0	3.85	.77

(N = 403)   a. On a five-point scale.

Average effectiveness ratings for these tools range from relatively high for evacuation plans and hurricane/storm hazard components to relatively low for capital improvement programs and basic land use/comprehensive plans. However, none were ranked below the midpoint (2.5) of the effectiveness scale.

Development Regulation

This category includes traditional land use controls. The most prominent, zoning and subdivision regulations, are currently in use in most responding localities. As shown in table 7.8, approximately 88 percent of the responding localities had zoning in place, and 86 percent had subdivision regulations. Approximately half of the respondents had shoreline setback provisions, while 38 percent and 27 percent, respectively, had dune protection and special hazard area ordinances.

Respondents generally rate such techniques as shoreline setbacks and dune protection ordinances as being more effective than traditional regulatory measures. This is partly because setbacks and dune protection regulations are more specifically related to storm hazards and are more difficult to circumvent, and partly because the results of these regulations are perhaps more apparent or visible to respondents. Special hazard area ordinances, while the least frequently used, were considered to be the most effective among these techniques.

Table 7.9   Capital Facilities Policy

	Number of Localities Currently in Use	Percentage	Average Effectiveness Rating[a]	Standard Deviation
1. Location of public structures and buildings (e.g., hospitals, schools) to reduce extent of risk to public investments	185	45.9	3.67	.93
2. Location of capital facilities to reduce or discourage development in high-hazard areas	126	31.3	3.43	.85

(N = 403)   a. On a five-point scale.

Capital Facilities Policy

One potentially effective growth shaping approach is through decisions concerning the construction and location of public facilities, public structures, and other public investments. Two entries were provided for capital facilities policy: locating public buildings to reduce risk to them and locating capital facilities to reduce development in high-hazard areas (see table 7.9).

Unlike the entries in the previous section, these two capital facilities entries are much more explicitly storm-hazard-related. Indeed, to circle one leaves little doubt that storm hazard reduction is the intended objective. While a majority of responding localities do not employ either of these policies, about one-third of the respondents do; this is a significant conclusion (see table 7.9). Survey responses do not indicate the precise form of such capital facilities policies. Are they explicitly developed and adopted by the governing body (that is, formal policies and development "rules" the jurisdiction follows) or are they more informal criteria that local planners and public officials use when making capital facilities decisions? This is a question left unresolved from the survey data.

Table 7.10 Taxation, Financial, and Other Incentives

	Number of Localities Currently in Use	Percentage	Average Effectiveness Rating[a]	Standard Deviation
1. Transfer of development potential from hazardous to non-hazardous sites (e.g., clustering, planned unit development)	84	20.8	3.46	.95
2. Reduced or below-market taxation for open space and non-intensive uses of hazard areas	44	10.9	3.00	1.21
3. Impact tax or special assessment to cover the additional public costs of building in hazard area development	7	1.7	3.71	.95

(N = 403)
a. On a five-point scale.

As we would expect, the policy of locating public structures outside of hazard areas, which is directly controlled by the government, is considered more effective than is orienting public facilities to discourage private development, which has a more indirect effect. However, both have relatively high effectiveness ratings, and the difference between them is not substantial.

Taxation, Financial, and Other Incentives

Three types of measures were included under this heading: reduced or below-market taxation, impact taxes or special assessments, and devices for the transfer of development potential. In the questionnaire each of these measures was specifically related to the mitigation of storm hazards. As shown in table 7.10, relatively few responding localities were using

Table 7.11   Public Acquisition

	Number of Localities Currently in Use	Percentage	Average Effectiveness Rating[a]	Standard Deviation
1. Acquisition of undeveloped land in hazardous areas	118	29.3	3.58	1.04
2. Acquisition of development rights or scenic easements	56	13.9	2.88	1.15
3. Acquisition of damaged buildings in hazardous areas	12	3.0	3.55	1.13
4. Building relocation program (moving structures)	9	2.2	3.33	1.12

(N = 403)   a. On a five-point scale.

these techniques. The most frequent, development transfer measures, were used by about one-fifth of the respondents (substantially less frequent than development regulations such as zoning and subdivision ordinances). Impact taxes or special assessments received the smallest number of responses (1.7 percent), with reduced or below-market taxation in second place (10.9 percent).

Relatively high effectiveness ratings were obtained for TDR and impact fees, although the generalizability of the latter score is questionable given the low number of observations involved.

Public Acquisition

As described in chapter 6, an effective mitigation approach is to purchase undeveloped land in high-hazard areas and to keep this land in public hands, preempting its availability for private development. One option here is to purchase the fee-simple title for the land (all the rights to the land), while another option is to purchase only the "development rights" (an easement restricting development). The former is a more traditional approach, and, as shown in table 7.11, a substantial number of respon-

Table 7.12 Information Dissemination

	Frequency	Percentage	Average Effectiveness Rating[a]	Standard Deviation
1. Hazard disclosure requirements in real estate transactions	103	25.6	2.93	1.07
2. Construction practice seminars for builders	62	15.4	3.24	1.06

(N = 403)
a. On a five-point scale.

dents indicated that such an approach was in use in their jurisdiction (29 percent). A number of respondents (13.9 percent) also indicated that they were using the second approach—the purchase of development rights or easements in high-hazard areas. Two other approaches are included in this section of the questionnaire: programs to purchase damaged buildings and structures in hazard areas and programs to relocate structures outside the hazard areas. An extremely small number of responding localities had such programs (only twelve and nine localities, respectively). Clearly purchase and relocation of structures in hazardous areas were not frequently used by these coastal localities.

Acquisition of undeveloped land and damaged buildings received relatively high average effectiveness ratings, with building relocation following close behind. Acquisition of development rights or scenic easements was considered of lower effectiveness.

Information Dissemination

Models of rational behavior suggest that individuals will make responsible decisions if they have access to all the relevant information. This belief has spurred interest in programs designed to inform the housing consumer, the developer/builder, and the general public about the risks associated with hurricanes and severe coastal storms. Two types of information programs were listed in the questionnaire: hazard disclosure in real estate transactions and construction practice seminars. As shown in table 7.12, approximately 26 percent of the responding localities indicated that they have hazard disclosure provisions in place, while approximately 15

Table 7.13   Development Management Measures
in Order of Frequency Used

Rank	Type of Measure	Survey Communities Using Measure	
		Number	Percentage
1	Zoning ordinance	354	87.8
2	Subdivision ordinance	347	86.1
3	Comprehensive/land use plan	340	84.4
4	Evacuation plan	272	67.5
5	Shoreline setback regulation	218	54.1
6	Capital improvement program	216	53.6
7	Location of public structures and buildings to reduce storm risks	185	45.9
8	Dune protection regulations	152	37.7
9	Location of capital facilities to reduce or discourage development in high-hazard areas	126	31.3
10	Acquisition of undeveloped land in hazardous areas	118	29.3
11	Special hazard area ordinance	109	27.0
12	Hazard disclosure requirements in real estate transactions	103	25.6
13	Recovery/reconstruction plan or policies	87	21.6
14	Transfer of development potential from hazardous to non-hazardous sites	84	20.8
15	Hurricane/storm component of comprehensive plan	80	19.9
16	Construction practice seminars	62	15.4
17	Acquisition of development rights or scenic easements	56	13.9
18	Reduced or below-market taxation	44	10.9
19	Acquisition of damaged buildings in hazardous areas	12	3.0
20	Building relocation program	9	2.2
21	Impact taxes or special assessments	7	1.7

(N = 403)

Table 7.14   Development Management Measures
in Order of Perceived Effectiveness

Rank	Type of Measure	Average Effectiveness Rating[a]
1	Special hazard area ordinance	3.85
2	Impact taxes or special assessments	3.71
3	Dune protection regulations	3.69
4	Location of public structures to minimize risk	3.67
5	Shoreline setback regulations	3.59
6	Acquisition of undeveloped land in hazard areas	3.58
7	Acquisition of damaged buildings in hazard areas	3.55
8	Evacuation plan	3.53
9	Transfer of development potential from hazardous to nonhazardous sites	3.46
10	Location of capital facilities to reduce or discourage development in high-hazard areas	3.43
11	Hurricane/storm component of comprehensive plan	3.33
12	Building relocation program	3.33
13	Construction practice seminars	3.24
14	Zoning ordinance	3.16
15	Subdivision ordinance	3.06
16	Reduced or below-market taxation	3.00
17	Recovery/reconstruction plan or policies	2.98
18	Comprehensive/land use plan	2.94
19	Hazard disclosure requirements in real estate transactions	2.93
20	Acquisition of development rights or scenic easements	2.88
21	Capital improvement program	2.53

(N = 403)
a. Based on a five-point scale.

percent indicated that construction practice seminars were being offered. The average effectiveness rating for hazard disclosure was relatively lower than for construction practice seminars.

Table 7.15   Relative Effectiveness of Mitigation Approaches:
Top Ten Measures in Terms of Average Effectiveness

	Average Effectiveness Rating	Type of Measure
1. More extensive elevation and floodproofing than required by NFIP	3.98	Building strengthening
2. Minimum elevation and floodproofing required under NFIP	3.86	Building strengthening
3. Special hazard area ordinance	3.85	Development management
4. Special storm-resistant construction standards	3.82	Building strengthening
5. Impact taxes or special assessments[a]	3.71	Development management
6. Dune protection regulations	3.69	Development management
7. Location of public structures to minimize risk	3.67	Development management
8. Building codes	3.62	Building strengthening
9. Shoreline setback regulations	3.59	Development management
10. Acquisition of undeveloped land in hazardous areas	3.48	Development management

a. Note that this is based on a very small number of cases.

Summary of Frequency and Effectiveness

The most frequently used of all techniques were the familiar zoning and subdivision ordinances and comprehensive plans, each used by over 300 respondents. Over 200 respondents were using evacuation plans, shoreline setback regulations, and capital improvement programs. Table 7.13 presents a summary listing of specific development management measures ordered according to the frequency of their use.

Those measures judged most effective were not those most frequently used. However, several of the more effective measures fell within the

Table 7.16   Ranking of the Mitigation Strategies Based on
Overall Importance in Reducing Local Storm Hazard

	Number of Rankings		
	Most Important 1	2	Least Important 3
1. Development management (N = 389)	211 (54.2%)	85 (21.9%)	93 (23.9%)
2. Strengthening building and facilities (N = 385)	100 (26.0%)	180 (46.8%)	105 (27.3%)
3. Structural reinforcement of coastal environment (N = 384)	84 (21.9%)	115 (29.9%)	185 (48.2%)

midrange of use. Table 7.14 provides a ranking of these development management measures by their perceived effectiveness.

Ranking the Three Mitigation Approaches

Table 7.15 ranks the top ten mitigation measures in terms of the average effectiveness ratings obtained in the survey and classifies them according to their overall type (building strengthening, development management, structural alteration of the environment). Three of the top four responses are measures found within the building strengthening category. Of all the mitigation measures more extensive elevation and floodproofing than that required under the National Flood Insurance Program received the highest average effectiveness rating (3.98). As well, the third highest measure, special hazard area management, while included under development management, is to a great extent actually another indication of localities implementing NFIP requirements. Of the remaining six measures five fall into the development management category and an additional one into the building strengthening category. No measures in the structural alteration of the coastal environment category were included in the top ten. Thus, both building strengthening and development management measures are considered highly effective, although ranking individual mea-

Table 7.17   Overall Effectiveness

	Frequency	Percentage
1. Very effective	48	12.5
2. Moderately effective	223	57.9
3. Slightly effective	92	23.9
4. Not effective	22	5.7

(N = 385)

sures does not provide information about the extent of effectiveness of the overall approach—that is, the combination of measures.

To assess the effectiveness of the overall approaches in reducing storm hazards, respondents were asked to order them (1, 2, or 3, with 1 the most important and 3 the least). Of the three approaches development management by far received the greatest number of "most important" responses (see table 7.16). Strengthening buildings and facilities received the most middle rankings, while structural reinforcement of the coastal environment received the highest number of "least important" rankings.

It should be remembered that this ranking is relative to the specific responding locality. That is, even in circumstances where development management is ranked third (last) by a respondent, the locality may have a solid and innovative development management program. Its lower ranking may be attributable, for instance, to the importance of structural improvements (for example, in the case where a large amount of the hazard area has already been developed).

Overall Effectiveness

In order to assess overall effectiveness of hazard mitigation efforts, respondents were asked to consider all of the strategies and techniques they have in use in their jurisdiction and to rate the combined effectiveness of these at reducing local storm hazards. Most respondents felt that local programs were at least partially effective (see table 7.17). Over 70 percent believed their combined programs were either moderately effective or very effective, while only a small 6 percent believed these programs were not effective at all. The majority of respondents (58 percent) placed their localities in the "moderately effective" category. This suggests that the

Table 7.18   Obstacles to the Enactment of Development Management
in Order of Frequency Cited

Rank	Frequency	Percentage	Importance Index[a]
1. General conservative attitude toward government control of private property rights (N = 359)	319	88.9	3.38
2. General feeling that community can "weather the storm" (N = 357)	309	86.6	3.09
3. Lack of adequate financial resources to implement mitigation programs (N = 347)	296	85.3	3.41
4. More pressing local problems and concerns (N = 351)	291	82.9	3.28
5. Opposition of real estate and development interests (N = 355)	286	80.6	3.06
6. Lack of trained personnel to develop mitigation programs (N = 345)	278	80.6	2.91
7. Lack of incentives or requirements from higher levels of government (N = 345)	278	80.6	3.02
8. Opposition of homeowners (N = 338)	252	74.6	2.64
9. Opposition of business interests (N = 337)	241	71.5	2.60
10. Absence of politically active individuals and groups advocating hurricane/storm mitigation (N = 339)	242	71.4	2.85
11. Inadequate or inaccurate federal flood insurance maps (N = 342)	215	62.9	2.49

a. Based on a five-point scale.

majority of localities have programs which have considerable effect in reducing storm hazards (something greater than "slightly effective"), but at the same time these efforts are far from being "very effective." Thus in most responding jurisdictions much room for increased effectiveness exists, a very important finding in terms of our recommendations in chapter 9.

Table 7.19   Arguments against Enactment of Development Management
in Order of Frequency

Rank	Frequency	Percentage	Importance Index[a]
1. Development management measures lead to increased developmental costs (N = 368)	315	85.6	3.18
2. Decisions about risks from coastal storms are best left to the individual (N = 346)	246	71.1	2.66
3. Development management measures dampen local economy (N = 355)	245	69.0	2.52
4. Particular development management measures are illegal or unconstitutional (N = 338)	225	66.6	2.42

a. Based on a five-point scale.

Obstacles to the Enactment of Development Management

An important question in this research is how politically feasible develop-ment management is likely to be in coastal jurisdictions. To better under-stand why such measures are more or less feasible, we asked respondents to identify local obstacles to the enactment of development management. This was accomplished by presenting respondents with a list of potential obstacles and asking them to assess their relative importance.

Two types of data from this question can provide a sense of which obstacles are most important. The first is the absolute number of respon-dents that indicated that a particular group or factor was important in their locality. Table 7.18 presents these obstacles in rank order according to frequency selected.

General conservative attitudes toward government control of private property rights was the obstacle most frequently selected by respondents (selected by 89 percent). This was followed closely by general feelings that the community can "weather the storm" (87 percent) and a lack of adequate financial resources to implement mitigation programs. Ranked fourth according to frequency selected is the obstacle posed by more

Table 7.20   Problems in Enforcement and Implementation
of Development Management Measures

Rank	Frequency	Percentage
1. Insufficient funds (N = 195)	116	59.5
2. Public opposition (N = 194)	89	45.9
3. Lack of support by public officials (N = 192)	83	43.2
4. Lack of qualified personnel (N = 195)	79	40.5
5. Insufficient data base (N = 195)	63	32.3

pressing local problems and concerns. Opposition of real estate and development interests rounds out the top five responses.

A second measure is the relative importance assigned to the obstacle by the respondent. This is indicated by the calculated average importance score, also shown in table 7.18. The order of the most important obstacles remains largely the same when degree of importance is considered. The absence of political advocates for storm hazard mitigation moves into the top five, while the feeling that the community can "weather the storm" drops out. Some reordering among the remaining four is also apparent. While lack of financial resources was rated third in terms of the frequency of responses, it moves to first when degree of importance is considered.

Arguments Against Development Management

To understand the nature of political opposition to development management programs, it is important to know the types of arguments typically made against their use. Survey respondents were asked to evaluate a short list of common arguments, indicating which were important and the extent of their importance.

As can be seen in table 7.19, the leading argument is that development management measures will lead to increased development costs. This is the clear leader both in terms of frequency of responses and perceived degree of importance. The traditional argument that decisions about storm risks are best left to the individual is second in frequency and importance, followed by arguments about the effects on the local economy and the legality of development management programs. Despite

Table 7.21   Undesirable Consequences Resulting from
Development Management

Rank	Frequency	Percentage
1. Increase in construction costs	106	83.5
2. Slowed economic growth and development	26	20.5
3. Reduced tax revenues	19	15.0
4. Reduced land values	14	11.0

(N = 127)

their relative ranking, all of these arguments appear to be important in a substantial number of the coastal localities in our population.

Enforcement and Implementation Problems

An important question concerns the extent to which high-hazard localities have experienced problems in enforcing and implementing their development management programs. Fifty percent of the respondents indicated that they had encountered problems enforcing or implementing the development management programs they had identified in earlier questions. Respondents were then presented with a more specific listing of possible implementation and enforcement problems and asked to indicate which had been encountered in their localities. Table 7.20 presents the results of this question, in rank order of frequency selected.

Clearly a major portion of the responding localities have enforcement and implementation problems, with certain problems, such as insufficient funds and public opposition, more important than others. Unfortunately this question does not permit the respondent to indicate the severity of these problems but only whether they exist or not. For instance, while insufficient funds may have been identified frequently as a problem, it may be a relatively small problem in each individual jurisdiction.

Undesirable Consequences of Development Management

Respondents were asked to consider whether the development management measures used in their jurisdiction have induced any undesirable

Table 7.22   Evacuation Knowledge: "Do You Know How Long
It Would Take to Safely Evacuate Your Jurisdiction?"

Population	Yes		No	
Less than 5,000	41	(10.3%)	38	(9.6%)
5,000–19,000	52	(13.1%)	85	(21.4%)
20,000–49,000	25	(6.3%)	38	(9.6%)
50,000–100,000	18	(4.5%)	33	(8.3%)
Over 100,000	41	(10.3%)	27	(6.8%)
Total	177	(44.5%)	221	(55.5%)

consequences or side effects. Roughly 66.7 percent indicated that no such consequences had resulted. The one-third of the respondents that had faced undesirable consequences were asked to identify from a list provided in the questionnaire which consequences occurred. The most frequent consequence, selected by more than 80 percent of this group, was an increase in construction costs (see table 7.21). The remaining entries ran a distant second, being selected by only 10 percent to 20 percent of the localities with such consequences. Again, however, this question does not take into consideration the severity of the consequences. While most localities may experience an increase in construction costs, the size of this increase was not reported and may not be known.

Evacuation Knowledge

In most of the localities receiving the questionnaire the issue of evacuation in the event of hurricane should be quite important. Surprisingly, however, when asked if they knew how long it would take to evacuate their jurisdiction, more than half (55.5 percent) indicated they did not (see table 7.22). A comparison of this response with the population size of the locality indicates that a large portion of those localities that do not know this information are small in size and thus expectedly low in local expertise and hazard management capacity. About 55 percent of the respondents that indicated they did not know how long it takes to evacuate were in jurisdictions of less than 20,000 in population. For those localities where respondents did know this figure, or were at least able to estimate it, evacuation times ranged from one hour to seventy-two hours.

Poststorm Adoption of Mitigation Measures

Respondents were asked whether or not their locality had been hit by a severe coastal storm (defined as a hurricane, tropical storm, or north-easter which caused substantial property damage) since 1970. Approximately two-thirds of the respondents answered this question in the affirmative (61.8 percent). If respondents answered yes to this question they were then asked to provide the name (if it had one) and date of the most severe and/or most damaging storm during this period.

More than a third of the respondents indicated that their localities had adopted more stringent development management measures following the occurrence of a storm. Approximately 33 percent of the respondents to this question adopted such measures following the most recent storm event, while 37 percent adopted such measures following the most damaging storm (32.9 percent and 37.2 percent, respectively). As might be expected, this percentage is somewhat higher in response to the more damaging storm. These findings suggest that storm events do significantly prompt development management adoption in coastal jurisdictions and that this is more likely to occur in response to more severe events.

Survey Highlights

This chapter has described the findings of a mail survey of hurricane-prone localities (containing V-zones under the National Flood Insurance Program) in eighteen Gulf and Atlantic coast states, plus Hawaii. A response rate of approximately 67 percent was achieved, yielding 403 usable responses. By definition these are communities which have a permanent population of at least 1,000.

The survey yielded a number of significant implications for storm hazard policymaking. Highlights of the more interesting and important of these implications are summarized below.

In contrast to the findings of much past research on natural hazards, storm hazard mitigation is of relatively high priority to elected officials in the localities surveyed. Over 46 percent of respondents indicated it was of high or very high priority to the local governing body in relation to other local issues, and over 70 percent indicated that it was of at least medium priority.

About one-half of the respondents (50.7 percent) indicated that their jurisdiction had adopted an explicit storm hazard reduction strategy, in addition to participation in the National Flood Insurance Program. The two most frequently selected objectives of this strategy (about 60 percent each) were (1) conserving the protective features of the natural environment and (2) increasing the ability of private structures and facilities to withstand storm forces. Guiding new private development into areas less susceptible to storm hazards was an objective in about 45 percent of the localities with an explicit storm hazard strategy.

About two-thirds of the responding localities are currently using shoreline protection works (bulkheads and seawalls), while sand-trapping structures (groins and jetties), sand-moving programs (beach nourishment and sand-scraping), and flood control works (dikes and channels) are each in use in about one-third of the localities.

Most localities have a building code in place and have met the elevation and floodproofing requirements of NFIP (about 90 percent each). A little less than half of the respondents indicated that they had adopted special storm-hazard-resistant building standards (47 percent). Only about 15 percent of the communities had adopted more stringent elevation and floodproofing provisions than those required under NFIP.

Most localities surveyed are using some type of development management. Approximately 70 percent indicated that they were currently using six or more of the twenty-one specific measures listed in the questionnaire. Roughly half of the communities fall in the six to ten measure range (55 percent).

Over 80 percent of the localities had enacted a comprehensive land use plan and zoning and subdivision ordinances. From 40 to 60 percent of the localities were using a capital improvement program, an evacuation plan, a shoreline setback, dune protection regulations, a policy to locate public structures and buildings in less hazardous locations, a policy to locate public facilities so as to discourage hazardous development, and the acquisition of undeveloped land in hazardous areas. Roughly 10 to 25 percent of the localities were using a hurricane/storm component in the comprehensive plan, a recovery/reconstruction plan or policies, a special hazard area ordinance, below-market taxation for open space, programs for the transfer of development potential from hazardous to nonhazardous parcels, the acquisition of development rights or scenic easements, hazard disclosure requirements in real estate transactions, and construction practice seminars for builders. Very few communities were using impact taxes or special assessments, acquisition of damaged buildings in hazardous areas, and building relocation programs.

Programs which strengthen buildings and facilities and development management programs are generally perceived to be more effective in reducing local storm hazards than programs which structurally alter the coastal environment.

The following ten development management measures were considered by respondents to be the most effective at reducing local storm hazards: special hazard area ordinances, impact taxes and special assessments, dune protection regulations, policies to locate public structures in safer locations, shoreline setback regulations, acquisition of undeveloped land in hazardous areas, evacuation plans, acquisition of damaged buildings in hazardous areas, programs which transfer development potential from hazardous to nonhazardous sites, and policies to locate capital facilities to reduce or discourage growth in hazardous areas. Several of the more conventional development management tools are considered to be less effective, including zoning and subdivision regulations, comprehensive/land use plans, and capital improvement programs.

Over 70 percent of the respondents believed their combined mitigation programs were either moderately effective or very effective.

In ranking the importance of different mitigative approaches, development management measures were considered to be most important in the majority of localities, followed by programs to strengthen buildings and facilities and programs to structurally reinforce the coastal environment, in that order.

From a list of eleven possible obstacles to the enactment of development management measures, the following five were most frequently identified, with each chosen by over 80 percent of those responding to the question: (1) the general conservative attitude toward government control of private property rights, (2) a general feeling that the community can "weather the storm," (3) lack of adequate financial resources, (4) the existence of more pressing local problems and concerns, and (5) the opposition of real estate and development interests. In addition, lack of trained personnel, lack of incentives or requirements from higher levels of government, opposition of homeowners and business interests, the absence of politically active individuals and groups advocating storm hazard mitigation, and inadequate or inaccurate flood insurance maps, while not as frequently selected, were indicated to be of high importance as obstacles.

An important argument against the enactment of development management identified by respondents is that such measures lead to increased development costs. Other arguments which were deemed important include: that decisions about risks from coastal storms are best left to the individual, that development management measures will dampen the local economy, and that particular development management measures are illegal or unconstitutional.

One-half of the respondents indicated that they had encountered problems in implementing or enforcing development management measures. Of these respondents the most frequently identified type of problem was that of insufficient funds. Public opposition, lack of support by public officials, lack of qualified personnel, and an insufficient data base were also indicated as problems by a significant portion of the respondents.

Approximately one-third of the respondents (33 percent) indicated that their localities had experienced negative consequences as a result of development management programs. The most frequent selection by an overwhelming margin was an increase in construction costs.

More than half of the survey respondents (55 percent) did not know how long it would take to evacuate their communities should a hurricane threaten. About one-half of these respondents were located in jurisdictions of less than 20,000 in population.

About 60 percent of the respondents indicated that their localities had experienced a hurricane or severe coastal storm since 1970. About one-third of the respondents in this group indicated that more stringent development management measures were adopted in response to these storms.

Notes

1. A list of localities containing V-zones was compiled from several sources. First, an initial list was acquired from the most recent FEMA "communities file"—the data set in which FEMA stores basic information required for NFIP administration. To obtain a more recent updating of this list, and to include jurisdictions which are currently being studied for V-zone designation (under the new wave height methodology), a second list providing the names of study consultants and localities being studied was used to supplement the communities file. FEMA officials indicated that between these two lists, 95 percent to 100

percent of V-zone localities would be obtained. As a double check, NFIP state coordinators in every relevant state were contacted and asked to provide an independent list of localities with V-zones in their state. This list was then compared with, and served to supplement, the above lists.

2. Each V-zone locality received a questionnaire in early June 1984. Approximately two weeks after this initial mailing a reminder letter was sent. After another two weeks, a second questionnaire with another reminder letter was mailed. Finally, for those localities which had not yet responded by late August, a letter asking them to indicate why they did not respond was sent. As of December 1, 1984, 420 survey responses had been received, for a preliminary response rate of 66 percent. From the final correspondence with those jurisdictions that had not responded, we attempted to learn whether we had inadvertently mailed questionnaires to localities which did not contain coastal storm hazards. From this we were able to eliminate fourteen nonhazard jurisdictions, bringing our overall survey population to 620. This in turn increased our overall response rate to about 67.8 percent. However, seventeen localities were deleted for consistency reasons, primarily because they contained less than 1,000 in population. This brought the final number of usable survey responses to 403 for a response rate of 66.9 percent (403 of 602).

3. It should be noted that because the data base here represents a population rather than a sample, tests to determine whether differences in effectiveness ratings are statistically significant have not been conducted.

References

Beatley, Timothy. 1986. *Influences on the Priority, Adoption and Effectiveness of Local Coastal Storm Hazard Mitigation.* Chapel Hill, N.C.: University of North Carolina, Department of City and Regional Planning.

Beatley, Timothy, David J. Brower, David R. Godschalk, and William M. Rohe. 1985. *Coastal Storm Hazard Reduction through Development Management: Results of a Survey of Hurricane-Prone Localities.* Chapel Hill, N.C.: University of North Carolina, Center for Urban and Regional Studies.

Drabek, Thomas, Alvin Mushkatel, and Thomas Kilijanel. 1983. *Earthquake Mitigation Policy: The Experience of Two States.* Boulder, Colo.: Institute of Behavioral Science, University of Colorado.

Rossi, Peter, James Wright, and Eleanor Weber-Burdin. 1982. *Natural Hazards and Public Choice: The State and Local Politics of Hazard Mitigation.* New York, N.Y.: Academic Press.

U.S. Army Corps of Engineers. 1975. *Guidelines for Identifying Coastal High Hazard Zones.* Galveston District.

8 Influences on Mitigation Priority, Adoption, and Effectiveness

Modeling Mitigation Decision Dynamics

Local decisions about the political priority of coastal storm hazard reduction and local decisions to adopt and effectively implement coastal storm hazard mitigation programs depend upon numerous social, political, and economic factors. In addition to case studies of individual hurricane-stricken localities (chapter 3) and surveys of all hurricane-prone localities (chapter 7), a third way to extend our understanding of the factors affecting local hazard mitigation is through statistical modeling of their influences on government decisions.

This chapter presents a causal model that tests the influence of critical factors on local mitigation decision dynamics.[1] The model analyzes influences affecting three outcomes of the decision process: (1) the *priority* of storm hazard reduction within communities, (2) the *adoption* of a development management program by local governments (a development management index),[2] and (3) the overall *effectiveness* of local mitigation measures. These outcomes are treated as dependent variables and data for them, as well as for the majority of independent variables included in the model, are obtained from the hurricane hazard survey reported in the previous chapter.

The model posits that priority, adoption, and effectiveness of mitigation and development management depend upon three types of influences: (1) *environmental* factors, (2) *policy catalyst* factors, and (3) *political conversion* factors. Significant environmental factors include measures of the political and cultural environment (extent of private property ethos, disaster culture), the economic and demographic environments (median home value, recreation/tourism-oriented economy, population size), and the physical environment (availability of nonhazardous sites, percent of the coastal floodplain already developed, percent of land within the floodplain, location on a barrier island). Significant policy catalyst factors include local measures (recent storm history, hurricane probability) and extralocal measures (status in the NFIP, number of years in the NFIP, state mitigation activity). Significant conversion process factors include characteristics of the local political system (absence of politically supportive groups, opposition of development interests) and technical capacity (planning respondent). In general form the model states that these three types of influences (independent variables) affect the three types of outcomes (dependent variables). Note that the dependent variables also affect each other (see figure 8.1).

Path analysis is the statistical technique used to analyze the relationships in the model. Path analysis combines the relationships among variables (expressed as regression equations) into a single conceptual framework and permits the computation of the indirect and direct effects which variables have upon one another, while controlling for other influences (Blalock 1961; Asher 1976; Pedhazur 1973). A three stage analysis was carried out testing influences on each outcome in turn.[3]

Many variables and relationships were tested, but only those that proved statistically significant were retained in the final model, which illustrates the significant paths or causal connections between critical variables. Table 8.1 presents those standardized regression coefficients

Figure 8.1   The Basic Model of Mitigation Dynamics

Influences   Outcomes
Independent Variables -------→ *Dependent Variables*

  1. Environmental Factors   1. Mitigation Priority

  2. Policy Catalyst Factors   2. Development Management
                                         Adoption

  3. Political Conversion Factors   3. Mitigation Effectiveness

Table 8.1   Mitigation Dynamics Model:
Statistically Significant Variables

	Dependent Variables[a]		
	Mitigation Priority[b]	Development Management Adoption[c]	Mitigation Effectiveness[d]
Environmental Factors			
Private property ethos	−.113	−.121	—
Median home value	—	.109	—
Recreation/tourism economy	.190	.175	—
Population size	—	.098	—
Availability of nonhazardous sites	—	—	.109
Percent floodplain developed	−.220	—	—
Percent land in floodplain	−.266	—	—
Barrier island location	—	—	−.127
Policy Catalyst Factors			
Recent storm history	.171	.097	−.157
Probability of hurricane	.195	—	—
NFIP program status	.151	—	—

a. Standard regression coefficients are statistically significant at the .05 level. Dashed marks indicate that variables were not statistically significant. The following variables were included in all three equations but did not prove statistically signficant in any: a seasonality index (percentage of local housing units that are seasonal), percentage population change from 1970 to 1983, new multifamily development in the 100-year floodplain, regional government activity, and planning personnel per capita. The opposition of homeowners variable was also included in the storm hazard priority and overall

or causal paths which were statistically significant at the .05 level. In the following sections relationships between each type of variable are discussed, and conclusions about the overall process then are presented.

Influence of Environmental Variables

Several environmental variables were found to be statistically significant. Environmental variables included political and cultural measures, economic and demographic measures, and physical measures.

Table 8.1   Continued

	Dependent Variables[a]		
	Mitigation Priority[b]	Development Management Adoption[c]	Mitigation Effectiveness[d]
Number of years in NFIP	.166	—	—
State mitigation activity	—	.174	—
Political Conversion Factors			
Absence of political support groups	−.202	—	—
Opposition of development interests	—	—	−.231
Planner respondent[e]	—	.124	—
Dependent Variable Cross Influences			
Mitigation priority	—	.141	.212
Development management adoption	—	—	.242

effectiveness equations but was not statistically significant. For a full explanation of
these variables, see Beatley 1986.

b. $R^2 = .3723$; adjusted $R^2 = .3356$.

c. $R^2 = .2134$; adjusted $R^2 = .1701$.

d. $R^2 = .2586$; adjusted $R^2 = .2070$.

e. The planner-respondent variable was included only in the development management
adoption equation.

Political and Cultural Measures

One of the most often mentioned influences on mitigation efforts is the
"private property ethos," involving objections to governmental regulation
of property. This exercises a significant negative influence both on the
priority of storm hazard reduction and the adoption of development
management measures.[4] It also exercises an indirect influence on the
effectiveness of a locality's mitigation efforts. This finding is consistent
with the more qualitative case study work reported in chapter 3.

This conservative, private property-oriented ethos clearly is an impediment to which proponents of coastal storm hazard reduction measures

must squarely face up. At the local level planners must find ways to heighten concern about storm hazards to make them consistent with the private property ethos. Recasting the mitigation problem in private sector/ private property terms should enhance its salience. Devising storm hazard mitigation solutions compatible with the protection of private property rights should enhance their political acceptability. For instance, regulatory proposals may have to involve adequate compensation for hazard area property owners who incur losses (for example, through TDR, land acquisition, etc.). The implications are similar for policymakers at higher levels.

Economic and Demographic Measures

Several variables within the economic and demographic environment category have significant influences in the causal model—population size, median home value, and recreation/tourist economic base. The economic base variable yielded relatively large positive influences on both the priority of storm hazard reduction and adoption of development management. This is an interesting result, counter to the expected finding. It was hypothesized that dependence on ocean- and hazard-oriented uses and activities would lead to a lower hazard priority, as well as to a lower tendency to adopt hazard mitigation programs which restrict these uses. This counterintuitive finding led to questions as to whether this particular variable was serving as a proxy for some other influence. Further analysis indicated a very high correlation between localities with a recreation/ tourist economic base and those which could be considered beachfront or oceanfront localities.[5] Thus it appears that one logical explanation is that this variable actually serves as a proxy for location with respect to storm risks, as these localities experience the cumulative effects of ocean derived hazards in much the same way that barrier island localities do.[6] It presents a contrast between tourist-oriented beachfront localities like Virginia Beach, Virginia, and nonrecreation/nontourist localities like Baytown, Texas, located further inland. If this interpretation is correct, it suggests that local planners in beachfront recreation-oriented jurisdictions are more likely to be successful at developing support for storm hazard reduction and the adoption of development management to accomplish it.

While the geographical location of a community is not a variable that can be manipulated, local planners in these jurisdictions should be aware of this influence on salience and be prepared to take advantage of it. Similarly, state and federal officials may wish to target their mitigation efforts here where storm hazard salience will tend to be greater. It also suggests the need to target efforts at increasing storm hazard awareness in coastal jurisdictions where the proximity to and presence of the storm hazard is not as obvious (for example, along sounds and bays where the piling-up effects of hurricanes and coastal storms can be devastating).

Population size was also found to have a positive influence on the adoption of storm hazard mitigation. The greater the population size of a locality, the more likely it is to have adopted development management measures, for instance. This is logical and suggests that such localities both have a greater experience and history of using such measures, and a greater relative need for them. The range of problems and public policy issues that must be addressed in these localities is much greater than in communities of smaller population size. Moreover, larger population size and larger planning staffs were highly correlated (and thus the latter variable was not included in the model), and it can be argued that the positive influence of population on mitigation adoption is at least partly a reflection of this. Population size did not, however, have a significant causal influence on either overall effectiveness or priority of storm hazard reduction.

The implications of the influence of the population variable are several. At the local level planners and policymakers in larger jurisdictions are more likely to find a more extensive package of mitigation tools already in place and at their disposal than are planners in smaller localities. These measures may be used in varying degrees to advance the goal of storm hazard reduction. Planners in larger places will generally have greater opportunities to integrate storm hazard reduction into the existing development management framework. Planners in smaller localities may have to start from scratch. For planners and policymakers at higher levels of government this finding suggests that different types of support services are required by localities of different population sizes. Planners in small localities are likely to need basic start-up assistance, which may range from the provision of model ordinances to assistance in land use mapping. Larger localities that are already doing a considerable amount of development management, and indeed which already have in place an extensive institutional and administrative framework, are going to find other types of assistance more beneficial. Assistance in the form of political and legal support for their efforts and ways of fine-tuning existing measures to storm hazard reduction objectives will tend to be of greater relevance and utility.

Consistent with expected outcomes, localities with higher median home values were more likely to have adopted development management measures. This can be explained in several ways. It may indicate the greater resources of these localities and thus their greater ability to formulate and enact such measures. It may also be that such measures are perceived to be of greater importance in such localities because the extent of property at risk is greater. It is also probable that more affluent communities are likely to exhibit a greater overall demand for the amenities that development management measures can bring about. This latter explanation is perhaps more plausible given that median home value did not yield a statistically significant influence on the priority of storm hazard reduction.

The influence of this home value factor implies that local planners in wealthier localities may have an easier time accomplishing hazard mitigation under the rubric of protecting the quality of life and the amenity values of the locality. They also are likely to find a greater level of resources and local support for development management. To the extent possible state and federal planners and policymakers should facilitate the incorporation of hazard reduction objectives into quality of life-oriented management measures in more affluent localities. In less affluent places hazard mitigation should be integrated with the economic development objectives which are more likely to be of local concern. At a state and federal level scarce mitigation resources should be directed toward demonstrating how development management can enhance economic growth in less-affluent localities that are less likely either to have the desire for or ability to develop development management programs.

Physical Measures

Variables in the physical environment had substantial influence on the priority of storm hazard reduction, as well as on the overall perceived effectiveness of mitigation efforts. The priority of storm hazard reduction is strongly influenced by the proportion of the jurisdiction which lies in the high-hazard floodplain area. The greater this proportion is, the higher will be the priority given to reducing the storm hazard. Where this proportion is smaller, the salience of mitigation will be lower.

From the analysis results a number of implications can be drawn. Local planners will have a harder time achieving local concern about the hazard threat and support for mitigation in jurisdictions where the hazard area is not large in relation to the locality's total land area. Additional efforts will be needed to enhance awareness in these localities. Policymakers at higher levels of government interested in increasing the local salience of storm hazards may be required to expend extra effort in these jurisdictions, assuming that the actual property and people at risk are not insignificant.

The analysis also indicates that the greater the proportion of the floodplain that is already developed, the lower will be the priority of storm hazard reduction. This supports the conclusions of Burby and French (1981) and Burby, French, et al. (1985). They suggest that where the hazard area is already heavily developed, there may be a prevalent belief that it is too late to do much mitigation. While this feeling may be largely accurate, opportunities for mitigation will still exist (for example, evacuation, reconstruction planning, structural reinforcement). Planners and public officials at all government levels should be aware of this tendency and adjust their strategies and policies accordingly.

Among the physical environment variables influencing overall effectiveness was the availability of nonhazardous development sites. The scarcer development sites outside the coastal floodplain, the less effective mitigation programs are considered to be. This is logical, as there would be little alternative in many localities but to permit the location of further development in the floodplain and, consequently, more property at risk. The result suggests that public officials should pay particular attention in such situations to encouraging "safer" development in these areas, for example, through better building standards, accessibility to storm shelters, ability to evacuate, and the like.

State and federal policymakers should be aware that in many localities where alternative nonhazardous parcels are not available, outside action by their agencies may be necessary to prevent development in hazardous areas of special value (perhaps to protect an important wetlands area or to ensure future public beach access, in addition to reducing storm hazards). These actions could range from the outright acquisition of such lands to their regulation through some mechanism such as Florida's Areas of Critical State Concern Program.

Location on a barrier island was found to have a negative influence on the overall effectiveness of existing mitigation programs. This is not surprising and indicates the pervasive nature of storm hazards there, while illustrating how difficult the barrier island mitigation problem is. It is logical that overall perceived effectiveness would be lower in these vulnerable but attractive areas. This finding supports the conclusion of barrier island experts (Platt, Pelczarski, and Burbank 1987) that state and federal policymakers ought to funnel additional resources and expertise into barrier island hazard mitigation.

Influence of Policy Catalysts

Several policy catalyst variables were statistically important in the causal analysis.[7] These variables were grouped under local and extralocal (federal, state, and regional) measures.

Local Measures

Recent storm history exercised the greatest cumulative influence and exhibited a statistically significant effect on the priority of storm hazard reduction, the adoption of development management, and overall effectiveness. This indicates the importance of storm events in enhancing the awareness of local officials and the public of the need for action to address these perennial hazards. Recent storms can create "windows of opportunity" during which adoption of mitigation programs will be more feasible. Thus planners in localities with a recent history of storm events will have an easier time. While this variable is not open to manipulation, the local planner can be prepared to take advantage of this natural increase in salience. For instance, disaster experts have argued for advance preparation of poststorm reconstruction plans, as well as mitigation provisions which will reduce the impacts of future events (Haas, Kates, and Bowden 1977; Rosenthal 1975). While implementing such programs may not be feasible before the hurricane or storm, they may be welcomed after the storm.

Because of the high salience and the receptive political climate that often accompany storm experiences, policymakers at higher levels of government may capitalize on such situations by (1) assisting and reinforcing the efforts of local planners and (2) taking direct state or federal mitigative actions that would normally be met with great opposition by local officials. The latter may include the acquisition of hazardous lands, the imposition of more stringent storm hazard planning requirements, or the movement of damaged structures to safer sites.

Of course, the reverse of this finding is that planners in coastal localities that are just as vulnerable to hurricanes and coastal storms will have a more difficult time in the absence of recent storm damage experience. The collective memory is often short and the planner may have to institute a general hazard awareness campaign before amassing support for storm hazard mitigation. Higher levels of government must continuously work toward increasing awareness of and concern for the storm threat.

Recent storm history also generates a sizable negative influence on the overall effectiveness of existing mitigation measures. This effect appears to be an issue of perception. Local officials and the public in general are in the best position to realize how ineffective their mitigation efforts really are in the aftermath of a hurricane or severe coastal storm. While this is not a variable that planners and policymakers can manipulate, again, the poststorm period may offer unique opportunities for enacting and implementing improved mitigation programs.

The probability of a hurricane strike, as expected, yielded a positive influence on the priority of storm hazard reduction. It is logical that localities where the chances of a hurricane strike are greater would in turn exhibit a greater hurricane hazard salience. This again suggests that location has a substantial effect on hazard salience. Local planners in these situations will, understandably, have an easier time reaching consensus about the need to address such hazards. Moreover, planners in these communities can focus their attention on translating salience or priority into tangible mitigation policies. Planners in localities where the hurricane probability is low will be required to spend more of their time on enhancing hazard salience. State and federal awareness campaigns can help here.

Extralocal Measures

Several extralocal policy catalysts were found to be significant in the model. Participation in the National Flood Insurance Program has a positive influence on storm hazard salience. While the direction of causation is debatable, it is plausible that involvement in this program will stimulate awareness and concern. Local planners should attempt to build upon this positive influence. Policymakers at higher levels should also consider the greater levels of storm hazard salience which may exist in localities with long histories of NFIP involvement.

As expected, the use of development management was greater in mitigation-active states.[8] Mitigation effects at the state level do in fact trickle down to the local level. As illustrated in chapter 5, states active in storm hazard mitigation are likely to exercise a number of different types of influences on local policymaking. These types range from actual requirements (for example, requiring that a local land use plan is prepared) to the provision of financial and political support. These results indicate that states should continue to perform these functions, albeit with perhaps more conviction and priority than has often been the case in the past. Planners and policymakers in states low in hazard mitigation efforts should strive for more activity and involvement.

Influence of Political Conversion Process

Several variables in the political conversion process were statistically significant.[9] These variables are grouped into those affecting balance of power and those related to technical capacity.

Balance of Power Measures

One of the largest path coefficients influencing the local priority of storm hazard reduction was obtained for the absence of politically supportive groups. The fewer such groups in the locality, the lower will coastal storm hazard priority tend to be. To overcome this impediment planners must nurture and encourage the participation of supportive groups in the political process. For instance, local environmental groups often have goals related to mitigation, and their support can enhance the salience of mitigation. Moreover, local groups, such as chambers of commerce or local taxpayer groups, can be encouraged to support reduction of storm hazards once they are able to see the connection to their own, more traditionally defined, interests. Local planners need to realize that concern about storm hazards may be eclipsed by other local issues with vocal supporters and that they must learn to cultivate political support. Officials at higher levels of government must also realize the clear importance of political support and orient their actions and outreach programs to develop and nurture these supportive political interests.

The largest and most definitive path coefficient from the overall effectiveness portion of the model is obtained for the opposition of development interests variable.[10] The greater this opposition, the less effective are mitigation programs. The case studies in chapter 3 support this thesis. The implications here are substantial. Local planners must work more closely with development interests to achieve effectiveness. They should recognize development concerns and seek to quell some of the natural antagonism which arises. For instance, local planners could streamline planning procedures to reduce the time it takes to gain development approval. The influence and power of development interests suggests that planners and policymakers may need to negotiate reductions in storm hazards from private development in a more quid pro quo manner. Take, for instance, new coastal setback provisions enacted in Myrtle Beach, South Carolina. Under these new regulations most new development must occur landward of a fifty-year erosion line. To relieve some of the burden of this setback requirement, a "setback impact allowance" is also incorporated. This provision allows a developer some relief from the additional sideyard setbacks required for buildings in development areas landward of the control line. The greater the proportion of the building lot affected by the control line, the greater will be the maximum height a building is allowed to be constructed before additional sideyard requirements are imposed.

Technical Capacity Measures

An early concern in designing the causal model was that the respondent's background, training, and governmental position would inject an element of bias into the results. Computing correlations between respondent position and the dependent variables did yield a significant relationship between planner-respondents and the development management index. Consequently, a planner-respondent dummy variable was included in the mitigation stage of the model to control for this bias. This variable exhibits a statistically significant positive influence on the adoption of development management.

Priority of Hazard Reduction and
Development Management Measures

Both storm hazard priority and the development management index were independent as well as dependent variables in the causal model. Storm hazard priority was found to exercise both a positive effect on the adoption of development management and the overall effectiveness of mitigation measures. The development management index was found to exercise a relatively strong positive effect on overall effectiveness, a relationship which did not exist for the other two major mitigation approaches—structural alteration and building strengthening. These relationships indicate, as well, that in addition to the direct effects exercised by the political, environmental, and other variables, indirect effects by these factors are also exerted through their impacts on the intervening variables of priority and adoption. For instance, while percent of the floodplain already developed does not exercise a direct effect on adoption of development management, it does exercise an indirect effect by influencing storm hazard priority, which in turn influences directly the adoption of development management.

The fact that the coefficient for priority of storm hazard reduction is not larger indicates that hazard mitigation measures often are adopted primarily to meet other equally legitimate local goals and objectives. Recognizing this has implications for planners and policymakers at all governmental levels who wish to encourage local efforts to reduce storm hazards. It suggests first that in many localities it may make more sense for planners to advocate mitigation programs for a variety of politically salable reasons. Moreover, it suggests that planners should look for ways to reduce storm hazards through mitigation programs which satisfy a number of local goals and objectives and respond to a range of local values. This might be described as "strategic dovetailing" (Beatley and Godschalk 1985). Coastal setbacks, for instance, are often a politically feasible form of coastal management because they respond to numerous local goals, including the protection of beach access and development of the local economy, in addition to reducing storm hazards. Planners interested in advancing the goal of coastal storm hazard reduction must also nurture the concern and interest of individuals and groups in the community who, while they may not be supportive of the goal of storm hazard reduction, will be supportive of programs which have as side-benefits the reduction of such local risks.

The development management index generates one of the largest and most significant path coefficients positively influencing overall effectiveness, confirming the descriptive results contained in chapter 7. Moreover, this finding confirms the intuitive expectation that the more extensive the development management package, the greater will be its effectiveness at reducing coastal storm hazards.

Critical Factors in Local Mitigation

Looking back at the results of the analysis, we can summarize the findings in terms of those factors that had a negative or blocking effect on mitigation decisions and those that had a positive or supporting effect. The significant *negative* environmental factors were percentage of the floodplain already developed (−.220), presence of barrier islands (−.127), and existence of a strong private property ethos (−.121; −.113). The significant negative policy catalyst factor was recent storm history (−.157).[11] The significant negative political conversion factors included the absence of politically supportive groups (−.202) and the opposition of development interests (−.231). Private property ethos negatively affected both priority and adoption dynamics. Percent of floodplain developed and absence of politically supportive groups negatively affected priority. Recent storm history, barrier island presence, and opposition of development interests negatively influenced effectiveness.

Many more factors contributed a positive effect. *Positive* environmental factors included median home value (.109), recreation/tourism economy (.175; .190), population size (.098), availability of nonhazardous sites (.109), and percent land in floodplain (.266). Positive policy catalyst factors were recent storm history (.171; .097), hurricane probability (.195), NFIP program status (whether or not the locality was in the "regular" program) (.151), number of years in NFIP (.166), and state mitigation activity (.174). The positive political conversion factor was planner-respondent (.124). Priority was positively affected by recreation/tourism economy, percent land in floodplain, recent storm history, hurricane probability, NFIP program status, and number of years in NFIP. Development management adoption was positively influenced by median home value, recreation/tourism economy, population size, state mitigation activity, and planner-respondent. Effectiveness was positively influenced by availability of nonhazardous sites.

The stage analysis also revealed significant positive influences. Priority of storm hazard mitigation had a positive effect on development management adoption (.141) and on overall effectiveness (.212). Development management adoption in turn had a positive effect on overall effectiveness (.242).

Underlying each community's mitigation decisions is a complex set of relationships among political, economic, and geographic factors. The findings from the causal model add to our understanding of the influence and importance of these factors on the priority of storm hazard reduction and the adoption and effectiveness of mitigation programs in hurricane-prone localities. Many of these factors are manipulable by policymakers, and even those that are not permit policymakers to understand better the causal framework and to focus their limited resources and energy on those factors which will have the greatest impact. Many of these findings support and reinforce the findings of other researchers in this area, while other findings provide new insight into the causal relationships which exist in coastal localities.

Notes

1. The model presented in this chapter is part of a larger model developed by Beatley (1986), as his doctoral dissertation at the University of North Carolina. Readers interested in details of the model specifications and the operational definitions of variables, as well as the outcomes of testing other relationships, may obtain this publication through University Microfilms. The conceptual structure of the model builds upon work on floodplain and land use analysis by Burby and French (1981).

2. The development management index variable is an additive variable of the specific development management measures identified in chapter 7.

3. Our model entails three stages, corresponding to each of the three dependent variables. In the first stage variables are tested for their influence on the priority of storm hazard reduction. Priority then becomes an independent variable in the second stage, which tests variables for their influences on the adoption of development management. Priority and adoption then become independent variables in the final stage, where influences on overall effectiveness are tested. Intermediate stages are not described here in order to simplify the statistical discussion and focus on the policy relevance of the findings.

4. A second political/cultural environment variable—disaster culture—also yielded a statistically significant coefficient. Disaster culture refers to the coastal resident's attitude that copes with hurricane threats through defiance and pride in ability to ride out the storm, rather than evacuating ahead of it (Moore 1964). The coefficient obtained for this variable was surprising, however, in that it was in the opposite direction than expected. It suggests, counter to our hypotheses, that the existence of such an attitude or philosophy will serve to enhance the adoption of development management programs rather than the reverse. A likely explanation for this result was that, as with opposition of development interests, this variable was measuring a response to the adoption of development management programs rather than a preexisting background condition. As a result, the variable was dropped from this stage of the model, although it is included in the other stages. A third environmental variable that was not statistically significant in any of the three stages was a seasonality index, reflecting seasonal population increases.

5. While a separate variable for beachfront location was not created, this observation was obtained from a direct printout and comparison of localities receiving high and low ratings on this variable.

6. This is an assumption, and it may be that local officials in these types of communities are actually more concerned about protecting tourists and recreational resources.

7. Policy catalyst variables that did not prove to be statistically significant in any of the three stages were: population change (1970–1983), new multifamily floodplain development, and regional government activity. Note that the variable evacuation time, included in earlier versions of this model, has not been included here.

8. As measured by whether or not a state-mandated coastal setback provision existed.

9. The political conversion variable of planning personnel per capita was also included in the model but was not found to be statistically significant in any of the three stages.

10. It should be noted that the conversion process variables of opposition of development interests and opposition of homeowners were not included in the adoption stage of the model. While these factors are still believed to negatively influence the adoption of development management programs, when they were included in prior analyses, they yielded coefficients in the opposite direction (that is, they were found to positively influence adoption). This was not logical, and it was concluded that these variables were measuring the results of local experiences with development management, rather than preadoption causal influences. In other words mitigation measures may need to be in existence before such opposition is apparent to the respondent. They were consequently deleted from this portion of path model but were included later in the effectiveness stage where this temporal problem does not exist.

11. Recent storm history had positive effects on priority and adoption and a negative effect on effectiveness.

References

Asher, Herbert A. 1976. *Causal Modeling*. Beverly Hills, Calif.: Sage Publications.

Beatley, Timothy. 1986. *Influence on the Priority, Adoption and Effectiveness of Local Coastal Storm Hazard Mitigation*. Chapel Hill, N.C.: University of North Carolina, Department of City and Regional Planning.

Beatley, Timothy, and David R. Godschalk. 1985. "Hazard Reduction through Development Management in Hurricane-Prone Localities: State of the Art." *Carolina Planning* 11, no. 1 (Summer): 19–27, 42.

Blalock, Hubert M. 1961. *Causal Influences in Nonexperimental Research*. Chapel Hill, N.C.: University of North Carolina Press.

Burby, Raymond J., Steven P. French, et al. 1985. *Floodplain Land Use Management: A National Assessment*. Boulder, Colo.: Westview Press.

Burby, Raymond J., and Steven P. French. 1981. "Coping with Floods: The Land Use Management Paradox." *Journal of the American Planning Association* 50, no. 4 (Autumn): 447–458.

Haas, J. Eugene, Robert W. Kates, and Martyn J. Bowden. 1977. *Reconstruction Following Disasters*. Cambridge, Mass.: MIT Press.

Moore, Harry E. 1964. *. . . and the Winds Blow*. Austin, Tex.: The Hogg Foundation for Mental Health.

Pedhazur, Elazar J. 1973. *Multiple Regression in Behavioral Research*. New York, N.Y.: Holt, Rinehart and Winston.

Platt, Rutherford, Sheila Pelczarski, and Barbara Burbank, eds. 1987. *Cities on the Beach: Management Issues of Developed Coastal Barriers*. Chicago, Ill.: University of Chicago, Department of Geography.

Rosenthal, John C. 1975. "Reconstruction After a Natural Disaster—A Need for Rapid Planning and Development." Paper presented to the AIP Conference, San Antonio, Texas.

9   Recommended Mitigation Policies and Strategies

The Importance of Coastal Storm Hazard Mitigation

If people were not attracted to the beauty and recreational potential of coastal areas, hurricane hazards would not be a problem. Yet because coastal areas are increasingly popular places in which to live and vacation, their population growth rate is three times that of the nation as a whole. Moreover, this growth and development is often attracted to the most hazardous and environmentally sensitive coastal areas—barrier islands. Barrier islands, and coastal areas in general, represent dynamic and environmentally complex ecosystems which, in their natural state, retreat before hurricanes and severe storms. Placing people and fixed property in these hazardous and dynamic areas spells the potential for catastrophic losses.

While the loss of human life associated with hurricanes has for a number of decades been on the decline, there is reason to believe that future death tolls may be much higher. As people flock to the coast, and as existing road and bridge systems become increasingly clogged, the ability to evacuate becomes severely constrained. Coupled with this is the fact that only marginal improvements in the prediction and forecasting of hurricanes can be expected in the future. Hurricane forecasting is an inexact science, and its shortfalls are accentuated by erratically moving storms, such as the recent Hurricane Elena where predicted and actual tracks were dramatically different.

Property losses also may soar. One projection estimated an annual loss from hurricanes in the year 2000 of $5.9 billion, topping all other natural hazard losses (Petak and Atkisson 1982). The private insurance industry has studied how they could respond to two successive $7 billion hurricane losses. Meanwhile, the anticipated rise in sea level could cause severe increases in coastal erosion over the next thirty to forty years, leaving much existing development awash (Titus 1984).

Future coastal catastrophes are not inevitable. While we have not found a way to avert the annual rash of Atlantic and Gulf coast hurricanes and severe storms, we have discovered ways to protect people and property from their most damaging effects. The most effective mitigation strategy is to manage growth and development so as to keep buildings and residents away from the most hazardous coastal areas where storm forces are the most destructive. While this sounds simple, it requires major changes and efforts within the organizations that make up our shared disaster governance system. These changes and efforts must take place in federal, state, and local governments, even though the visible outcomes appear only in local coastal communities. They are applicable to all storm-threatened shorelines, including not only those of the Gulf and Atlantic, but also those of the Pacific and Great Lakes.

This chapter sets forth our conclusions about the types of changes that are needed and the necessary efforts to carry them out at each level of government. While our major research focus is on the local level, we also have studied the federal and state contexts which shape and support local mitigation action. Despite our optimistic findings about the high level of local concern, the path-breaking programs of a few areas, and the increasing mitigation efforts by some federal and state agencies, we are painfully aware of the many remaining gaps in implementing a comprehensive national mitigation policy. This chapter first sketches the outlines of an effective national policy and then suggests effective implementation strategies. Looking at implementation from the bottom up, we first review what needs to be done by coastal local governments, and then what federal and state governments can do to spark effective local programs.

Coastal Storm Hazard Mitigation Policy Goals

To be effective, coastal storm hazard mitigation policy must influence a very complex policy arena. Such a policy must deal with both public and private decisionmakers within a multistate coastal region where economic incentives for hazard area development often overpower conservation incentives for preserving the natural environment and public safety incentives for mitigating storm hazards. Salient characteristics of this arena include the high-impact/low-probability form of the hazard, the intergovernmental setting for action, the dynamic structure of the shoreline hazard area, the growing need to move people and buildings out of harm's way, the traditional expectations about federal disaster relief responsibility, the catalytic role of public investment in coastal facilities, and the controversial need to intervene into the private development market to protect the public health and safety.

Having studied this arena and past policy in detail, we conclude that an effective national policy must be based on three actions:

1. Establishment of a comprehensive set of *coastal storm hazard mitigation performance standards*, against which state and local plans and programs can be assessed. Such standards would specify acceptable evacuation and shelter capacities relative to exposed populations; prestorm and poststorm development intensities within high-hazard areas; limits on public investments that increase risks of property damage; circumstances when relocation of exposed structures should be considered; conservation and enhancement of natural protective systems such as beaches, dunes, and wetlands; and minimum mitigation plan and program elements. These standards would be devised through a process involving representatives of all affected interests, perhaps using the negotiated rulemaking procedure employed in some recent federal programs (Susskind and McMahon 1985). Among these representatives would be state, local, and federal officials, coastal builders and developers, coastal scientists and planners, public and private insurance providers, and environmental conservationists.

2. Reorientation of *federal expenditures related to mitigation* to reward state and local programs that meet the performance standards. Such expenditures would use sliding scales based on the degree of compliance to determine federal flood insurance premium rates, public disaster assistance payments, coastal area infrastructure subsidies, beach nourishment assistance, and perhaps even economic development grants. The underlying principle would be that public funds would not be used to increase the level of vulnerability to coastal storm hazards. Only if this positive approach did not prove equal to the task would sanctions be invoked to

require compliance. This reorientation would require a major policy analysis by a qualified staff to identify the effects of various expenditures and to recommend alternative means of tying expenditures to conformance with mitigation standards.

3. Incorporation of the mitigation standards into the *state and local development management plans and programs* that actually guide coastal development. With the reinforcement of clear performance standards and positive expenditure incentives, state and local planners and policymakers could adopt and implement integrated development management and hazard mitigation plans. The presence of a consistent national policy based on protection of the public health and safety would help overcome the arguments against public intervention into the private development process within hazard areas. Defining the standards in terms of performance criteria rather than fixed specifications would allow for creativity and latitude in adopting the mitigation principles to a variety of state and local circumstances and needs. A mitigation network, including a national conference, workshops, newsletters, and demonstrations, could provide information exchange, research, and education support.

This sketch of fundamental needs for a comprehensive policy suggests a direction for reform of the present patchwork of policies affecting mitigation. It does not work out all the details of a new policy; many other actors must be involved in formulating that policy if it is to be accepted and implemented. In the meantime a number of individual actions can be taken by the governments involved to improve mitigation effectiveness, while we await such a new policy. The rest of this chapter addresses our recommendations for local, federal, and state strategies to improve mitigation practice.

Effective Local Mitigation Strategies

The single most effective local strategy for hurricane and coastal storm hazard mitigation is to incorporate mitigation objectives into a *multi-objective development management program*. Development management measures to reduce storm hazards can be "strategically dovetailed" with other local concerns and objectives to enhance their political salience and feasibility (Beatley and Godschalk 1985). For instance, the acquisition of hazard zone open space may not be politically or economically feasible when hurricane and storm hazard mitigation objectives are considered alone but becomes feasible when other local objectives, such as the need for recreational facilities and beach access, are considered as well. Development controls which reduce the density of development in high-hazard oceanfront areas may be difficult to justify exclusively on storm hazard reduction grounds but again may be feasible where other local goals (for example, aesthetic, recreational, traffic management) are advanced as well. Support for excluding seawalls and other forms of coastal armoring may be difficult to gain on the basis of their negative impacts on sand supply dynamics but becomes feasible in league with a beach preservation campaign.

Each locality must adopt a development management program suited to its particular circumstances. For instance, preferential taxation of open space may be an effective incentive to reduce development in hazardous sound and riverine areas but may not work in barrier island contexts where agricultural uses are minimal and the development value of land is very high. Capital facilities planning may not be an appropriate development management strategy in localities where all or most areas are already serviced (that is, where the potential for opening up new areas for development does not exist) but may work well in localities where large areas of undeveloped land exist.

Where communities face a lack of evacuation capacity, they could consider adopting ordinances limiting development in hazard areas to the capacity of evacuation routes, similar to Adequate Public Facility Ordinances that limit development to the capacity of major roads. They could set up hazard area impact fees or special taxing districts to pay for needed evacuation or vertical shelter improvements. In this way those who benefit from development within hazard areas would pay for the necessary protection, rather than transferring the costs to the taxpayer at large.

Local development programs need not be complex to be effective. A relatively simple yet properly written and strongly enforced zoning or subdivision ordinance, in company with a basic land use plan, may be all that is necessary to guide development away from hazard areas, especially in smaller jurisdictions. If provided with an adequate delineation of hazard areas and shoreline processes, such as erosion rates, then the small jurisdiction can build its mitigation program on a solid base of protecting the public health, safety, and welfare.

In larger or more complex localities, development management programs may need to draw from the full range of available techniques described in this book: (1) land use planning; (2) development regulation; (3) land and property acquisition; (4) public facilities/infrastructure policy; (5) taxation, fiscal, and other incentives, and (6) information dissemination. Each of the tools and techniques within these approaches involves certain benefits and limitations. We found many hurricane-prone localities not only using these techniques, but also rating them of higher effectiveness than traditional structural and other approaches to hurricane hazard mitigation.

Both simple and sophisticated development management programs are most effective when they acknowledge and protect the intrinsic mitigative features of the natural environment. For instance, sand dunes provide a degree of natural protection from storm waters and should not be allowed to be disturbed by development. Buildings should be placed not only well back from the shore, but also so that they do not undermine the natural integrity of the dune system. As another example, development management programs should be designed to protect the integrity of estuarine areas because these features of the coastal ecosystem serve as natural sponges, retaining and absorbing hurricane floodwaters.

Overcoming Local Adoption and Implementation Obstacles

Local mitigation programs can be difficult to adopt and effectively implement. Our survey and case study findings identified a number of local obstacles to hazard mitigation and development management. One of the most important problems is the lack of political leadership and a political constituency supporting hazard mitigation. Finding ways to encourage elected officials to embrace often thorny hazard mitigation issues and building coalitions of local interests willing to lobby for hazard mitigation and development management is crucial. Supporters must be prepared to face well developed opposing arguments.

Negative arguments tend to be of two types: (1) those which deal with the objective, usually economic, impacts of development management programs and (2) those which deal with normative and value issues, usually concerning individual rights. One argument of the first type holds out the specter of deleterious economic effects associated with development management programs. Restricting the amount and density of commercial and residential development on the beachfront, so the argument goes, will serve to significantly undermine the local tourist/recreational economy. Yet, in contrast to what we would expect from this argument, experiences by coastal localities with development management indicate that such programs instead enhance community attractiveness. Development management is in effect an approach to protecting the "goose that lays the golden eggs." However, often this first argument is only a smoke screen for the concerns of shorefront property owners. They see that while overall community economic benefits may increase, property values may shift inland to less hazardous second- and third-tier lots and away from their first-tier shorefront property. Depending on the political influence of these shorefront property owners, which can be substantial in small resort towns, existing land use patterns can be nearly impossible to change (Sturza 1987).

A common normative argument is that government has no legitimate right to interfere with the normal risk-taking behavior of individuals who wish to build and live in hazardous locations. This argument overlooks the government's obligation to protect the public safety. First, in most cases individual decisions to build in a particular coastal location, and in a particular way, can have many negative impacts on neighbors and the community as a whole. These external effects range from clogging evacuation routes to increasing flood damages to other structures (for example, debris turning into battering rams) to swelling disaster response and recovery costs. Since most individuals lack complete understanding of the nature and magnitude of storm risks, government intervention is justified (Beatley 1985). Recent surveys of Galveston Island residents, for example, indicated that they were grossly uninformed about the time it would take to evacuate the island in the event of a hurricane (Ruch and Christensen 1981). The obligation of government to protect the health, safety, and welfare of the public demands a strong mitigation function.

In many coastal localities opposition from real estate and development interests represents a substantial obstacle to the adoption and effective implementation of development management programs. Where the power of such interests is strong, public planners and others interested in promoting hazard mitigation may be forced to strike practical balances between development demands and mitigation needs. They may need to negotiate a quid pro quo arrangement, where developers may be permitted to build at somewhat higher densities if they incorporate mitigative features into their project locations and site designs. They may need to use development management techniques that clearly incorporate private interests. For instance, Transfer of Development Rights (TDR) may be a particularly feasible technique because it does not restrict the absolute amount of coastal development but simply reshuffles its location while allowing the hazard area owner to realize a monetary return from selling his development rights. Another possible approach is the use of the investment amortization concept in hazardous locations, similar to nonconforming uses in zoning ordinances. Property owners would be allocated an economic life span for their hazard area buildings, and after that period if they are destroyed by a hurricane, they would not be permitted to be rebuilt. Finally, another possible approach is to write into hazard area property deeds a statement that the shoreline is a moving edge and that owners who build there without sufficient room to move their buildings back from the approaching water (due to erosion, sea level rise, or storm damage) ultimately may lose their development rights. This would put waterfront property owners on notice that the beaches may move, leaving them without a buildable lot, as on the Galveston Beach after Hurricane Alicia.

Funding for local mitigation also constitutes an important obstacle. Coastal localities need dependable sources of income for their mitigation programs, particularly if they involve acquisition of land or development rights, relocation, or beach nourishment. They also need appropriations for continuing staff, technical studies, planning, and management. This funding may well come from the beneficiaries of mitigation programs. Coastal localities can establish special hazard area assessment districts or impact fees to fund mitigation. In North Carolina, localities can levy a hotel/motel occupancy tax for, among other purposes, coastal erosion control measures. While state and federal funding should not be overlooked, those local activities benefiting from hazard area locations also should bear a fair share of mitigation costs.

The technical capacity of localities is very important. A competent, energetic planning staff is crucial both to initiating a mitigation program and ensuring that the provisions of the program are implemented and enforced. A second technical aspect pertains to the knowledge and data base available to a community when formulating a development management mitigation program. It would be difficult, for instance, for coastal localities in North Carolina to manage and regulate development near shifting ocean inlets without an adequate understanding of their historical movement and natural dynamics. Developing this necessary data base takes special skills and resources. Myrtle Beach, South Carolina, for instance, conducted a shoreline erosion study which then served as the basis of a fifty-year erosion setback requirement. As a further example, the Nags Head, North Carolina, hurricane hazard property analysis was quite important in helping the town identify particular areas where development management should be focused, both prior to and following a hurricane or severe coastal storm. In addition this study helped convince local politicians of the vulnerability of the town and the need to plan for coastal storm hazards.

Planning for Poststorm Reconstruction

Our research indicates that despite the devastation and trauma associated with being hit by hurricanes, localities also enjoy opportunities to rebuild in ways which reduce the future chances of damages and loss of life. Public and private structures can be relocated, densities in high-damage areas can be reduced, and roads and sewer lines can be elevated (see the case studies in chapter 3; see also Haas, Kates, and Bowden 1977). Yet, we have found that few coastal localities are prepared to take advantage of these opportunities. More specifically, they lack the legal, institutional, and planning tools to effectively manage the political and economic forces at work following such a disaster.

Strong pressures exist to rebuild a devastated community in a rapid manner. Homeowners wish to restore their homes quickly and to return to a sense of normalcy; local businesses want to resume operations and reduce the loss of commercial revenue; and local government officials desire to minimize the impacts of storm damage on the tax base. An influx of outside funds, from insurance payments to federal disaster assistance, serves to fuel these rebuilding forces. Moreover, public officials are apt to assume natural "helping" roles, seeking to facilitate a rapid rebuilding and return to normalcy. Coastal localities must anticipate the presence of these powerful reconstruction forces and develop a planning and institutional framework to effectively guide and manage them so that important mitigation opportunities are not lost.

A number of development management measures that can be used in the aftermath of a hurricane or severe storm have potential for effectively guiding reconstruction. The poststorm redevelopment moratorium can be used to prevent premature reconstruction and can provide time for public reconstruction decisionmaking. The Texas Open Beaches Act, which prohibits rebuilding seaward of the vegetation line following a storm, is an example of using changes in the natural environment to guide reconstruction. The damage triage, which focuses resources on damaged areas most likely to benefit from them, is useful in managing redevelopment. Substantive decisions concerning appropriate mitigation actions can be addressed in advance of a hurricane through the preparation of a local poststorm reconstruction plan. Such a plan provides policy guidance which can relieve the heavy decisionmaking demands placed on public officials during reconstruction and serve as a politically useful device for resisting pressures from home owners and businesses for premature rebuilding. The reconstruction task force also holds much promise in assisting in the identification of specific mitigation opportunities during reconstruction. While the experience with such an institutional mechanism is not great, enough experience does exist to support its utility. Convened following a storm, the reconstruction task force can serve to effectively oversee poststorm damage assessments, implementation of the reconstruction moratorium, and application of the poststorm reconstruction plan, among other functions.

In addition to the immediate opportunities to rebuild in mitigative ways, the occurrence of a hurricane or severe coastal storm may create a supportive climate for the adoption of long-term mitigation measures. Our research findings indicate that recent storm experiences serve as positive causal influences on the adoption of hazard mitigation. Planners and public officials must be prepared to take advantage of these "trigger events" and the changes in the political climate that may result from them. The public awareness and political priority of storm hazard mitigation as a local issue may increase substantially in the aftermath of a hurricane, and this receptive local climate should be capitalized upon.

Federal Policy Support for Local Hazard Mitigation

To support local mitigation the most important change needed in federal policy is to *end public subsidies to private development in hazard areas.* Past federal programs often have encouraged and subsidized private development in vulnerable coastal areas. These subsidies have been provided through a number of programs including the provision of federal flood insurance (the National Flood Insurance Program), the federal funding of capital projects in coastal areas (for example, highways, sewer and water facilities), and the provision of disaster assistance funding for the rebuilding of damaged public facilities. Depending upon local needs and circumstances, different federal subsidies can determine the feasibility of risky development for both individuals and development firms. As we have seen, under the federal flood insurance program an individual building a home in a highly hazardous coastal location can receive insurance payments to rebuild it after innumerable flooding events. Acting in tandem, federal disaster assistance monies can be used to rebuild the public facilities, such as roads and sewer lines, that serve this development. Before the storm federal road and bridge subsidies can facilitate barrier island development, and federal flood insurance can facilitate projects lying in coastal floodplains.

Breaking the Build-Destroy-Rebuild Cycle

Only recently has the federal government acknowledged the need to get out of the business of subsidizing risky development and to break the past cycle of building-destruction-rebuilding. Congress took a major step in this direction when it enacted the Coastal Barrier Resources Act in 1982. This act prohibits the issuance of federal flood insurance and the provision of federal project grants for development in designated "undeveloped" barrier island units. It also places restrictions on the provision of disaster assistance in these areas. The act represents a positive effort to minimize the extent to which the public subsidizes risky development and represents a model for future policy (Godschalk 1987).

There are other changes which should be made in federal policy to minimize public subsidies to risky development. Federal provision of disaster assistance needs careful reconsideration both at a conceptual and programmatic level. These provisions grew out of a perceived need to offer financial assistance to individuals and state and local governments *overwhelmed* by a particular disaster. The law states that a presidential disaster declaration is only to be made in circumstances where the resources and capacity of the state to handle the disaster are exceeded.

Yet, this clear criterion often is ignored in practice. A case in point is Hurricane Diana, which struck the North Carolina coast in 1983. This storm did relatively minor damage, generating all told only $80 million in estimated damages. While a presidential disaster declaration was requested and easily granted, this did not appear to be a case where the resources of the state to deal with the disaster were exceeded. Substantial modifications to FEMA's disaster assistance regulations were proposed in 1986, which would have made it more difficult to declare a presidential disaster. These proposed changes would require FEMA to measure the fiscal capacity of states and localities in a disaster area. If the total damages in the state were less than a fixed proportion of state general revenues (adjusted by a comparison with national per capita income), a disaster declaration would not be recommended by FEMA. A state's past efforts at hazard mitigation would also be considered. These efforts to make states and local governments more responsible for mitigating damages from hurricanes and other natural disasters were not adopted, due in part to extensive state and local government opposition.

Many states and localities will seriously confront the inadequacies of their development policies only when they must bear significant responsibility for damages occurring in hazardous areas. Rather than tying disaster assistance to a state's ability to pay, we suggest that the disaster assistance cost-sharing ratio be related to the state's mitigation efforts, as mentioned earlier in this chapter. The change to a 75 percent federal/25 percent state and local cost-sharing ratio for public assistance funds increased state and local contributions and awareness of their responsibility. Basic principles of equity suggest that, as coastal states and localities benefit from hazard area development and have as well the powers necessary to prevent it from occurring in the first place, they should be expected to use their powers for the public benefit. If they chose not to do so, then they should not expect to receive large disaster payments in compensation for their inaction.

In future policy debates concerning the federal obligation to provide disaster assistance, it would be useful to consider a conceptual distinction between a true "disaster" and a regular, periodic natural event. There has always been a sense in which disaster assistance has been viewed as being "deserved," that is, that society has an obligation to provide for the needs of individuals in circumstances where unexpected and unavoidable tragedies occur. Such a position would support disaster assistance for a community devastated, say, by a tornado—a random and unavoidable event. Yet this logic does not apply in the same way to coastal storm hazards. Do residents of Dauphin Island, Alabama, for instance, "deserve" to receive federal public assistance funds to rebuild their roads after every hurricane or storm? In this context many hurricanes and coastal storms are not so much unanticipated national disasters as they are *recurring* events which should be mitigated by, or alternatively largely paid for by, local governments rather than the federal government. The objective should be to avoid compensating those who knowingly subject themselves to repeated storm damage.

Beefing Up Mitigation

The federal government, and specifically the Federal Emergency Management Agency, should strengthen its poststorm hazard mitigation requirements. At a minimum, adherence to and implementation of previous Section 406 mitigation plans should be a stringently applied requisite for receiving disaster assistance. FEMA's proposed disaster assistance regulations attempted to provide for this. In addition, FEMA should consider the imposition of mitigation requirements following a disaster, even when an earlier 406 plan does not exist. An excellent point at which this can occur is immediately following the issuance of the Interagency Hazard Mitigation Team's preliminary report. These Interagency Mitigation Teams provide a quick and creative analysis of the mitigation opportunities which exist following a hurricane and typically recommend specific actions that should be taken by state and local governments to seize these opportunities. FEMA should increasingly hinge the provision of postdisaster assistance on the good faith efforts of states and localities to implement these recommendations.

Certain FEMA public assistance regulations have come under fire in the past for their negative effects on mitigation efforts. These past regulations virtually required public facilities and structures to be rebuilt as they were prior to the disaster. If a community wished to rebuild a public road or sewer in a safer location, but the costs of this reconstruction were substantially greater than rebuilding in the same spot, the community was prevented from even using its own funds to pay the additional expenses. The proposed new "disaster-proofing" criteria would have corrected this problem by permitting the locality to spend whatever amount of its own funds would be necessary. Facility mitigation efforts during redevelopment should be strongly encouraged under future federal policy.

The postdisaster use of the Interagency Hazard Mitigation Team should also be applied to predisaster mitigation exercises. FEMA should make such expert teams available to coastal localities for a prestorm hazard mitigation "audit." The team would operate much as it does in the aftermath of a hurricane but would focus on the identification of current, prestorm mitigation opportunities, as well as on opportunities that localities should be prepared to take advantage of following the next storm. Such a program could lead to better mitigation planning on the part of local governments and long-term reductions in the loss of property and human lives. Visits by the predisaster audit mitigation teams could be funded on a cost-sharing basis among the state and locality and FEMA.

Finally, the technical underpinning for mitigation should be strengthened. More funding is needed for the Hurricane Preparedness Planning Program. These analyses of the vulnerability of both people and property are needed as soon as possible in order to enable local decisionmakers to incorporate them into their development management and hazard mitigation efforts before the storm. Coastal flood hazard maps, believed by some to understate the degree of actual storm risk, need to be updated. Provision of this data base is a critical form of federal support for effective local mitigation.

Giving Relocation a Chance

FEMA has at its disposal some underused programs which could fuel major local mitigation initiatives if given a chance. The Section 1362 flooded properties purchase program is perhaps the most promising of these. Under this program the federal government can provide funds for the purchasing of land and damaged structures in the aftermath of a serious hurricane or flooding event. The intent is to prevent the rebuilding of such structures if it is likely that they will be flooded and damaged in the future. Relocating these residents to safer locations is a fiscally responsible action for FEMA to take, as future flood insurance claims will be reduced and the extent of future federal liability for such damages will be lowered. The Baytown, Texas, relocation project following Hurricane Alicia (described in chapter 3), illustrates the potential role this approach could play in reducing future storm damages.

The major problem in implementing the 1362 program has been inadequate funding. Relatively small amounts of money have been appropriated for this program in the past, relative to the need. This 1362 funding level must be increased substantially; the action could be viewed as shifting funds from future disaster relief payments to current hazard mitigation which will reduce the need for future disaster relief. A second problem, related to the first, is that 1362 monies do not go very far in coastal areas because of the high market value of property in these locations. Some FEMA officials have indicated that they do not recommend use of the 1362 approach in coastal areas for this reason. The reverse of that argument is that such high property value is also indicative of the higher value of the property which would be safeguarded against future hurricanes and storms. These 1362 funds should be used selectively in coastal hazard areas, perhaps in league with other state and local programs, such as beach access, where cost-sharing arrangements would increase the impact of limited federal dollars. A final problem is the requirement of "substantial damage" before 1362 applies, relegating it to reactive uses after the disaster has occurred. If eligibility were broadened to include structures with documented high probability of *future* substantial damage, more could be done to prevent loss. Coupled with priority for projects with cost-shared funding that were covered by an adopted mitigation plan, section 1362 could become a major incentive to act prior to extensive losses.

In May 1986 the Coastal States Organization approved a strong policy statement in favor of relocation for existing structures in high-hazard coastal areas. Specifically, it recommended studying a number of possible alternatives for accomplishing this including, "but not limited to, making relocation of eminently endangered structures an eligible expense under the federal flood insurance program, setting aside a percentage of flood insurance premiums for mitigation and loss prevention programs, establishing a trust fund for loss mitigation programs, integrating relocation into recreation and open space acquisition programs, and reviewing state and local regulatory and planning programs that facilitate or impede damage prevention" (Coastal States Organization 1986, p.2). Recommended in the policy statement, as well, is the initiation of one or more large-scale demonstration projects to test the cost and feasibility of relocation and other damage prevention strategies, and the elimination of public financial investments, tax laws, and other programs which reduce the incentive for property owners to avoid future disaster losses. This strong statement by the coastal states indicates a strong consensus about the need for relocation and the political importance of programs like 1362.

Another way to address this problem was proposed by Congressman Walter Jones of North Carolina as an amendment to the 1987 Housing Act.[1] Under this proposal state and local governments could declare a structure eminently endangered, and then its relocation would become an eligible insurance loss claim, provided it was relocated behind the thirty-year erosion setback and the cost was not greater than 40 percent of its insured value. If it were not relocated within a reasonable time and then suffered damage, its claim would be limited to the same 40 percent. The benefits of this approach are that it does not require an appropriation since it is financed through insurance premiums, it holds future premiums down by limiting future claims, and it is directly related to other mitigation methods, such as coastal setbacks.

Consistent with increased use of the 1362 program, FEMA should consider reinstating its informal policy of constructive total loss. This policy —permitting an insurance claim for the full value of a damaged structure that is not to be reoccupied, even where an actual total loss does not exist—would reduce the amount of future coastal property at risk. While this policy lost favor several years ago, it is time for FEMA to reintroduce the concept into its mitigation arsenal.

Reorienting the Flood Insurance Program toward Mitigation

The availability of federally subsidized flood insurance is often seen as a major incentive for hazardous coastal development. While this in many ways could be described as a "chicken and egg" issue, our research indicates that major changes in the way in which the NFIP is administered are, indeed, in order. At a broad philosophical level we believe that FEMA should attempt to manage the NFIP more like a conventional, private insurance company, with careful scrutinizing of high-risk policyholders. Insurance premiums should reflect differential risks, and the efforts of individuals, states, and localities to reduce storm risks should be reflected in these rates.

FEMA should also ensure that mitigation requirements are strongly enforced, including insurance cancellation for both individuals and governments if mitigation requirements are not met. FEMA's attempts to recover insurance payments from localities through subrogation suits should be continued in the future. Localities wishing to participate in the NFIP should understand that FEMA will hold them accountable for any past negligence in enforcing or implementing NFIP requirements. FEMA should also adopt a more stringent position with respect to providing public assistance to nonparticipating communities following hurricanes and storms. Following Hurricane Elena, for instance, the Florida community of Cedar Key was provided full disaster assistance even though it was not participating in the NFIP at the time of the storm. This type of leniency will discourage localities from participating in the NFIP in the first place or from fully enforcing its land use requirements.

We support FEMA's efforts to tie local mitigation effort to reductions in individual policy premiums. Coastal policyholders might be given a lower flood insurance rate, for instance, in a locality where mitigation and posthurricane reconstruction plans had been prepared. Even lower rates might be given to policyholders in localities which had enacted restrictive coastal development regulations.

FEMA should not be timid in identifying levels of risk beyond which it will not insure. It should consider the extent to which insuring structures in V-zones, for example, is simply an unacceptably high risk. Consistent with this philosophy, occasions may arise where, just as an automobile insurance company might cancel a policy, FEMA should consider terminating unacceptably risky existing policies (for example, after successive major storm damage events). The knowledge of such a possible action could encourage more responsible coastal development, just as it encourages safer drivers in the case of automobile insurance.

Stronger State Mitigation Programs

A major conclusion of our study is that state governments play vital roles in promoting safer patterns of coastal development. States can directly regulate coastal development, providing consistent coastwide mitigation. For example, North Carolina's permitting system for development in Areas of Environmental Concern (AECs) represents an effective state action to safeguard coastal development. As part of this system North Carolina has enacted a rigorous coastal setback provision, substantially reducing the vulnerability of development along their shores to storm hazards and erosion.

States can frame and guide local planning and development regulation. Through the imposition of local planning requirements states set common planning "ground rules" that all localities must adhere to. Increasingly these mandatory planning requirements incorporate explicit consideration of hurricane and coastal storm hazards. The North Carolina CAMA hurricane hazard mitigation and reconstruction standards, and the provisions of Florida's 1985 growth management package, illustrate the type of rule-setting appropriate in coastal states. Such state-mandated planning requirements also change the texture of local politics in favor of planning. That is, supportive individuals and groups in the community can now point to the state requirements as a rationale for undertaking such activities, whereas prior to such requirements the local political costs of supporting such provisions might be high. State requirements act as a sort of "political lightning rod," serving to redirect political opposition and antagonism away from local officials.

State standards also can ensure equity in coastal development management. A single locality contemplating the adoption of mitigation measures may consider it unfair that other coastal localities are not required to undertake similar actions. A set of common state standards ensures that all coastal localities enforce the same mitigation standards.

States can encourage and facilitate local mitigation through funding and technical support. This assistance ranges from providing planning monies to providing field support for local delineation and monitoring of hazard areas to the provision of funding for acquisition of coastal high-hazard lands. At the state level it is possible to justify the technical and legal staff work necessary to develop model hazard management tools for use by localities in the field. In order to provide these support services on a reliable, long-term basis, states need to find sources of continuing funding for them. One possible approach is the creation of a state trust fund for hurricane and coastal storm hazard mitigation. Ideally such funds would be collected from coastal activities benefiting directly from their coastal locations.

State infrastructure and public investment policies can have a substantial influence on local coastal development patterns in the same way that federal programs do. Coastal states must begin to acknowledge these influences and take actions to ensure that such state investments do not undermine local and state mitigation programs. Florida has been the most active in this area, most recently through the coastal infrastructure policies contained in its 1985 growth management package. States should begin to develop policies which restrict public investment in high-hazard areas, much as the Coastal Barrier Resources Act does at the federal level.

State-created regional agencies also can facilitate hurricane and coastal storm hazard mitigation. Coordinating local government actions through a regional agency helps to overcome the problems of political and geographic fragmentation often found in coastal areas. The most extensive experience with regional agency involvement in coastal storm hazards planning has been in Florida, primarily in the area of regional evacuation planning. However, regional agencies have increasingly been active in ensuring that local development management decisions adequately incorporate storm hazard planning. These experiences, and the limited experiences of other regional agencies such as South Carolina's Coastal Commission, suggest that these governmental units can play important roles. They can provide technical expertise and manage data bases for development management and hazards planning; they can provide institutional mechanisms for coordinating the mitigative efforts of a number of localities; and they can help to enhance the political salience and legitimacy of hurricane and storm hazard mitigation and development management.

Averting Coastal Catastrophe: A Final Word

In the final analysis, whether or not the United States suffers a crushing coastal storm disaster in the future is both in and out of our hands. The probability of a killer hurricane striking a coastal area is not reducible by human action. The likelihood of massive erosion from sea level rise allowing a hurricane surge to inundate a coastal area is tied to forces we do not know how to control. What we can manage is how we build on the coast. The clear answer to the question of how to mitigate potential future coastal disasters is to manage coastal growth so as to keep people and property out of harm's way. This demands that mitigation policy be taken more seriously throughout the shared governance system responsible for coping with disaster. At the local level mitigation must be integrated into day-to-day development management decisions. At the federal level policies that encourage development in vulnerable coastal hazard areas must be turned around, and programs spurring local mitigation must be devised. And at the state level political and budgetary priorities must account for coastal disaster mitigation. Nothing less is justifiable in the face of the size of the threat.

Notes

1. This was adopted on Feb. 5, 1988, as Section 544 of the Housing and Community Development Act of 1987, PL 100-242 (100 Stat 1850).

References

Beatley, Timothy. 1985. "Paternalism and Land Use Planning: Ethical Bases and Practical Applications." In *The Restraint of Liberty*, edited by Thomas Attig, Donald Callen, and John Gray. Bowling Green, Ohio: Bowling Green State University.

Beatley, Timothy, and David R. Godschalk. 1985. "Hazard Reduction through Development Management in Hurricane-Prone Localities: State of the Art." *Carolina Planning* 11, no. 1 (Summer): 19–27, 42.

Coastal States Organization. 1986. "Policy Position: Existing Development in High Hazard Areas." Washington, D.C.

Godschalk, David R. 1987. "The 1982 Coastal Barrier Resources Act: A New Federal Policy Tack." In *Cities on the Beach: Management Issues of Developed Coastal Barriers*, edited by Rutherford Platt, Sheila Pelczarski, and Barbara Burbank. Chicago, Ill.: University of Chicago, Department of Geography.

Haas, J. Eugene, Robert W. Kates, and Martyn J. Bowden. 1977. *Reconstruction Following Disaster*. Cambridge, Mass.: MIT Press.

Petak, William, and Arthur Atkisson. 1982. *Natural Hazard Risk Assessment and Public Policy*. New York, N.Y.: Springer-Verlag.

Ruch, Carlton, and Larry Christensen. 1981. *Hurricane Message Enhancement.* College Station, Tex.: Texas A&M.

Sturza, R. P., II. 1987. "The Retreat Alternative in the Real World: The Kill Devil Hills Land-Use Plan of 1980." In *Cities on the Beach: Management Issues of Developed Coastal Barriers,* edited by Rutherford Platt, Sheila Pelczarski, and Barbara Burbank. Chicago, Ill.: University of Chicago, Department of Geography.

Susskind, Lawrence, and Gerard McMahon. 1985. "The Theory and Practice of Negotiated Rulemaking." *Yale Journal of Regulation* (Fall).

Titus, James G. 1984. "Planning for Sea Level Rise Before and After a Coastal Disaster." In *Greenhouse Effect and Sea Level Rise,* edited by Michael C. Barth and James G. Titus. New York, N.Y.: Van Nostrand Reinhold.

Appendix. Survey Questionnaire

Instructions: Please answer the following questions for your planning jurisdiction. Note that we have used the term *severe coastal storm* throughout. This is meant to include hurricanes, northeasters and tropical storms. The term *development management* includes programs and policies which control or influence the location, density, timing and type of development which occurs in a jurisdiction. The term *hazard reduction* refers to decreases in the potential loss of life and/or property damage from a hazard such as a severe coastal storm.

If there are any questions which you cannot answer, please feel free to consult with others who may be able to provide the answer. Where detailed information is called for, but unavailable, please estimate.

1. How would you rank the priority given by your jurisdiction's governing body to the threat of severe coastal storms in comparison with other local issues? (circle one)
   1) Very High Priority
   2) High Priority
   3) Medium Priority
   4) Low Priority
   5) Very Low Priority

2. Approximately what percentage of your jurisdiction's land area lies in the 100-year coastal floodplain (i.e., V-zones and A-zones subject to coastal flooding under the National Flood Insurance Program)? (circle one)
   1) Less than 5%
   2) 5-19%
   3) 20-49%
   4) 50-79%
   5) 80-100%

3. How much of the 100-year coastal floodplain (i.e., V-zones and A-zones subject to coastal flooding) in your jurisdiction is now *developed* (land which has been converted from its natural state)? (circle one)
   1) Less than 5%
   2) 5-19%
   3) 20-49%
   4) 50-79%
   5) 80-100%

4. What is the *most common type of land use* now in your jurisdiction's 100-year coastal floodplain (i.e., V-zones and A-zones subject to coastal flooding)? (circle one)
   1) Single Family Detached
   2) Multi-Family
   3) Commercial (Including Private Recreational, Hotel/Motel)
   4) Industrial
   5) Public Recreational/Park Land
   6) Other (Specify)

5. What are the types of *new development* that have occurred in the 100-year coastal floodplain (i.e., V-zones and A-zones subject to coastal flooding) in the *last five years*? (circle all that apply)
   1) Single Family Detached
   2) Multi-Family
   3) Commercial (Including Private Recreational, Hotel/Motel)
   4) Industrial
   5) Public Recreational/Park Land
   6) Other (Specify)

6. Approximately what percentage of the *total dollar value* of new development occurring in your jurisdiction in the *last five years* has located in the 100-year coastal floodplain (i.e., V-zones and A-zones subject to coastal flooding)? (circle one)
   1) Less than 5%
   2) 5-19%
   3) 20-49%
   4) 50-79%
   5) 80-100%

7. How abundant are residential development sites outside of the 100-year coastal floodplain (i.e., V-zones and A-zones subject to coastal flooding)? (circle one)
   1) Very Scarce
   2) Scarce
   3) Moderately Scarce
   4) Abundant
   5) Very Abundant

8. Does your jurisdiction have an *explicit* storm hazard reduction strategy in addition to participation in the National Flood Insurance Program? (circle one)

1) No
2) Yes

9. If yes, which of the following are its *objectives?* (circle all that apply)

1) Guiding new *private* development into areas less susceptible to storm hazards
2) Locating new *public* facilities and structures in areas less susceptible to storm hazards
3) Relocation of existing *private* development into less hazardous areas
4) Relocation of existing *public* facilities and structures into less hazardous areas
5) Increasing evacuation capacity
6) Provision of adequate storm shelters
7) Increasing ability of *private* structures and facilities in hazardous areas to withstand storm forces
8) Increasing ability of *public* structures and facilities in hazardous areas to withstand storm forces
9) Structurally altering and/or reinforcing the coastal environment (e.g., seawalls, bulkheads)
10) Conserving protective features of the natural environment (e.g., dune protection)
11) Other (specify)

We would now like to ask you several questions about the specific programs and policies in place in your jurisdiction which may contribute to the reduction of coastal storm hazards. *Please answer these questions even if your jurisdiction has no explicit storm hazard reduction strategy.*

Information is requested on three types of programs: those which *structurally alter the coastal environment* and increase its ability to resist storm forces; those which *strengthen buildings and facilities* to better withstand storm forces; and those which reduce storm hazards through *development management* designed to control or influence the location, density, timing and type of development.

10. Following are programs which *structurally alter the coastal environment.* Indicate which of the following *are currently in use in your jurisdiction* and, if they are used, to what extent they reduce local vulnerability to storm hazards (from 1 = Don't reduce hazards at all to 5 = Reduce hazards very much).

1) Sand-trapping structures (e.g., groins, jetties)
2) Sand-moving programs (e.g., beach nourishment, beach scraping)
3) Shoreline protection works (e.g., bulkheads, seawalls, revetments)
4) Flood control works (e.g., dikes, channels, retaining ponds)
5) Other (specify)

11. Following are programs and policies which *strengthen buildings and facilities* to better withstand storm forces. Indicate which are *currently in use in your jurisdiction* and, if they are used, to what extent they reduce local vulnerability to storm hazards (from 1 = Don't reduce hazards at all to 5 = Reduce hazards very much).

1) Building code
2) Special storm-resistant building standards (e.g., wind-resistant standards)
3) Minimum elevation and flood proofing standards required under National Flood Insurance Program
4) Elevation and floodproofing standards more extensive than required by National Flood Insurance Program
5) Floodproofing of public facilities and structures (e.g., sewer and water, roads, utilities)
6) Other (specify)

12. Following is a list of plans, programs, and policies which *guide and manage development*. Indicate which are *currently in use in your jurisdiction* and, if they are used, to what extent they reduce local vulnerability to storm hazards (from 1 = Don't reduce hazards at all to 5 = Reduce hazards very much).

Planning
1) Comprehensive or land use plan
2) Hurricane/storm component of comprehensive or land use plan
3) Capital improvements program
4) Recovery/reconstruction plan or policies
5) Evacuation plan

Development Regulation
6) Zoning ordinance
7) Subdivision ordinance
8) Dune protection
9) Shoreline setback
10) Special hazard area ordinance

Public Facilities Policy
11) Location of capital facilities to reduce or discourage development in high hazard areas
12) Location of public structures and buildings (e.g., hospitals, schools) to reduce extent of risk to public investments

Taxation, Financial, Other Incentives
13) Reduced or below-market taxation for open space and non-intensive uses of hazard areas
14) Impact tax or special assessment to cover the additional public costs of building in hazard zone
15) Transfer of development potential from hazardous to nonhazardous sites (e.g., clustering, planned unit development)

Public Acquisition
16) Acquisition of undeveloped land in hazardous areas (e.g., for open space)
17) Acquisition of development rights or scenic easements
18) Acquisition of damaged buildings in hazardous areas
19) Building relocation program (moving structures)

Information Dissemination
20) Hazard disclosure requirements in real estate transactions
21) Construction practice seminars for builders
22) Others (specify)

13. Please *rank* the following three approaches according to their overall importance in reducing storm hazards in your jurisdiction (i.e., 1 = most important; 3 = least important).
    1) Structural Reinforcement of Coastal Environment
    2) Strengthening Buildings and Facilities
    3) Development Management

14. How would you rate the *combined* effectiveness of the programs and policies identified in questions 10, 11, and 12 at reducing storm hazards in your jurisdiction? (circle one)
    1) Very Effective
    2) Moderately Effective
    3) Slightly Effective
    4) Not Effective

15. Have you had any *problems in enforcing or implementing* the development management programs and policies listed in question 12? (circle one)
    1) No
    2) Yes

16. If yes, which of the following have been problems? (circle all that apply)
    1) Insufficient Funds
    2) Lack of Qualified Personnel
    3) Insufficient Data Base
    4) Public Opposition
    5) Lack of Support by Public Officials
    6) Other (specify)

17. Have any *undesirable consequences* resulted from the development management programs and policies listed in question 12? (circle one)
    1) No
    2) Yes

18. If yes, which of the following have been experienced? (circle all that apply)
    1) Increase in Construction Costs
    2) Reduced Land Values
    3) Reduced Tax Revenues
    4) Slowed Economic Growth and Development
    5) Other Consequences (specify)

19. We are interested in learning more about the *obstacles to the enactment* of development management measures which reduce storm hazards in your jurisdiction. Have any of the following been obstacles in your jurisdiction? (Circle appropriate numbers: 1 = not important to 5 = very important.)

1) Opposition of business interests
2) Opposition of real estate and development interests
3) Opposition of homeowners
4) Absence of politically active individuals and groups advocating hurricane/storm mitigation
5) More pressing local problems and concerns
6) General feeling that community can "weather the storm"
7) General conservative attitude toward government control of private property rights
8) Lack of adequate financial resources to implement mitigation programs
9) Lack of trained personnel to develop mitigation programs
10) Lack of incentives or requirements from higher levels of government
11) Inadequate or inaccurate federal flood insurance maps
12) Other (specify)

20. Following are some *arguments* often cited in opposition to the enactment of development management measures to reduce storm hazards. How important have these been in your jurisdiction? (Circle appropriate numbers: 1 = not important to 5 = very important.)
    1) Development management measures dampen local economy
    2) Development management measures lead to increased development costs
    3) Decisions about risks from coastal storms are best left to the individual
    4) Particular development management measures are illegal or unconstitutional
    5) Other (specify)

21. Has your jurisdiction been hit by one or more severe coastal storm *since 1970* (i.e., hurricanes, tropical storms, and northeasters which have caused substantial property damage)?
    1) No
    2) Yes

22. If Yes, please indicate below the name and date of the *most recent* and *most damaging* hurricane/storm during this period. (If most recent is also most severe, write the word "same.")

23. Were stronger or more stringent measures to manage development adopted following either or both of these storms?

24. How familiar are you with sources of state government assistance to localities for storm hazard management? (circle one)
    1) Very Familiar
    2) Somewhat Familiar
    3) Neither Familiar nor Unfamiliar
    4) Somewhat Unfamiliar
    5) Very Unfamiliar

25. Has your local government received any of the following types of storm hazard management assistance from state government in the past five years? (circle all that apply)

1) Floodplain Maps
2) Hydrologic Data
3) Information on the National Flood Insurance Program
4) Help with Storm Drainage Problems
5) Help with Disaster Preparedness Plans
6) Help in Administering Hazard Area Regulations
7) Grants or Loans for Construction of Storm Protection Works
8) Grants or Loans for Acquisition of Hazard Area Property

26. During the past year, has your local government had any of the following types of contact with state government personnel concerning storm hazard management? (circle all that apply)
1) Personal Visits (Face-to-Face Contact)
2) Telephone Contacts
3) Correspondence Related to Storm Hazard Management
4) Received Technical Reports on Hurricane Hazard Mitigation
5) Other (Specify)
6) None of the Above; No Contact during Past Year.

27. Overall, how would you rate storm hazard management assistance available from state agencies? Is it . . . (circle one)
1) Adequate to Meet Local Government Needs
2) Barely Adequate to Meet Local Government Needs
3) Inadequate in Relation to Local Government Needs
4) Don't Know

28. Is there a *regional agency* involved in local storm hazard mitigation in your area (e.g., a council of government, regional planning agency)? (circle one)
1) No
2) Yes

29. If Yes, have they . . . (circle all that apply)
1) Prepared a regional evacuation plan
2) Prepared a regional hazard reduction plan
3) Modeled or simulated potential storm impacts for the region (e.g., using a SLOSH model)
4) Assisted your jurisdiction in developing a storm hazard management plan
5) Other (specify)

30. Please indicate the approximate *peak* and *permanent* populations for your jurisdiction in 1983.

31. Do you know approximately how long it would take to *safely evacuate* your jurisdiction, assuming peak population, should a hurricane threaten? (circle one)
1) No
2) Yes   If Yes, how long: _____ hours

32. What is the approximate number of full-time staff in your planning department?

33. What was the total value of all building permits issued in your jurisdiction in 1983?

34. How many square miles are there in your jurisdiction?

35. Rate the following according to their importance to your jurisdiction's economic base. (Circle appropriate numbers: 1 = not important to 5 = very important.)

    1) Tourism and Recreation
    2) Manufacturing
    3) Service and Trade
    4) Retirement
    5) Fishing
    6) Agriculture
    7) Other (specify)

36. What is your position in local government?

37. How many years have you worked in this jurisdiction?

38. Do you have any futher comments about the use of development management to reduce storm hazards?

Finally, would you please provide your name, address and telephone number below. This will allow us to keep in touch with you. The information you have provided on this survey will be kept in the strictest of confidence and we will not cite or identify you in any way in our findings. *Only aggregate data will be cited.* We would be happy to send you a copy of our research findings. If you would like to have a copy, please check the box below. (We will send it to the work address you list below.)

Thanks Again for Your Assistance! Without your help this research would not be possible. Please place the completed questionnaire in the enclosed business reply envelope and mail it back to us. No postage is necessary.

Index

About the Authors

Timothy Beatley is Assistant Professor in the Division of Urban and Environmental Planning in the School of Architecture at the University of Virginia. Beatley's primary teaching and research interests include coastal planning, urban growth management, and environmental policy and politics. He is also strongly interested in the subject of ethics as it relates to planning and public policy and has written extensively on this subject. He holds a Ph.D. in planning from the University of North Carolina at Chapel Hill.

David J. Brower is Associate Director of the Center for Urban and Regional Studies at the University of North Carolina at Chapel Hill. He is a lawyer and a planner interested in the management of urban and regional growth to accomplish public and private goals. His research has included the investigation of growth management to mitigate the impact of natural hazards, conserve natural ecosystems, and achieve social equity. He is also President of Coastal Resources Collaborative, Ltd., Chapel Hill and Manteo, North Carolina, and counsel to Robinson & Cole, Hartford, Connecticut.

David R. Godschalk is Professor of City and Regional Planning at the University of North Carolina at Chapel Hill, where he teaches land use and environmental planning. Dr. Godschalk's work has focused on development management for cities, regions, and coastal areas. He has done research on carrying capacity, hazard mitigation, dispute resolution, citizen participation, and computer information systems. A registered architect, he has been editor of the *Journal of the American Institute of Planners*, chairman of the Department of City and Regional Planning at the University of North Carolina, and a member of the governing boards of the American Planning Association, the American Society of Planning Officials, and the Association of Collegiate Schools of Planning. He holds an A.B. from Dartmouth College, an architecture degree from the University of Florida, and master's and doctoral degrees in planning from the University of North Carolina. He currently serves on the Chapel Hill Town Council.

Godschalk, David R.
Catastrophic coastal storms: hazard mitigation and development
management / by David R. Godschalk, David J. Brower, Timothy
Beatley.
p.   cm.—(Duke Press policy studies)
Bibliography: p.
Includes index.
ISBN (invalid) 0-8223-0558-X
1. Coastal zone management—South Atlantic States. 2. Coastal
zone management—Gulf States. 3. Shore protection—Atlantic Coast
(U.S.) 4. Shore protection—Gulf Coast (U.S.) 5. Hurricane
protection—South Atlantic States. 6. Hurricane protection—Gulf
States. I. Brower, David J. II. Beatley, Timothy, 1957–
III. Title. IV. Series.
HT392.5.S65G63   1988
333.91'716'0973—dc19